Phineas C. Headley

The Harvest Work of the Holy Spirit

illustrated in the evangelistic labors of Rev. Edward Payson Hammond

Phineas C. Headley

The Harvest Work of the Holy Spirit
illustrated in the evangelistic labors of Rev. Edward Payson Hammond

ISBN/EAN: 9783337285678

Printed in Europe, USA, Canada, Australia, Japan

Cover: Foto ©Lupo / pixelio.de

More available books at www.hansebooks.com

THE
HARVEST WORK

OF

THE HOLY SPIRIT,

ILLUSTRATED IN THE EVANGELISTIC LABORS

OF

REV. EDWARD PAYSON HAMMOND.

EDITED BY REV. P. C. HEADLEY,
AUTHOR OF "WOMEN OF THE BIBLE," "JOSEPHINE," "KOSSUTH," ETC.

"Say not ye, There are yet four months, and then cometh harvest."—John iv. 35.

BOSTON:
HENRY HOYT,
No. 9 Cornhill.

Entered according to Act of Congress, in the year 1862, by

HENRY HOYT,

In the Clerk's Office of the District Court of Massachusetts.

PREFACE.

A general and sufficient reason for the publication of such a work is found, in the following extract from the British Standard, by Rev. Dr. Campbell, of London, referring to Mr. Hammond's labors in Scotland: "One theatre of his operations was Dumfries, where a work of a very extraordinary character was carried on for a lengthened period. All sects and denominations united, and there was such a movement both in and around the town as, we believe, was never previously heard of. The largest church edifices were too small to accommodate the meetings which were held both day and night. The facts of the enterprise were recorded in a very interesting pamphlet, which was sent us, and which we publish in successive portions in the *British Ensign*. We have reason to believe that the narrative was read with very deep interest, and that it has been extensively useful.

"Mr. Hammond next appeared in Glasgow, where he labored with equal zeal, energy, and success, surrounded, encouraged, and sustained by ministers of the various denominations. The account of his doings there, and those of his zealous associates, have now reached us in the form of a handsome volume, entitled 'Good-will to Men: a narrative of Evangelistic labors, and of the blessed results which attended them during his visit to Glasgow, in the Spring of 1861: with an introductory note by the Rev. Dr. Hetherington, Professor of Theology, Free Church, Glasgow.'

" Amid the many interesting things in the volume, the most important, we think, is the report of the *soiree* and presentation to Mr. Hammond, in Glasgow, prior to his departure. His own speech on that occasion, made just on his return from Italy, is one of very deep interest. We shall endeavor to make room for it in the next number of the *British Ensign*."

The present volume was suggested by the writer, and its design is not to honor man, but God; to furnish Christians and all friends of revivals, for their own estimate of truth and duty, of evangelistic labors and the great awakenings on both sides of the Atlantic, sketches of the wonderful and blessed harvest-scenes within a few years past.

The editor of these unpretending pages entered upon his work, hopeful of God's guidance and blessing, because, whatever the difference of opinion of men and measures, all must feel that the whole question of religious effort — the grand enterprise of a world's conversion, compared with which all other objects become insignificant, is one of general concern. And we believe the facts here given are authentic. They were taken either from formal narratives referred to, scrap-books containing the reports of local papers, prepared by a lady in Scotland, or from written correspondence. All the works upon revivals at command have been consulted, and the reader left as far as possible to judge of principles, facts and results, rather than invited to accept the views of any one connected with this volume. It has been the constant endeavor to keep, in its proper relation to the truthfulness and usefulness of the book, the name of him whose recent labors are embodied in it; and it is now sent forth with the prayer, that it may contribute to the advancement of God's kingdom, and the encouragement of those who long for its triumphant coming.

The introduction by Rev. J. J. Carruthers, D. D., of the Payson Church, Portland, who entered warmly into the revival movement, and was greatly favored with the divine presence in his congregation, will be found rich in Christian thought, and enlarged views of the word's spiritual harvest.

INTRODUCTION.

The aggressive power of the Church of Christ has been, as yet, very partially developed. The associated missionary operations, which happily distinguish the present age, leave almost untouched the talents committed to Christ's people — the moral resources provided by the Head of the Church for the evangelization of the world. The great mass of Christian disciples are but little affected, by the known condition, and the coming destiny of the multitudes by whom they are surrounded. These are perishing by thousands and by millions, for lack of that knowledge which Christians have, and which, by every consideration of fealty to Christ, and charity and faithfulness to men, they are bound to communicate to others. What mean the divinely selected and employed emblems of their moral relation to the impenitent and unrenewed — the light of the world, the salt of the earth, the leaven secretly, silently, but surely leavening the whole lump — if they do not imply the duty and privilege of morally influencing those with whom they are brought into immediate contact? Does it, can it comport with such symbols of diffusive action, that those who know the grace of God in truth should constantly associate with Christless, hopeless and unholy relatives, friends, and fellow-citizens, without conveying to these, in any way, the convictions and forebodings entertained as to their actual condition in the sight of God, and their rapidly approaching destiny? Christians have hearts to feel, and eyes to weep, and tongues to utter the emotions of affectionate and earnest sympathy in reference to all that affects the temporal circumstances of their friends and neighbors; but how is it that so few hearts are touched, so few tears shed, and so little said or done, for interests so far outweighing in importance the aggregate of all interests temporal and earthly? Surely, it is high time that Christian disciples of our own and of other lands, should awake out of sleep, ponder deeply their solemn and untransferable responsibilities, and give not merely their prayers and their pecuniary contributions, but themselves to the work of converting sinners and saving souls from death.

To break this criminal, dishonorable and destructive slumber, and to bring the burden of conscious responsibility to bear, with adequate pressure, on the hearts and lips and lives of those who are bought with a price and are not their own, has ever been one leading object of those evangelistic labors, which, with their expected and realized results, are recorded in the present volume.

Another principal and ever-prominent object of these labors is to preach to children all the words of this life; to invite and urge them to come, in penitence and hope, to Christ; and thus to secure their present and perpetual welfare. So wisely and wondrously adapted is the truth, as it is in Jesus, to the very earliest stages of mental development, that a little child can know enough of its own sinfulness and of Christ's grace and power, to become wise unto salvation. A too common incredulity on this point has been effectually overcome, by facts perpetually occurring in connection with the labors here detailed. The best, most precious, and most promising fruits of these revivals are seen in the conversion, salvation, and growing sanctity of childhood and early youth.

Multitudes, even in our own land, never hear the gospel of the grace of God. In many so-called sanctuaries, this gospel is supplanted by deadly error, and tens of thousands are living and dying in utter destitution of the power of godliness, and in habitual disregard even of the forms of Christian worship. Can these be reached, are they, in any number, ever reached, by the ordinary agencies and appliances of the Christian Church? — and, if not, ought we not gratefully to welcome a means and mode of action, which have proved so potent in the hand of God, in calling back the prodigal to his Father's house, and conducting the sheep, lost but found, to the fold of the good shepherd? Ought not the Church, by her chosen and approved Evangelists, to go forth to the highways and hedges, and compel these outcasts to come in, and share the bounties of redeeming grace? The well-chosen title of this book will secure the Christian reader, at the outset, from all mistake as to the convictions and expectations of the friend and brother, whose labors of love are here brought to view. He serves the Lord Christ, and ever seeks from Him direction, all needed aid, and all desired success. He recognizes and relies on the promised agency of the Holy Spirit; and, inasmuch as this is ever inseparably associated with the prayer of faith, he always and everywhere insists on this, as the *sine qua non* of success in his momentous enterprise, that fervent, inwrought prayer shall precede, accompany, and follow every effort to persuade sinners to flee from the coming wrath, and seek the open, accessible, and sure refuge of the cross.

May the circulation and perusal of this volume instrumentally lead to more of that Harvest-work, which comes of the good seed of the kingdom, fructified and ripened by the Sun of Righteousness, and by the dew and rain of Heavenly grace!

J. J. CARRUTHERS.

Portland, Me., Nov. 10, 1862.

CONTENTS.

PREFACE..
INTRODUCTION...

CHAPTER I.

What is a Revival?—The relation of Revivals to the growth of the Church—Hindrances to their occurrence and progress—Testimony of Rev. James Caughy—Rev. E. Porter, D. D.—Farewell words of John Angell James—The work of the Evangelist—The present position and duty of the Church. 13

CHAPTER II.

Mr. Hammond's early home, and Conversion—Preparation for his work during his course of study—Sails for Europe—Terrific scene at sea—His providential introduction to the labors of an Evangelist—Awakening in Musselburgh—Results.......................... 37

CHAPTER III.

Revival in Gifford—Haddington, its historical interest, and the awakening—Mission to the West of England—Great open air meeting at Huntly—The work in adjacent towns, Aberdeen, Dunfermline, Tillicoultry—The Mining District, Motherwell and Wisham—The closing year's record 76

CHAPTER IV.

The work of God in Annan—Testimony of secular papers, statements of incidents—The Soldier, the Infidel—The means of success in reviving souls................. 100

CHAPTER V.

Glasgow—the awakening there — Mr. Hammond's method of conducting the Religious Services and style of preaching—Children's Meeting—Meeting for Cabmen —Letters—Summary 142

CHAPTER VI.

A Tour on the Continent — Letters from Geneva and Milan—Letter from an officer of the Exmouth — Presentation Meeting in Glasgow — Meetings at Moffat, London, Liverpool — Voyage in the Great Eastern— Conversions among Soldiers...................... 179

CHAPTER VII.

Commencement of labors in Boston—Services at the Salem Street Church — Records of the work — Cases of Conversion — Revival in Portland — Interesting cases of conversion........................... 216

CHAPTER VIII.

A week in Bethel — An unusual scene — Gorham, among the White Mountains — Bath — Statement of Rev. J. O. Fiske—South Paris—Farmington.. 237

CHAPTER IX.

The Old Colony—Church of the Pilgrimage—The Winter and Spring of 1862 — Facts and Incidents, Lewiston, Maine — The cloud like a man's hand — The mighty outpouring—Letters— Farewell—Brunswick—College scenes... 258

CHAPTER X.

Revival meeting in Portland — Seven Pastors give an account of Revivals in their parishes — General propositions drawn from the narrative.................... 290

HARVEST WORK OF THE HOLY SPIRIT.

CHAPTER I.

What is a revival? The relation of revivals to the growth of the church. Hindrances to their occurrence and progress. Testimony of Rev. James Caughy. Rev. E. Porter, D.D. The farewell words of John Angell James. The work of the Evangelist. The present position and duty of the church.

The terms revival, awakening, and reformation, with other forms of expression in popular use, mean the same thing — an unusual measure of the Holy Spirit among the people, beginning " at the House of God." Although the indispensable agent in regeneration was always abroad, and, since Abel bowed at his altar, has led every soul to Christ saved by his sacrifice; and there were at long intervals, times of great refreshing as in the reign of Hezekiah ; yet, is it evident, that under the new economy of grace, the revival period in the church commenced at Jerusalem, on the day of Pentecost. The most spiritual branch of Zion has had and must have the harvest seasons, when, like the fields of the prosperous husbandman, the scenes of joyful ingathering of the ripened grain, display the richness and abundance of God's goodness and mercy.

Rev. Dr. Hetherington, Professor of Theology in the Free Church College, Glasgow, in his introtion to "Good Will to Men," gives the following explanation of the word revival:

"The word itself is often used in Scripture, and, as so used, it generally implies the reproduction of a spiritual life which had almost died away. It is not, however, strictly synonymous with the term *conversion;* for while *revival* implies the renewal of a life which had almost died away, *conversion* strictly means the conferring of a spiritual life on those who were previously 'dead in trespasses and sins.' In truth, it so happens that revivals and conversions commonly accompany each other; so that, where *conversions* are frequent and striking, many will be re-quickened or *revived.*"

In the glowing language of Rev. Wm. Reid, editor of the British Herald:

"God in his wise and holy Providence, answers prayer 'by terrible things in righteousness,' and close upon the back of a judgment period, the Holy Spirit descends upon a whole community as 'a rushing mighty wind'—like 'floods upon dry ground,' or 'like rain upon the mown grass;' and the great heart of society begins to heave and palpitate as the heart of one man, and myriads of careless sinners are arrested, alarmed, filled with anxiety about salvation, and turned simultaneously to look on Him whom they have pierced, and mourn those sins that pierced Him and brought Him to the dust of death.

"The quiet conversion of one sinner after another, under the ordinary ministry of the Gospel, must always be regarded with feelings of satisfaction and gratitude, by the ministers and disciples of Christ; but a periodical manifestation of the simultaneous conversion of thousands is also to be desired, because of its adaptation to afford a visible and impressive demonstration to a world lying in wickedness, that God has made that same Jesus, whom they have rejected and crucified, both Lord and Christ; and that, in virtue of his Divine Mediatorship, He has assumed the royal sceptre of universal supremacy, and 'must reign till all His enemies be made His footstool.'

" And, considering that He is 'by the right hand of God exalted,' as the rightful though rejected Sovereign of the world, is it not reasonable to expect that, from time to time, He will repeat that which, on the day of Pentecost, formed the conclusive and crowning evidence of His Messiahship and Sovereignty; and, by so doing, startle the slumbering souls of careless worldlings, gain the attentive ear of the unconverted, and, in a remarkable way, break in upon those brilliant dreams of earthly glory, grandeur, wealth, power, and happiness, which the rebellious and God-forgetting multitude so fondly cherish? Such an outpouring of the Holy Spirit would form, at once, a demonstrative proof of the completeness and acceptance of His once offering of Himself as a sacrifice for sin, and a prophetic 'earnest' of the certainty that He 'shall appear the second time without sin unto salvation,' to 'judge the world in righteousness,' and 'give to every man according as his work shall be.' And, in every age of the Church, the God of our salvation has graciously bestowed the Holy Spirit in His demonstrative power, that He might glorify Jesus, by discovering Him in all His fulness to the regenerated souls of multitudes of His ransomed people. When 'the promise of the Father' was first realized on the solemn day of the first Pentecost, after the ascension of Jesus to the right hand of power, an all but universal awakening was experienced, and thousands of Jerusalem sinners were simultaneously convinced of sin and converted to God. We read that 'about three thousand souls' repented, and were baptized 'in the name of Jesus Christ for the remission of sins,' and received 'the gift of the Holy Ghost,' as the result of one exhibition of the Cross and Sceptre of the glorified Emmanuel. With one voice we exclaim, 'How blessed!' But how very many of us are, at the same time, entertaining the idea, that although it was peculiarly needful, then, as a testimony for Jesus, and to solemnize the inauguration of the new dispensation, which is termed emphatically 'the ministration of the Spirit,' yet such a remarkable outpouring of the Holy Ghost, and such a vast number of simultaneous conversions, are not to be expected in subsequent ages. But, by harboring such a thought, we entertain an opinion, which both Scripture and ecclesiastical history unite to disclaim: for the Word of God leads us still to expect the Holy Spirit, 'like *floods* upon the dry ground;' and such 'times of refreshing' and wide-spread, simultaneous conversion have repeatedly occurred in the history of the Church, as to prove conclusively, that extraordinary religious awakening and simultaneous conversion ought not to be regarded as peculiar to the day of Pentecost, but as part of the ordinary working out of God's great purpose of grace, for the conviction and conversion of the ungodly, and for ultimately 'bringing many sons to glory.' The history of the Church in our own land bears ample and frequent testimony to such periodical awakening and remarkable revival."

We shall not attempt a narrative of the "times of refreshing," since that Pentecostal baptism of the Spirit, peculiar only in a few miraculous manifestations, to authenticate, and give a fitting inauguration to the new and glorious working of His power; nor of the mighty outgoings of the conquering Emmanuel in England, Ireland, Scotland, and on the continent, in centuries past; but turn for illustration of the facts recorded in the Sacred Annals, to our New England history, and also that of the Middle and Southern States. From the earliest settlement of the country, the churches were enlarged and strengthened by the special visitations of the Spirit.

But, within the last century and a half, there have been the most frequent and amazing exhibitions of His wonder-working presence. The "Letters on Revivals," by Rev. E. Porter, D. D., late Professor of Theology at Andover, "Thoughts on the Revival of Religion in New England, A. D., 1740," by Jonathan Edwards, and Joseph Tracy's more elaborate work, "The Great Awakening," contain stirring narratives of the mighty manifestations of the Spirit in our country, which commenced in 1739, whose beginning, in some cases, was "attended with overwhelming power." Rev. Dr. Griffin, then of Newark, N. J., describes, with graphic pen, the marvelous descent of the Holy Ghost upon all the people, so that, regardless of time, the children even hung upon his lips until he was sometimes compelled to leave them.

In Vermont, "on a sudden, the Spirit of the Lord appeared to come like a rushing mighty wind. Almost the whole place was shaken at once; scarcely was there a family in which some were not earnestly inquiring what they should do to be saved; scarcely a countenance without evident marks of solemnity."

Whitefield came to America, in 1739, and went with flaming zeal and great success, through the Northern and Southern States. Yet was he met by decided opposition in and out of the Church. Associations of ministers passed resolutions against his evangelistic labors. Still he labored on, finding congenial spirits in the Tennents, also "sons of thunder," in proclaiming the gospel message. There were extravagances incident to human weakness in many places, but the good fruits made the tares seem inconsiderable in the contrast. The churches were raised to a higher plane of religious experience and duty.

Of the phenomena in general, attending the revivals, Dr. Porter writes:

"In many instances, less promising at first, there was a gradual progress for three, six, and even eighteen months, before any visible decline; and in some of these, a steady current of divine influence, rising and swelling, amid continued showers of heaven, bore down all opposition. The churches, which were visited with these more protracted seasons of mercy, generally, perhaps, received the most solid accession to their strength, if not in numbers, at least in the intelligent, shining, enduring piety of those who were added to their communion. It ought to be observed, that, while in some places divine influence was continued, for several years, like the dew that descended on the mountains of Zion, in others there was an apparent suspension and renewal of such influence, resembling successive revivals, several times in the same year."

Among the Evangelists, who assisted pastors during these revivals, conspicuous are the names of George Whitefield, Gilbert Tennent, and Asahel Nettleton. Associated with the similar scenes since that period, are Rev. Dr. Kirk, now of Boston, whose success was very similar to Dr. Nettleton's; and, also, Rev. Charles G. Finney. The annals of 1831 especially, and 1857 and 1858, are familiar to the present generation, and need no farther mention here, than that, under the rebukes of God's providence, bringing Christians to their knees, the great religious movement arose directly in the hearts of the people, with no other visible means besides those in ordinary use, excepting the meetings for daily prayer. That but a small portion of the blessing offered was secured, and loss sustained for the want of deeper humiliation, more entire consecration and discriminating presentation of the evangelical system, none can doubt. Notwithstanding, it was a priceless benediction to our land, preparing it in some degree for the life-struggle of freedom, and many of her sons, for the Christian hero's death on the battle-field. And here we may add, that when Christians in England express their surprise, that the great awakening did not visibly affect the anti-slavery cause, they overlook the fact that a religious influence which would revolutionize government, virtually controlling its politics, must transcend anything Britain or America can hope for till very near the millennial period, when a nation shall be born in a day. Until then, we shall have to mark the effect of revivals upon churches and communities where they occur, and the general progress in religious thought among the masses, silently and almost unconsciously preparing them for great changes in political and commercial life, and giving an impulse through the under currents of feeling, to the popular reforms which spring from the gospel of Christ,— the soul of all true progress in the world. There can be no more important inquiry to a Christian mind, than that which is directed to the obstacles in the way of the gracious visitation of the Spirit to save the souls of men, and those which interfere with his work, when already commenced. Like the destroying angel's mission, the question goes at once to the sanctuary and the very altars of God. On this subject we quote from Dr. Porter's Letters on Revivals, whose wisdom and piety is known to all the churches. After specifying defects in the pulpit, he writes: " that, where there were no revivals at the period to which I've referred, it was generally the fact, either that the whole truth was not exhibited in the pulpit, or at least with pungency and fidelity, or that the proper tendency of preaching, though good in itself, was frustrated by something decidedly amiss in pastoral influence."

Dr. James W. Alexander, of the Presbyterian Church, New York City, who so recently departed to his rest above, urged with great force upon the clergy the singleness of aim in securing the salvation of souls; and with the venerable Dr. Ide, of Medway, expressed his strong preference for extempore preaching, as designed to reach more directly the people, and accomplish the work of the gospel ministry. Dr. Thomas H. Skinner, of the same city, has always, by various discourses and example, presented similar views, recognizing the necessity of revivals, and the work of the Evangelist.

Indeed, the ministers, greatly blessed in winning the souls to Christ in all denominations, have not differed on this question of means and results, excepting on minor points of labor.

We shall quote an eloquent passage from Rev. James Caughy, the Nettleton of the Methodist church, an eminently successful evangelist. In his "Revival Miscellanies," a work of great power, addressing a friend upon the objections usually made to revival efforts, he says:

"Christianity has her subjects of beauty, harmony, and grandeur. In many instances, she would seem to invite the inquiring mind into the investigation of ' truth in the abstract ;' where taste may be regaled, and where the lover of polite literature may luxuriate in the wide field of her boundless wealth. That there is much in such intellectual disquisitions ' to soothe the mind,' ' please the fancy, and move the affections,' I do admit; but I do not forget, that there may be much also to gratify human vanity. Could you see my papers, which are folded up and put away, you could not believe such subjects have been by me 'always and wholly disregarded;' but they are totally unfit for the *present services*, and those great truths which are adapted to them I conscientiously prefer, even at the risk of having 'certain persons of an intellectual character form an unfavorable opinion of the mind and education of the stranger.'

"My work, in these *special services*, is to cast away from me every discussion that would serve to retard the great purposes of my mission, and to preach those mighty truths of the Gospel that will awaken and convert men. If some of my hearers do not, or will not understand my 'object and aim,' I cannot help it. We may say of fine sermons, during a revival, as Hector said to Paris: 'It is not your golden harp, nor curled hair, and beautiful painting, that will stand you in the field;' and, as an old divine says: 'Neither is it the wrought scabbard, but the *strong blade;* not the bright color, but the *sharp edge* of it, that helpeth in danger, and hurteth the enemy.' I have, my dear sir, drawn the sword, and have thrown away the scabbard. Let jesters and speculators 'have their say,'— that sword shall make havoc, by the power of the Holy Ghost, among 'the king's enemies;' and before I leave this chapel, I hope to be able to point to a great cloud of witnesses,— a host of *new converts*,— and say, 'Behold the fruits of my ministry!' These are of more value to me in the church of God than thousands of hearers applauding my sermons, and not a sinner, perhaps, converted to God!"

We add, as most solemn and touching counsel, the last work of a justly distinguished pen, passages from the Review of the Life of Richard Knill, whose tracts are well known, by John Angell James, with whom Mr. Hammond had an interview, at his home in Birmingham, just before this last testimony was written. It is also an interesting fact, that Rev. Dr.

Carruthers, whose earnest words are found in this chapter, was predecessor to Mr. Knill, in the Scottish Missionary Church of St. Petersburg, Russia. The venerable author writes of Dr. Knill:

"We now take up the inquiry after the means, by which he attained to so great a measure of usefulness. It is evident that it was, in a great degree, to be attributed to *his intense desire after it.* He set out in life with the adoption of that mighty, impulsive, and glorious word, USEFULNESS; and usefulness, with him, means converting sinners. He yearned for the salvation of souls. It was, with him, not merely a principle, or a privilege, but a passion. For this he longed and prayed in the closet, wrote in the study, labored in the pulpit, conversed in the parlor, and admonished, counselled, and warned wherever he went.

* * * * * * *

"It is, I think, an error into which many of our modern ministers, whose education has been carried to a high pitch, have fallen, that every thing is to be done by the head rather than the heart. We know very well, that the true method is to reach the heart through the head, and that men must be made to feel by being shown why they should feel, and what is to make them feel. But in very many cases, especially in the least educated, the head is to be reached by appeals to the heart. We often hear the remark, 'Yes, it was a clever sermon, but it wanted heart.' * * * *

"The passion for the conversion of souls, which he manifested in the pulpit, and which led him to seek it with such earnestness there, he brought with him out of the sanctuary, and carried into more private spheres, as the great object of life and principle of action. Like the enthusiastic botanist, geologist, he was ever in pursuit of his object, and looking out for fresh means of gaining it. It was his felicity to have rarely to say,

'*I have lost an opportunity.*' How few, how very few of us have attained to this watchfulness for occasions of usefulness.

* * * * * * *

"Whether it was the servant girl that waited upon him in the house of a friend, or the host and hostess themselves, or the fellow-traveller in the railway carriage, or the porter at an inn, or a person he usually met on the road, or a sailor on the sea-beach, he had a tract or a word — generally an apt word — for each. In every one, he saw an immortal being on his passage to eternity, and he longed to be the instrument of his conversion. Oh, what multitudes would be converted to God, and how changed would be the face of society, if all ministers and all Christians were thus set upon the work of saving souls! And why should they not be?

"He had an ardent, and, if we may so say, an outgoing soul. Then there was dauntless moral courage, and an unflinching boldness of address.

"By many, I know, the introduction of religion in the way of personal address, especially if the person he treated as unconverted, is considered as a breach of good manners and a mark of vulgarity; and too many pious people, and ministers, also, yield to this conventionalism, and pass through life without ever attempting thus to do good. But can this be right? Is it not a cowardly, guilty silence? If we have found the secret of happiness for both worlds, should we not in all proper ways seek to make it known to others?

He was eminently a man of prayer, and did everything in the *spirit* of prayer. His communion with God was close and constant. He came from the closet strengthened for his work in the pulpit and in the city, and went back to his closet, not only for repose and refreshment, but to be strengthened and prepared for further labor. This made him 'strong in the Lord and in the power of His might.' And why are any of God's servants feeble in action, but because they are weak in devotion? We live in days when Christians are far less in the closet than they should be. The study and the counting-house encroach upon the closet. We are preaching-men and business-men, but not so much as we should be, praying-men.

"In the retrospect of a long life, now drawing to a close, during which I have watched, of course, the career, and observed the mode of action, of many of my brethren, I have noticed great diversity in the results of their ministry; and I have most assuredly seen, that where they have been intensely earnest for the salvation of souls, and have sought this by a style of preaching adapted to accomplish it, God has honored their endeavors by giving them success. If, without impropriety, I may refer here, as I believe I have done elsewhere, to the service which, during fifty-four years, I have been allowed to render to our Great Master, I may declare my thankfulness in being able, in some small degree, to rejoice that the conversion of sinners has been my aim. I have made, next to the Bible, Baxter's 'Reformed Pastor,' my rule as regards the object of my ministry.

"I sometimes venture to hope that it has kindled in me a spark, but oh, how dim! of that spirit which actuated Mr. Knill. In regard to all that constitutes earnestness, I blush before his statue, as it rises before me in this volume, and confess my short comings in the work of the Lord. Standing, as I now do, in the prospect of the close of my ministry, of the eternal world, and of my summons to the presence of the Great Lord of all, the salvation of souls, as the object of the ministry, appears to me, more than ever before, in all its awful sublimity. Everything else, as compared with this, seems but as the small dust of the balance; and though, perhaps, not altogether an idler in the vineyard of the Lord, it is now my grief that I have not been more devoted. To my younger brethren I say, You are engaged in the greatest work in the universe; for in preaching for the salvation of souls, you are brought into fellowship with God in His eternal purposes of mercy to the children of men, with our Lord Jesus Christ in His redeeming work upon the cross; with the Holy Spirit in His mission to our world; and with prophets, apostles, and martyrs. Heaven, through eternity, will resound with the praises of your diligence, or hell with lamentations and execrations upon your neglect. Happy will it be for you, and happy for your flocks, if the perusal of this volume should help you to find and to wear the mantle of Richard Knill."

While these weighty words were passing through the press, the great and good man suddenly finished his course, and joined the church triumphant — leaving to his ministerial brethren, and to all, this affecting entreaty and benediction.

In the churches, the grand difficulty has always been unfaithfulness to covenant vows — either as stated by Dr. Porter, neglect of discipline indispensable to healthful growth and moral power, or the practical opposition, if not open to revivals, and scepticism in regard to the doctrine of the final and eternal punishment of the impenitent, which have made, and do make, the world doubt the reality of religion. The want of believing prayer, is the fatal weakness toward God. Prayer, whose qualities are sincerity, which leads to appropriate effort — fervor, which wrestles with God, and perseverance, which takes no denial; prayer and fasting before God. Says Edwards, in his "Thoughts on the Revival of Religion in New England," "There is no way that Christians in a private capacity can do so much to promote the work of God, and advance the kingdom of Christ, as by prayer. By this, even women, and children and servants may have a public influence. God is, if I may so say, at the command of the prayer of faith." Edwards dwells warmly upon the Scriptural duty and privilege of private and public fasts. Christians must go through Gethsemane, to the cross, with their burden of souls. The divine appointment of Evangelists in the early history of the church, none will doubt; nor we think can it be shown that their office has ever been set aside.

Dr. Porter, after presenting very forcibly the primary importance of the pastoral relation, recognizes the value, if not necessity, of successful helpers in gathering God's harvest: " In a large congregation, where the ordinary labors of the ministry are as great as one man can possibly sustain, a failure of his health, or a revival among his people, may render it indispensable that he should have help in his work for weeks or months successively. Such help has often been furnished by the occasional labors of other pastors, who have had a short leave of absence from their own flocks. But perhaps the only adequate provision for such emergencies would be, that a few men, of rare endowments for this particular service, — men of God, distinguished for judgment, fervor of piety and suavity of temper, — should be held in reserve to labor where they are most needed, as assistants to stated pastors." We think the following resolutions drawn by the Rev. Mr. Balkam, of Lewiston, Me., a city blessed with a remarkable outpouring of the Spirit in connection with the labors of an evangelist, expresses the truth on this subject:

"1. God honors the established ministry of the Christian religion by employing, in the conversion of sinners, usually, the truth, as preached by his faithful ministers.

"2. The establishment of such a ministry, however efficient and successful in any branch of the church, has by no means exhausted the instrumentalities of salvation. The prerogative being still His, to project, even into the most cultivated portions of his vineyard, new and additional means.

"3. Masses of precious truth, imparted by many an able and faithful pulpit, sometimes lie inoperative, at least in that which is most essential, because unquickened by the Spirit — by importunity of prayer — by devout ardor of sympathy — by fervor of appeal — and by variety of motive made intense and almost irresistable. To do this may demand, for a time, men and measures not usually employed.

"4. Evangelists are of divine appointment, and have their peculiar work. That work is never in derogation of, but always collateral and auxillary to, the established ministry; being designed merely to supplement its officers and labors, and thus be tributary to the conversion of souls, the spread of the Redeemer's kingdom, and the glory of His name."

At the meeting of the General Assembly of the Free Church, in Edinburgh, May, 1860, the statement of the Rev. Julius Wood, D. D., formerly moderator, in whose church Mr. Hammond labored, fills a most important place in this connection. It is given respecting the phenomena of revivals, in a report of that body, as follows :

"Dr. Julius Wood, Convener of the Committee on Religion and Morals, then gave in his report. He said — This, in some respects, is the most important and interesting report that was ever laid on the table of the General Assembly. If, as has been said, 'a living soul is of more value than a dead world.' what joy has there been in Heaven over souls, that have been made alive in Scotland, since we met here in General Assembly a year ago! In consequence of instructions from the last General Assembly, the Committee on Religion and Morals transmitted a circular to every minister and probationer in a charge or station throughout the Free Church. In reply to that circular I have received 168 returns — 169, for one has reached me since the Assembly met. These 169 returns are from 66 Presbyteries of the Church, all the Presbyteries except 5. From some Presbyteries we have received only one return, from other Presbyteries we have received several. Of the 169 returns, 86 report decided awakening and revival in the congregations of which they report. These 86 congregations are to be found in 42 Presbyteries of the Church. Thus in 42 Presbyteries we have reported, decided awakening or revival; and in the other 83 congregations which are to be found in 26 Presbyteries, we are gratified by being told that, whilst there is no decided awakening or revival, there is in almost every instance, without exception, increased attention to, and interest in spiritual things. We find, indeed, that since the returns were sent in to me, awakening has taken place in a number of localities. Some of these returns were sent in two or three months ago; and I find, that since then there has been a decided work of the Lord going on in those places, whilst at that time they were able only to report a considerable interest in religious things. In many of our congregations, there was a gradual increase of the spirit of prayer and increased expectation of revival, which was quickened when we had tidings of the Lord's great work in America and Ireland. These tidings both excited gratitude to God, and raised expectations that He would not pass us by; and, when we used the Scriptural means for obtaining the blessing, they were blessed to us by God. There was increased attention to the preaching of the Word, increased attention at prayer meetings, and an increase in the exercise of prayer in our social circles, in our families, and in secret. And, when the Lord had thus prepared us for receiving the blessing, it pleased him to pour it out very remarkably and very abundantly. *I cannot help observing, that one great means of awakening seems to have been, the communicating of intelligence of what the Lord had done in other places. I find in almost all the reports, that this was done with the most blessed results. The information interested the people, and brought the thing home to them; they felt that it was a reality;* and it excited a desire to partake of the benefit, and led them to use the means God has appointed for obtaining the benefit. I believe we can scarcely ascribe too much influence to the communication of religious intelligence, in bringing about the results in which we this day rejoice. The revival throughout the country began in every variety of way, and through every variety of instrumentality, sometimes under the quiet ministrations of the stated pastor, sometimes through the visit of a stranger from a distance; sometimes it was a convert, who went and told his simple story of the Lord's goodness to him. I find, in many of the returns, mention made of such men as North, Grant, Radcliffe, Hammond, Forlong, and Weaver. God seems to have honored the labors of these men in a marvellous way. The work was sometimes carried on by a single remark made by one individual to another — by the repetition of a text of Scripture — by a message from one friend to another — or by a letter written from the scene of revivals to friends or relatives. I believe that the day of judgment only will reveal, how much the work has been forwarded by the letters of Christian men and women, written in the warmness of their hearts to friends and relatives at a distance ; for no sooner is a sinner brought to Christ, than his first thought is — ' I will tell my relatives and friends what Christ has done for me.' The convert cannot rest, until he has made known to those in whom he is interested the Lord's work upon him. I find from the report, that in a number of places there was considerable excitement. I do not wonder at that, Moderator. When men for the first time find themselves on the brink of hell, with nothing between their souls and perdition but the frail, fleeting breath in their nostrils, I do not wonder that they should feel alarmed and excited — when they feel themselves for the first time to be under the wrath and condemnation of a righteous and holy God. My wonder is, that there is not more excitement — that people still unconverted can hear of sin and hell, of a Saviour and heaven, without feelings of emotion. Ah! that excitement; people are afraid of it, and sometimes it comes with a mighty power, as if it would sweep everything away before it ; but when one is enabled to cast himself humbly upon God, and to enter into the work earnestly, it is not such a formidable thing after all. Our God is a God of order ; and if we cast ourselves upon his strength, and take counsel of Him, I believe He will enable any man of ordinary prudence and courage to guide these excited meetings for his glory, and for the good of souls. Then I am very glad to be able to state, that, from almost all the reports I am able to gather, there has been a great change in the manners and habits of the people. Where the awakening has been anything like general, there has been upon general society an awe and restraint ; and I find testimony borne by employers to the effects that have been produced upon their workmen. One will say, if you doubt the reality of the revival, ' Come to my workshop, and you will see what it is ; if you knew my men before, come and see what they are now, and you will see that something has been at work that has produced a most salutary change.' The police reports, too, are exceedingly favorable; the chief constable of one of our largest counties, which includes a good many towns, told me that there is a diminution of considerably more than one-third, upon all that class of crimes including violence, &c., such as assaults and disorderly conduct. Now I do not venture to lay down any rules in regard to this great movement. I remember a most intelligent Irish Presbyterian minister saying, that, when the north of Ireland was visited, he formed his plans in anticipation of the wished-for revival in his own place. But when it came these were all swept away, and he was just forced to do the Lord's work in the Lord's way. I believe, the only rule lies in the two great commandments — ' Thou shalt love the Lord thy God with all thy heart,' and ' Thou shalt love thy neighbor as thyself.' God will carry us through this and nothing else. At the same time, there is much room for wisdom and prudence. Much may be done by any loving-hearted man, blessed with a fair share of moral courage, if he throw himself into the work. I can never forget the weighty words uttered by a member of this house — Superintendance, Suggestion, and Substitution. If we take these for our guide and go into the work in dependence on the Spirit of God, He will enable us to glorify Him and benefit the souls of men. With regard to young converts, when they go and state quietly to their fellow-men what the Lord hath done for them, I believe that is a legitimate employment for them. I do not think it a good thing for them to be long employed in this way, however. When one of them has stated his experience in a few meetings, it would be wise in him to retire and cultivate fresh knowledge, and learn a spirit of duty to God."

An American divine, in the midst of a powerful outpouring of the Spirit recorded in this volume, answered the objections of some cautious minds, by a communication which we give from the Christian Mirror:

"Will you kindly insert in your next issue the following remarks of Dr. Chalmers? They are found in the New York edition of his sermons, vol. 1 pp. 116, 117. Although we are forbidden to call any man Master upon earth, there are some with whom, in matters of religion, human names have great weight, and for their sakes as well as others it may be well to give publicity, at this time, to these observations.

Yours, sincerely,

J. J. CARRUTHERS.

"He recently observed, in discoursing on the knowledge of Jesus Christ, and him crucified, that some were visited with an alarming sense of danger, and were long kept in a state of pain and perplexity, and had much of disquietude upon their spirits, ere they found their way to a place of rest or a place of enlargement. * * But we further observed, that, though this was frequent in the history of conversions, it was far from universal. And why should it? There is a message of pardon from heaven at our door, and its very first demand upon us is, that we should give credit thereto. If any one claim upon us be preferable to another, surely it is the claim of Him who cannot lie, that we shall believe in his testimony. Are we to hold the truth of God in abeyance, aye, and until we have walked some round of mental discipline and experience, that may liken the history of our transition from darkness to light to that of some fellow mortal who has gone before us? Are we to postpone our faith in an actual report brought to us from the upper sanctuary, till we have brought the frame of our spirits to its rigid adjustment, by having travelled over a course of certain feelings and fluctuations?

* * * * * * *

We know that there is a peace where there is no peace; and, better than this sleep of death, were the disturbance of loud and perpetual alarm, from which there might be no respite to the sinner, till forced to betake himself to the only effectual hiding-place. But better, most assuredly, still, that you saw the hiding-place to be open now, and that, without the interval of a single moment, you have fled for refuge there, and that the soul had no sooner broken loose from the tranquility of nature, than it instantly fastened on the anchor of hope that was most sure and steadfast. At this rate, there would be no season of intermediate darkness. Converts would experience now what was oft experienced in the days of the Apostles. Their belief would instantly come in the train of the gospel testimony — and their joy would instantly come in the train of their belief."

It needs no argument to prove that the church of Christ occupies a place in her march of conquest, of peculiar interest. The world is unsettled as never before, theologically and politically. Error unshackled is abroad, confronting, in its most daring and subtle forms, "the truth as it is in Jesus." Governments are shaken, and lawlessness grows defiant on every hand. God's judgments are abroad, and the fragments of the shaken order of things fill the air. But comparatively unemployed and unfelt, are the energies of His dear Zion. A writer has well said, "she is two-fold in her character, — having under the one visible form, the church of the world, and within that circle of destructive influence, the Church of Christ." Covetousness, which is idolatry, has hoarded God's silver and gold, — ambition has devoted the best talent and highest position to sectarian controversy, — pleasure-loving has taken under Christian patronage, amusements and frivolity, with the plea of cheerfulness, which have paralyzed her spiritual strength, and practically wiped out the line of separation from the world. Unbelief and licentious charity have disguised and modified the evangelical system; in other words, the gospel of the Son of God, as it fell from his lips armed with the retributive sanctions of law, and melting appeals of the cross. Nor has she been true to liberty and humanity. We know that these statements have a limited application; but sin must be felt, and put away from the Church of Christ; then in the might of an entire consecration to her Lord, with wrestling prayer, and the sword of the Spirit in her hand, will she become "fair as the moon, clear as the sun, and terrible as an army with banners." Jehovah's fan is in his hand, and he will thoroughly purge the floor. And it is fitting, that we, who bear His name who has declared that "judgment must begin at the house of God," should inquire of him upon our knees: "Who may abide the day of his coming, and who shall stand when he appeareth?"

Oh! shall the hosts of God's elect dictate to the Spirit of God when, how, and by whom he shall work in the redemption of a world straining on its fetters, and sighing for deliverance?

The captives in material chains, and the slaves of sin, moving in a great caravan to the shades of a mornless night, must stir the heart of the church to wrestle and to labor, as never before since time began. We believe they will; and that soon her victories will attract the interest of the nations, as do now the triumphs of the crimson field of martial combat.

Forcibly says an eminent American divine: —

"The time is coming, when his successes shall be reported with more than the rapidity of Napoleon's victories; when the press shall teem with intelligence of Christian movements in the world; when the steamer shall furrow the deep to speed the tidings of His power; when the electric wires shall thrill with heavenly life, to convey from city to city, and from continent to continent, the news of revivals of religion, and of ' nations born in a day.' The kingdom of Christ is yet to be the one thing thought of in the world, and at every market, in every exchange, in every bulletin; at the street corners men shall speak of the glory of His kingdom, and talk of His power one to another, making known His mighty acts, and the glorious majesty of His kingdom."

CHAPTER II.

Mr. Hammond's Early Home and Conversion — Unconscious Preparation for his Work during his course of Study — Sails for Europe — Terrific Scene at Sea — His Providential Introduction to the labors of an Evangelist — The awakening in Musselboro' — Its Results.

It is no part of the design of this volume to write a biography, or commend to popular favor by direct approval, or to defend against the criticism and prejudice of any, the name around which necessarily gathers much of the human interest of the narrative; but to give to the public whatever will present, in a clear and satisfactory light, the work of God, as promoted by the labors of the most successful Evangelist, in this country, recently before the churches. And this naturally includes some notice of the early history and training of God's servant for His service.

Edward Payson Hammond was born in Ellington, a quiet town in the Valley of the Connecticut, Sept. 1st, 1831, but passed his boyhood and youth in Vernon, Ct. He was a child of prayer, consecrated to God by parental piety; especially was he nurtured with holy fidelity under the wing of maternal love. At the age of seventeen, he attended school at Southington, where had been a powerful revival of religion, including in its sweep nearly all of the youth of the place.

Mr. Hammond, in his addresses, sometimes refers to the story of his conversion, and relates it thus:—

"The first Sabbath of my stay in Southington was the communion. This was held between the services, and all who were not Christians were in the habit of going out. As I looked about, it seemed that all my friends and relatives, and new acquaintances were gathering around the table of the Lord. Among the few who passed out were none whom I knew.

"The thought of the judgment day flashed across my troubled mind. And the awful scenes of that final separation passed like a panorama before my view. On returning to my boarding-place that night, a lady handed me James' 'Anxious Inquirer' to read. I glanced my eye hastily over a few of its pages, but thought it too dry a book for me, and I angrily threw it down. But this did not extract the arrow of conviction that had pierced my heart. I felt that I was a sinner, hastening on to the great judgment day unprepared. Little did I know of the earnest pleadings that were daily ascending from a mother's fond heart.

"Day by day my convictions deepened. My heart rebelled against God. I disputed his undivided claim to my heart. I was willing to give a portion of my affections, but I was not ready to give up all for Jesus, and say,

"Just as I am,
O Lamb of God I come."

and thus,

"Against the God that built the sky,
I fought with hands uplifted high,
Despised the mansions of his grace,
Too proud to seek a hiding-place."

"Yes, 'too proud' to come as a lost, guilty, helpless, hell-deserving sinner to Jesus. As yet 'ignorant of God's righteousness and going about to establish 'my 'own righteousness.' (Rom. x : 3.) For two long weeks I wept and prayed, and read my Bible, all the while treading 'under foot the Son of God.' (Heb. x : 29.)

"Vindictive justice stood in view,
To Sinai's fiery mount I flew;
But justice cried, with frowning face,
This mountain is no hiding-place."

"During these dark days I read 'James' Anxious Inquirer.' I looked upon it no longer as a 'destroyer of my peace,' but as a guide to happiness—to Christ and heaven. I used to study it by the hour with my Bible, looking out all the passages referred to. I thus saw more and more of my awfully deceitful and polluted heart.

"At *first*, it was thoughts of the *judgment day*, and the *sight* of the *wicked going away into everlasting punishment*, that alarmed me; but afterwards it was the *sight* of *myself* that alarmed me most.

"I then began to realize that *reformation* was not enough, that a great, an entire, a *radical* change must be experienced if I would enter heaven.

"When to the law I trembling fled,
It poured its curses on my head,
I no relief could find;
This fearful truth increased my pain,
The sinner must be born again,
And whelm'd my tortured mind."

"It was then the *pit* of *sin* in my own heart alarmed me more than the pit of hell, into which I had been so lately gazing. The desperate enmity of my guilt before God I began to realize. My burden seemed heavier than I could bear. But another, a *third* sight I was called to gaze upon which pierced my soul with a new and *keener* arrow,— Godly sorrow. I was led by the Holy Spirit to look on Him whom my sins had 'pierced, and . . . . . mourn.' (Zach. xii. 10.) I began to understand those words in Acts v. 31, 'Him hath God exalted with his right hand to be a Prince and a Saviour, for to *give repentance*.' I shall never forget that calm Autumn morning when I fell upon my knees in my little closet and repeated the hymn my mother had taught me.

> "Alas, and did my Saviour bleed,
>   And did my sovereign die?
> Would He devote that sacred head
>   For such a worm as I?
>
> Was it for crimes that I had done,
>   He groaned upon the tree?
> Amazing pity! grace unknown,
>   And love beyond degree!"

"It was then, in the light of Calvary's cross, I began to feel that 'godly sorrow' for sin that 'worketh repentance to salvation.' I then saw that God 'might be just, and the justifier of him which believeth in Jesus,' (Rom. iii. 26,) and that I must

> "Cast my deadly doing down,
>   Down, down at Jesus' feet;"

and with tears in my eyes I exclaimed, in the words of the last verse of the hymn which I was repeating,

> "But drops of grief can ne'er repay
>   The debt of love I owe,
> *Here, Lord, I give myself away,*
>   *'Tis all that I can do.*"

"It was then the blessed Holy Spirit, that had so long been striving with me, took of the things of Christ and showed them unto me — my blind eyes were opened. I saw that God was satisfied with what *Christ* had done; that Jesus had paid the debt, and I had only to trust him for it all — and I could sing with all my heart,

> "My God is reconciled,
>   His pardoning voice I hear,
> He owns me for his child,
>   I can no longer fear."

"I then knew the meaning of the promise in Ezek. xxxvi. 26, 'A new heart, also, will I give you, and a new spirit will I put within you.'

"As there was no revival at the time, and no preaching that I remember made any special impression on my mind, I can but feel that my conversion was the direct work of the Holy Spirit in answer to the wrestling, agonizing prayers of my dear mother.

"Some of the 'fruit of the Spirit' (Gal. v. 22,) were at once mine. 'Love, joy, peace,' filled my heart.

"I remember that I sat down at once and wrote mother that I had 'found Jesus.'"

He subsequently completed his preparation for College at Phillips' Academy, Andover, Mass. There, as wherever he went after his conversion, God blessed his faithfulness to the conversion of souls in the Institution, and in neighboring villages in which, with other students, he established meetings.

He entered Williams College in 1854. Without neglecting his studies, as his instructors testify, he labored earnestly and successfully for the conversion of his classmates. Among them was Henry Hopkins, the President's son, now Chaplain in the army, with whom he attended meetings in Pownal; where together they went forth, weeping, "bearing precious seed," and they returned, "bringing" their "sheaves with" them. The little company of seven or eight Christians was increased to a prosperous church. In the Spring of 1855, he went, in behalf of the American Sunday School Union, among the Alleghany mountains, and planted several Sunday schools during his vacation, which in some instances proved to be the nucleus of churches.

Prof. Chadbourne, one of the faculty of Williams, now of Bowdoin College, thus wrote, to one of the associate Professors, of his pupil, after his return from Europe. We quote it, because it meets objections made to methods of labor which are strongly marked with the individuality of the worker, which will be farther noticed hereafter.

"You will be glad to hear of our old friend and pupil, Mr. Hammond. He is now laboring in Bath, and I think it must be evident to all that the blessing of God attends his labors. He came to me last week to lend him a helping hand, as he is much exhausted with his continued labors. He is the same that he was when a student, except that he has gained wonderfully in power; the same good nature, the same fervent piety and zeal for the salvation of souls. He is not like other men, and it is folly for other men, to judge of him by their standards. The only true test, and one it seems to me, that ought to satisfy every one, is, the great blessing that accompanies his labors. Some good men find fault, and wonder at his success, and think him over excited, but we who have known him so long, know that the same zeal stirred his heart when a Freshman in College, that stirs it now. God is making good his promise, to honor those that honor him. His success is wonderful, because God gives it to him! And before I dare to criticise, I must wait till I find a style of labor that God more signally blesses. I gave our dear brother all the advice I dared to give, with all the freedom of an old instructor towards his pupil; and would that those, who are now my pupils, would receive advice, in the same spirit of meekness and thankfulness. But I did not dare advise him to try to change his style of labor, nor to be more like this or that distinguished minister, because, among all the names that are precious in the churches, I could think of no one whom God has more signally blessed in turning men from sin, than he has this young man, now three years out of College. And while I rejoice in the loyalty and bravery of Col. Garfield and others of our old pupils who are fighting the battles of our beloved country, I will rather rejoice that I have been a teacher of this valiant soldier of Jesus Christ, who is doing so much to bring back this whole world, from its rebellion against God; and in this, I know you will heartily join me."

He received the degree of A. B., along with an appointment for Commencement, in 1858, and in 1861 the degree of A. M.

The desire and intention to be a missionary had been cherished by the young disciple; but God otherwise ordered his useful life. In the year 1858, he became a student in Union Theological Seminary, New York, and in that great city, continued with unflagging zeal his home missionary work among the destitute.

Having planned a trip to Europe, he sailed in the noble ship Edinburgh. A few days later, the vessel struck an iceberg, and startled all on board by the shock. We quote Mr. Hammond's description of the solemn scenes which followed:—

"At first we rejoiced with trembling, hoping that the ship had not sprung aleak. The pumps were sounded, and in ten minutes the words, "she leaks!" rang from stem to stern. Numbers fainted. Some were soon found upon their knees, crying for mercy; one, who had a little before been scoffing at prayer and God's word.

"At midnight, during the fearful storm which ensued, when the first and second compartments of the mighty ship were filled, and the ship, at an angle of 45°, was every moment in danger of being engulphed with the mountain waves, when hope had fled, and the impenetrable darkness, like the pall of death, enveloped us, as I was hastening along the deck, amid the pelting rain, to my work at the pumps, my ear was startled as the bell tolled the hour, with the watchword, " All's well!" Four times it echoed along the sides of the sinking ship. But not a voice responded, ' Let us eat, drink, and be merry, for 'all's well!'" for all knew too well they were lying words. Had we believed these words, and ceased to work for our lives, in one hour's time none would have been left to tell the tale of our finding a watery grave. And I could but think of the sinner's trusting in a false hope, with the waters of sin silently, yet surely, hour by hour, engulphing his soul, hastening to the 'father of lies,' as he whispers 'all's well!' And I then resolved that if the Lord spared my life, I would strive more faithfully to obey his command, ' *Say ye to the righteous that it shall be well with him*,' ' *woe unto the wicked; it shall be ill with him.*' Isa. iii. 10, 11.

"We barely reached St. John's, Newfoundland, the next night, at dusk. We continued to bail and pump to the last moment. And I thought of those solemn words (1 Peter iv. 18), ' And if the righteous scarcely be saved, where shall the ungodly and the sinner appear.' The experience of those solemn hours, when near going into eternity, I would not forget. How earnest our united prayers, as the little band of Christians intuitively gathered and said to Jesus, in pleading tones, ' Master, carest thou not that we perish?' Acts iv. 38."

A poetical description of the perils and rescue, written for his mother, has been so often repeated by Mr. Hammond as a very affective illustration, especially the cry, " all's well!" that it will interest many readers; and a part of it is here added to the record of the disaster.

" A nobler ship than ours,
　　Man's eye hath seldom seen,
　As proud amid the cannon's roar
　　She sailed with queenly mien.
　Our hearts with hopes beat high,
　　Of joys full many in store,
　And so across the deep we hie,
　　For Scotland's bonnie shore.

" With us there were no seers ;
　　And none on board could ken,
　When blighted hopes would change to fears,
　　Far from our journey's end :
　So o'er the restless tide
　　We sped with joyous glee,
　No fears that aught of ill betide —
　　Shadows of danger flee !

" Our gallant ship bounds on,
　　Amid the flashing spray,
　While sparkling rainbows in their dance,
　　Attend us on our way.
　So on the sea of life,
　　Do th' rainbow words of love,
　Bedeck the worn and wounded heart,
　　With a beauty from above.

" The sunlight now is gone,
　　And we are left in gloom ;
　The blinding fog comes on anon —
　　Hope still bestows its boon.
　But hark ! what means that shout
　　From th' watchman at the prow ?
　As wildly now he shrieks — " A Port ! "
　　See terror on each brow.

" Well may the stoutest shriek,
   And cry for mercy now ;
An iceberg of the Northern deep
   Has struck our noble bow.
Joy first lit every eye,
   As towering o'er our left,
That monster grim went angry by,
   As of his prey bereft.

" Soon o'er its massive form
   Was cast a veil of mist,
Thus quickly from our view 'twas borne,
   As wind and tide might list.
But hark, with loudest skricks,
   From lip to lip it flew ;
Oh! ho! our ship; she leaks! she leaks!
   Ah! then was terror new!

" All eyes then to the boats
   With anxious looks were turned ;
How waned our fondly cherished hopes!
   What thoughts within us burned!
The bravest were appalled —
   The timid stood aghast —
As if by winged lightning called,
   Grim death before us passed.

" How floods the mind with thought
   Of loved ones o'er the main !
How deep with keenest sorrow fraught,
   Lest ne'er we meet again.
But orders then were brought
   The pumps to quickly man,
Then with the raging sea we fought,
   Like warriors in the van.

OF THE HOLY SPIRIT.

"For many a weary hour,
   We toiled with all our might,
While orisons arose to heaven,
   Midst th' darkness of the night.
Anon our faith did fail,
   As flew the cry 'she gains,'
And many cheeks grew ghastly pale,
   Amid the drenching rain.

"But every nerve was strained,
   Our fifteen score to save,
For o'er our hearts cold horror reigned
   At thought of wat'ry grave.
But palsied be my tongue,
   If I forget to praise,
The women in that noble band
   Who toiled our hopes to raise.

"For in that darkness drear,
   'Midst wild wind's awful shriek,
Their cheerful voice, we loved to hear,
   Their praises then we'll speak.
Our prayers at length were heard,
   'Twas a brighter, happier hour,
When smiled on us the peaceful sun,
   And clouds no longer lower.

"It seemed our Father's frown,
   Passed with the gloom away,
We freely breathed, and praised His name
   Whose smile around us lay.
For Oh, at his command,
   Had winds increased their rage,
Far from the ocean's beaten strand,
   We 'd sunk beneath the wave.

"But now we're safe in port,
  By no unfriendly shore;
For here we find *free* hands, *warm* hearts;
  We ask for nothing more.
When far away we hie,
  Across the deep blue sea,
Our thoughts will hither quickly fly,
  With faithful memory."

Spending a few weeks in England and Scotland, Mr. H. went to Ireland to witness and enjoy the wondrous displays of divine grace on that Island.

At Ballymena, he addressed large audiences, triumphantly vindicating the American revivals from the charge circulated abroad by their enemies, that they had proved a failure. We take the following passage from a report of his remarks as published in one of the papers of that city.

"Since coming to this land I have been more deeply convinced than ever of the reality of the existence of a personal evil spirit. We read in Job of a 'day when the sons of God came to present themselves before the Lord, and Satan came also among them.' And, from what I have, with perfect astonishment, heard this day, I find that, as the sons of God *here* have gathered together Satan also has come among them. And I find, too, that he often pursues the sames course with nations and communities as with individuals. We all know the awful struggle he has with those who are striving to escape from his power to the arms of Jesus. But when, at last, the 'evil spirit is cast out of a man,' he does not entirely quit the field, but *is* ever on the alert, either to regain the mastery, or to destroy the influence of the one who has now become his enemy. And, if he find the life blameless, he still has a great calumny to whisper in the ears of the unbeliever. He then impugns his *motives*. He asks—'does Job fear God for naught?' Now this faintly illustrates the movement of the great arch-enemy of man with regard to America. When he found hundreds of thousands all over the land escaping from his grievous bondage, and declaring themselves no longer the 'servants of sin,' but free men in Christ Jesus, he, with all his allies, were sorely troubled; and they looked about them to contrive some means to destroy the influence of this great movement, that ' it spread no further among the people.' They were not long in concluding that their old policy was the most expedient; and so the *motives* of God-fearing men were maligned—the inconsistencies of young converts were closely watched, and greatly magnified; and those cases where the ' good seed ' chanced to fall ' by the wayside,' or ' among thorns,' or upon ' stony ground,' were eagerly sought out; but those where it brought forth ' an hundred fold ' were passed by as not answering the desired purpose. He strove to make wicked men with us believe that it was all excitement, and would soon pass away; and when the Spirit of God with its mighty convicting and converting power, in its progress from west to east, came among *you*, Satan was not long in finding out his friends here, who were ready to spread abroad the report that the ' Revival in America is a failure.' But I am glad of the opportunity to stand up here to assert that this is but another of the fabrications of the great ' Father of lies.' He was a liar from the beginning; and the more we know of him leads us to believe that he will never change for the better in this respect. The Revival is *not* a failure, but a *glorious triumph over the powers of darkness.* You have only to read the books that have been published in America giving reliable accounts of the glorious results of the work, to be convinced that the Revival is anything but a failure. No doubt there have been cases where persons have been deceived in regard to the ground of their hope; some whose ' hands Satan has cut off.' Here Mr. H. told of two men who were speaking together of the evidence of their hope. The first said he should be saved, for he had hold of Christ. 'Ah! but what will you do,' said the second, 'if the *devil cut your hands off?*' 'What then,' asked the first, 'is *your* hope?' '*My* hope,' said he, 'is that *Christ has hold of me*.' So, continued Mr. H., no doubt some were deceived in trusting too much to their own efforts, and not relying entirely upon Christ for salvation. But I must say that few, if any, cases of backsliding have come under my own observation. He would not number among these cases those who were convinced of their lost condition, but were unwilling to trust in Jesus as their only Saviour. Such there were, and always have been. Mr. H. spoke of the *effects* of the work being the same there as exhibited here. The converts manifested the same love for Christ, and the same earnest desire to engage in his cause. Ministers of different denominations were seen there as here to-day, upon the same platform. The causes, he believed, too, were the same — namely, the Spirit of God through the 'Word' operating with Divine power upon the heart. The phenomena manifested as the result of such agency were different, but the ultimate effects were the same. With us the parties affected *rose up* when oppressed with the burden of guilt, and asked Christians to pray that it might be removed. With you they are often stricken to the ground, like Saul on his way to Damascus; and I have seen cases in your midst as marvellous to me as the conversion of Saul. Mr. H. then spoke of prayer as being the chief instrument, on the part of Christians, in calling down the blessing of heaven—dwelling at some length upon the power of prayer and encouragement to honor God by asking great things of him."

The two weeks' experience in Ireland were a fresh preparation and impulse in the life-work of saving souls. Returning to Scotland after a tour on the Continent, Mr. Hammond failed to receive remittances from America, and was disappointed in his expectation of sailing for his native land. Unexpectedly God's kind Providence, opened the way for resuming and prosecuting his Theological studies in the Free Church College, in Edinburgh. Extracts from his letters and remarks by Dr. Alexander, will give the interesting facts of his introduction to evangelistic labors in Scotland. Mr. H. writes:

"For a few weeks I devoted myself entirely to intellectual pursuits, and I found the literary atmosphere of Edinburgh very congenial. But after all my conscience reproved me for doing nothing for Jesus. I felt that I might at least teach a Sunday School class, or something of the kind, or perhaps supply some pulpit on the Sabbath, as I had done while in New York. I called on two or three of the Free Church ministers, but they knew of no opening.

"Dr. W. L. Alexander, the leading minister of the Congregational Church in Scotland, spoke of a forlorn hope in Musselburgh, six miles from Edinburgh."

Mr. H. went to M. We select the following testimony to the genuineness and power of the work in Musselburgh, from a letter addressed to Rev. Mr. Reid, Editor of the British Herald.

Dr. Alexander, on several public occasions, made similar emphatic remarks.

"I think no impartial and grateful person will say that the soil in Musselburgh has been one favorable to the growth of a vital spiritual piety. The indifference of the people to religion, and immobility under the most earnest preaching of the Gospel seemed to come out more strikingly as a characteristic of the place than in other towns. Such at least had been for a long time the impression on my mind, and therefore it was with mingled joy and wonder, that I heard of the interest that had been awakened there by the preaching of the Gospel. When I heard of and saw crowded gatherings of people evening after evening during the week, assembled to hear plain, earnest, and faithful addresses on the concerns of their soul; when I saw the deep, unmistakable earnestness of groups of inquirers ; when I listened to the sobs and cries of men and women — some of them as unlikely to be moved to such displays of emotion as can be well conceived ; when I found that night after night, the work of conversion was apparently going forward; and many who had been not only careless but profligate were giving evidence of being born again ; and when I heard of large meetings during the day, and numerously attended meetings in the street for religious purposes, I felt that indeed new and strange things had come to pass ; and I could only bow my head and say, 'It is the doing of the Lord and it is marvellous in our eyes.'

"Besides the general interest which the movement as a quickening to spiritual life and earnestness, of a torpid and lifeless community presents, there are many special features of interest arising from individual cases.

" I will only add that the work seems still to be going on ; and I would earnestly entreat the prayers of all the people of God, into whose hands these details may come, on behalf of the work itself — on behalf of those who have been impressed, and those who have been brought to Christ, and on behalf of those who are carrying on the labors by which God is reviving his cause there, especially Mr. Hammond, whose labors have been most abundant, and to whose zeal, tact, perseverance and great self-denial the whole that has been accomplished, is, under God, mainly due. He came among us an unknown stranger from a distant land, though bringing with him credentials of the most satisfactory kind. He will return to his own land when his work here is finished, bearing with him the love and confidence of all who have made his acquaintance, and leaving his name embalmed in the grateful recollections of many who shall praise God through eternity that ever his feet were directed to the shores of Scotland.

I am, dear Sir,
Yours in Christian bonds,
W. LINDSAY ALEXANDER.

In the Scottish Congregational Magazine, for May, 1860, we find a very interesting report of the anniversary meetings of the Congregational Union of Scotland, at Glasgow, during which a convention was held in the City Hall, to hear addresses on the great revival then in progress. It was. Mr. Hammond's public introduction to his work. A large audience was present. Ralph Wardlaw, Esq., presided; and after speeches by Rev. Mr. Cox, of Edinburgh, and Rev. Mr. Nichol, of Rhynie, Rev. W. L. Alexander, D. D., of Edinburgh, was next introduced to the meeting. He said:

"Christian friends, the duty which I have to discharge on the present occasion is a very pleasant one, and will be very quickly discharged. I have simply to introduce to the meeting a very much esteemed brother, who is a stranger among us; who has come to us from a far distant country, in the providence of God; who has been honored to do a very great and important work in connexion with one of our churches; and who, at my suggestion and request, (which was cordially met by the local committee,) has come through to give us some account of the work of the Lord in which he has been an instrument in that place. In introducing my friend, Mr. Hammond, to the meeting, I may say, in the first place, that I look upon his visit to this country and his residence in Edinburgh, as entirely Providential. He has been brought to us without, in the first instance, intending to come to us. He was employed in New York very actively during the revival there; and about twelve months ago it was thought desirable, that he should take a voyage to this side of the Atlantic. When he left home, his intention was simply to visit this country and return; but circumstances induced him to spend the winter in Edinburgh as a student of theology. It was about the beginning of last winter that he made himself known to me. In the meantime, the brethren at Musselburgh, feeling that they had no arm of flesh to trust to, had been thrown very much upon earnest supplication that God would mercifully appear on their behalf. Just at this crisis, one day Mr. Hammond called upon me, and he said to me — 'Now that I am engaged with my studies here, that is my chief business; but I feel as if it would be necessary for my soul that I should be engaged in some kind of evangelistic work.' He had hardly uttered the words when the thought rushed across my mind — 'Here is a man sent to me for Musselburgh.' I suggested to him that there was a place which had occupied my thoughts for some time back, and that if he would go down on Sabbath day and preach to them, I thought he might revive their hearts, or, at any rate, keep the place open. He consented at once.

"What I am about to state has been found interesting to Christian people in other places, and have no doubt will be found interesting to every Christian present this evening. I will give expression to one or two feelings that have been excited in my mind with regard to the Musselburgh meeting. The first thing that struck me in going out there was the increased number of attendants. I went out upon a week evening and preached in a place where I hardly ever saw a full house upon a Sabbath day, and I found myself called upon to address a congregation that crowded the place from wall to wall, and even filled up the steps leading to the pulpit. That struck me as very remarkable. It immediately satisfied my mind that some very great work was going on there. Another thing that struck me very much was the multitude of young persons — of children, who were in the meeting, and who seemed interested in the work that was going on then and there. I may mention that before going into the meeting, I had been in the vestry, which I found quite full of children. Mr. Hammond was in the midst of them, and he must allow me to say I was struck, and it was the first time I had ever heard him speak, with the few words he said to the children and with the way in which he adapted himself to them. I found he talked as well to their understanding as to their hearts with great facility, and he showed that he possessed what I think a very happy quality, inasmuch as I do not possess it in the least myself, — when he did not seem to interest them so much by talking to them, he began to sing to them, and they joined at once in the song. I was struck, further, after I had been preaching, on going into the vestry, with the number of young lads, ragged-looking collier lads, fisher lads, and that class of young men who, from my knowledge of Musselburgh, seemed to me really almost beyond the reach of evangelistic efforts — I had a sort of feeling that they were a hopeless class altogether. There they were, however, in the room, listening with the greatest attention. When I went in they were engaged in singing. After they were done singing, the whole company went down on their knees. They had been accustomed to do so in prayer; and that was part of Mr. Hammond's system, I was going to say tactics. One of the party engaged in prayer. I looked at the man. I know him well enough; I knew him of old. He was a man who was pretty well known in the town as a very rough character indeed, and he still retains upon his outward appearance something of his original roughness. His prayer was very short; I don't think it lasted for three minutes. It was the prayer of a man who had never been taught by any human being to pray. There was not a single expression in his prayer that we are accustomed to hear in prayers. He had evidently been taught by his own meditation, and by the Spirit of God, to pray. Some of his expressions were very striking. I do not know that I ever felt so touched by a prayer as I was by that, though it was so short and simple. It was very striking, coming from a person who had never learned to pray; indeed, whose only approximation to a prayer before probably was taking his Maker's name in vain. Allow me to mention also what struck me very much — the work among the children. I confess I had something of the unbelieving state of mind upon that subject to which reference has been made. Having never come in contact myself with anything of the kind, I frankly confess I had not just the same cordial belief in the conversion of very young children as I have now. I happened, when I was out there one evening, to leave my great-coat in one of the small vestries, and feeling the night air a little chilly I thought I would put it on. When I went to the vestry door I found it bolted. I was going to retire, when the door opened, and a very little girl appeared. I asked if there was anybody in? She said — 'Yes, Sir.' Whispering, I said — 'I was going in for my great-coat, but I will not disturb you; but who is it?' She said — 'A wheen o' us lassies.' I said — 'I will not go in then; could you get me my coat?' She said — 'It's here, Sir, but I canna get up to't.' I was going away when she said — 'You might come in.' So I went in, and there I found some six or eight — I forget exactly how many — little girls like herself upon their knees, and one of them was engaged in prayer when I stepped in. Whether she had overheard us talking at the door, or supposed that some person had come in, I don't know, but her voice faltered, and she concluded very quickly. I hardly heard her; but immediately she had concluded, another girl began to pray without their rising from their knees, and a very simple, very child-like, but very beautiful prayer it was. I stood listening to that child's prayer, and the tears rushed down my cheeks as I listened; I could not help it, because I felt that I was reproved, that I had doubted the work of God in that particular, and now He had brought me face to face with the work itself. After she had concluded her little, short prayer, they rose up, and very abashed the poor little things looked when they saw I was standing in the midst of them. I began to talk to this little girl who had been engaged in prayer, and I said to her after I had reassured her a little — ' Well, now, I heard you thanking God for pardoning your sins, and for the peace of mind you have; I suppose you feel that you have been converted?' And she said — ' Yes, Sir,' with great quietness and great assurance of mind. I said — ' Now, how did that come to pass? you didn't always think of these things.' 'Oh no!' she said, 'I never cared about these things at all.' ' Well,' I said, ' just tell me how it came to pass that you did come to care about them.' She said — ' I came to the meetings, and attended them for a while, but I did not care much about what was going on. One night I went with some others into a room. There were a good many women there, and some of them were greetin' about their sins; and a lady was present who spoke to them and told them about their sins, and told them how they were to get pardon of their sins; and,' she added in her simple sort of way — ' the thought just came into my mind that I was a sinner too.' I said — ' And did you go away with that thought?' ' Yes,' she replied. I said — ' Did that grieve you?' Looking up in my face with a most earnest and striking expression, she said — ' Eh, Sir, I was in an awfu' way!' In this state she continued, she said, for a good while. I asked — ' How did you find peace of mind?' ' Oh, Sir,' she said, ' It was something that Mr. Hammond said when he was preaching.' I asked—'What gave you peace of mind?' Turning on me again the same intense and earnest look, she exclaimed—'Oh there is nothing *can* give peace of mind to the sinner but the blood that was shed on Calvary.' Now, I just put it to any experienced minister whether a statement like that does not show that this child knows the way of salvation, and affords evidence of having experienced the grace of God in truth. For my own part all my doubts and unbelieving suspicions were gone. I may just mention that, as this talk was going on, there was a little boy in the corner of the room — so little a fellow that he had just emerged from the condition of petticoats, and had not reached the dignity of a jacket; his whole costume being in one piece from his neck to his heels. He was standing in the corner of the room, and sobbing very hard. The only idea that came into my mind was that the little fellow was sleepy, and that he wanted to go away home as it was now about ten o'clock. I said to one of the girls that he was wearied, and that some one had better take him home. She said — 'Oh no, Sir, he is not wearied; he is crying for his sins.' I went to the little fellow and I spoke to him; however, he was really past speaking to. He was in a state of great distress whatever was the cause. I said to one of the girls — 'Perhaps you could speak to him better than I could;' and she said to me — 'Well, yes, Sir, I will speak to him, but he does not belong to this place.' I said — 'Indeed.' 'No,' she said, 'puir fallow, he has walked all the way frae Prestonpans to-night.' Now this was a dark wintry night, and yet this little creature had walked by himself about four miles to get to the meeting. I asked about him the last time I was out. This little girl told me that she believed he was going on in the right way, but that he did not come to Musselburgh now as there was a revival in Cockenzie in his own neighborhood. This was a very striking instance to me, and I was struck also with the manifestation of a kindly interest in him on the part of his juvenile companions. I said — ' This poor little fellow cannot go home at this time of night.' ' Oh,' says one little girl. ' I'll no let him gang hame ; I'll tak' him bame wi' me.' This struck me as like the time of the beginning of the gospel at Jerusalem, when they had all things in common, and every man received into his house those from a distance who were converted to the truth. Mr. Hammond has referred to some who went down to Musselburgh from Edinburgh. One servant girl went down, and she got into conversation with one of those little girls, or the little girl got into conversation with her, — I don't know which — and the little girl began to preach Christ to her as the Saviour of sinners, to the utter amazement and astonishment of this grown-up woman. She said to her, " Lassie, where did you learn this ? ' After a little while the little girl, to her still further astonishment, said — " If you will kneel down, I will pray with you.' And to use the woman's own words ' she just drappit doun on her knees and I couldna but gang doun too." And the little girl prayed; and the woman, strongly moved, when they rose up, exclaimed, ' Lassie, wha ever learned you to pray ? ' The child's answer was — ' Naebody learned me ; I think the Lord just pits't into me.' That was the means of that woman's conversion ; she is now one who gives evidence of being really converted."

We introduce a few of the remarks of Mr. H. in reply, because they reveal facts of interest.

" He said that, when he first commenced his labors amongst the people at Musselburgh, they were very few in number. He found also that the great mass of the people in the neighborhood were not church-going people, and though they were ready to promise to attend the church, they were too ready to break their promises. At last a few began to come out. One night a mother came to him and asked him to speak with her son, as he seemed to be very anxious about his soul. Night after night inquirers came in crowds, for a while there were few to assist in pointing inquirers to Christ. Some people came out of curiosity, and many Christian men of various denominations, who came 'to see,' remained to pray, and help on the good work. The Provost of the town, and prominent members of the various churches, felt that it was their common cause. The nightly meetings had been kept up for eight weeks, and the church had been generally well filled, and sometimes crowded. A number of people had come from a distance to attend the meetings. A most respectable lady, at a place thirty miles distant, had heard of the work at Musselburgh; and, without knowing an individual in the place, she came and took lodgings that she might attend the meetings. A request was sent in, stating that she had come so far that she might know the truth as it is in Jesus. For a number of days she was in deep distress of mind; but in the course of a week she began to have hope; and she had since written, stating she was now happy, and striving to do something for Christ amongst her neighbors. It had been delightful to see men of all denominations coming up to assist in this good work of the Lord. It was truly refreshing to get letters, from those unknown before, offering to come and preach the Word of Life to those anxious to know what they must do to be saved; and Dr. Cunningham and Prof. Smeaton, with whose advice he had undertaken the work, had manifested much interest in the movement. It was delightful to see so many from different wings of the bannered hosts of the Lord coming up to battle against the powers of darkness. In these revival times the followers of our great Captain cease to look with an evil eye upon those wearing different regimentals, and, with their faces fixed upon the banner of the cross, press forward to the victory. Mr. H. referred to the necessity of the meetings sometimes being kept till late.

Every soldier in Edinburgh Castle during a time of peace is expected to be within the gates before a given hour; but let an enemy invade the land, old rules are then set aside, and no thought is taken of the winged hours, not even if the whole night is spent in the conflict. 'This,' said he, ' is a time of invasion. The Holy Spirit has in many places been graciously poured out. The minions of darkness are alarmed and martialed in battle array; and now is the time, calmly, yet fearlessly, and trusting in Him whose right arm alone can gain the victory, to go forth to the conflict.' He repeated the words of a prominent member of the Free Church — ' Would that in all our Churches the number of those anxious for the salvation of their souls were so great, that it was necessary to remain up till midnight to point them to Jesus.' Some might call this excitement, but those who had impartially witnessed the revival in Musselburgh were convinced that it was a deep and solemn work of the Holy Spirit."

Rev. Wm. L. Gage, formerly Unitarian minister in Massachusetts, also spoke; and we here give, instead of his speech, an extract from a letter written several months later, for the Congregationalist, Boston, from a sick-room. He did much by voice and pen to prepare the way for revival labors in America:

" ' Go to Musselburgh,' said Dr. Alexander, ' and save this church, and if you succeed there, you can succeed anywhere.' Mr. Hammond went. And not only did he go, but he prospered. In only two or three weeks he had vitalized every member of the little flock and had set them to work. In a week or two more, he had revival meetings every evening, and the church was crowded. He had little or no encouragement from the other clergymen of the place, for they had never witnessed a revival before, and had no nearer view of Whitefield's preaching in the reign of George II. But, unaffected by the want of co-operation, Mr. Hammond worked on, introduced our American melodies, the unwonted sounds to those who have never listened to a more rapidly moving air than Wells, or Dundee, introduced our inquiry meetings, and our bright, sharp and prompt methods of conducting the religious services. The effect was immediate. Inquiry meetings were instituted and were thronged. In a month from the time when a special interest was awakened, a hundred felt that they had found their Saviour. He was continuing his studies at Edinburgh, preaching every night amid the excitement of a revival. For a month, the length of my stay there, I was intimate with the young evangelist. I preached for him fifteen times, and was with him under all circumstances. We often occupied the same room at night; we were together recipients of the same generous hospitalities, we communicated to each other our inmost thoughts. I was utterly unable to make his place good in a revival meeting, and the most that I could do was to stand in his stead and give him time to rest. But I had ample opportunity to study his character, and it is my deliberate conviction, that I have never met a man who was more devoted, heart, mind, soul and strength, to the cause of Christ. He was recklessly prodigal of his health. He labored without salary, and with no grounded expectation that a purse would be made up for him. He was remembered, it is true, and during my visit at Edinburgh I was charged with the delightful duty of presenting him publicly with a valuable set of theological writings, and a liberal sum was subscribed in his behalf. Mr. Hammond is by no means deficient in scholarship, nor in the lighter graces of culture. He is now a graduate of Williams College He is a young man of reading, and even of literary aspirations. But first and foremost in him is his devotion to the work of an evangelist. I write all this entirely out of his knowledge, and only from the wish that he may not meet in Boston the cold hand and unsympathizing face of misjudged prejudice, but that he may be helped by all those who wish well, I will not say to the revival system, but to a man of integrity, power, fervor, and of the most humble mind, and purest aspirations."

Rev. Wm. Arnot, of St. Peter's Church, Glasgow, remarked at the great "Presentation Meeting" in the same place a year later:

"If I understand aright the position which I have been invited to occupy this evening, the two points which I ought to touch are the work and the wages of an evangelist. I am prepared to assume fully the responsibility of dealing with these two things in their application to our present circumstances. These I count the main pillars of the cause, and on these I am ready to take my stand without faltering. . . . While I hold myself neutral on some points, I see clearly that a large portion of the people who oppose them have no ground to stand upon. When a soldier or diplomatist who has gained a name comes in their way, they are in haste to feast and honor him. Soldiers who have fought and won they feast; and, failing these, so keen is their relish for the work, that they will catch and feast a stray soldier who has neither fought nor won. Now to the two points which I count my own. And first, the work of an evangelist. Where do evangelists come from? They just cast up, and that is all that can be said about the human side of the question. On the upper side, the answer is short and easy — if they are true evangelists, they are the gifts of Christ to his weary heritage. When God intends to trouble the waters I must not, under color of order, limit him in the instruments which He shall employ. He may employ a ministering angel, or a ministering man, or a ministering child; or He may do the work by political revolutions or material earthquakes. It is not my part to determine beforehand how he ought to do it, but to wait reverently and gladly on what he has done. And after the work is done, it is not difficult even to see some of the reasons why the Head of the Church employs a stranger chiefly in such an awakening. It is dangerous to be set upon such a height of public observation as this awakening necessarily sets him on; if it is dangerous for him, a stranger, what would it have been for some of us who have for a generation been in a position of honor in the community, and who are rooted in the almost hereditary affections of large congregations? Every man must judge for himself on this point; but for my part, I gladly acquiesce in the providence of God herein, believing that I see Divine wisdom even in the incidental circumstances of the work. Consider further how much practical power and success have depended upon certain authoritative private thrusts at the conscience — probing directly the present spiritual state of the individual. He is in a better position for doing that work than I would be, or than most resident ministers. The very fact that he is a stranger increases his power in that direction. That sort of thrust is like stretching a beam over a chasm, and expecting it to bear a weight. The length of the beam lessens its strength. The shorter beam is the stronger, simply because it is short. Every stumble that a resident minister makes during a thirty years' ministry among the same people is like a knot in the wood — a place at which it will give way if he venture to lean much upon it. No doubt, an evangelist might settle down to a thirty years' ministry on the same spot, and be so kept, by God's almighty and miraculous grace, that he would not only make no weakening stumble, but that the people would not at any time take up a causeless prejudice against him. This and all things are possible with the Lord; but they are not common in the world — perhaps I may say more, they never happen. M'Cheyne had that strength, and exerted it. He spoke with authority, and spoke home. He spoke with amazing effect to the conscience in his quiet words. Would this peculiar power have been weakened if his life had been lengthened? I cannot tell; all I know is, that it was not tried. It may be, indeed, that we are on the verge of brighter days and higher attainments for the Church. I can think, with hope, of the time being near when the weakest of Israel shall be as the house of David, and the house of David as the Angel of the Lord. I am hopeful for the future; but I speak of the history of the past. We shall gladly forget the things behind, if we are carried onward and upward. Let no one fear for a moment that the recognition of this extraordinary evangelistic work supersedes the ministry. It supports the ministry in two points of view; first, it gives us more work in the way of directing the awakening and watching the converts; but, further, it will make our sermons more appreciated, and more in request. A man who has been awakened by an extemporaneous, unstudied address, does not want to sit and hear such addresses always. He has an appetite now for careful, systematic teaching; your well-prepared sermon, that went over him like water off a goose's back, now goes into him like rain into thirsty ground. I speak not only by reasoning on the nature of the case, but also by experience of the fact. Where many are awakened by miscellaneous fervent appeals, there the ordinary ministry is more needed and more valued. Although a hundred such men as Mr. Hammond were let loose on Glasgow, my occupation would not be gone. By-and-by, if they were successful, their occupation would be gone — their occupation as awakening evangelists; and if they should remain, they would require to fall into the regular methods of the ministry. I thank God for this work; and I honor the worker. And when a faithful man comes up to my side, and whispers, are you not afraid you spoil him? I answer, there is danger on that side, I am alive to it; but I must not do one evil to escape another. I should fear to offend the Lord, if I did not acknowledge his servant. Last and not least, he helped us to interest the children. I do not say that he suggested the idea, for some of us have been trying it for many years; but he has given us something new in method, and has shown us how to put life in the old method. The employment of music to enlist the sympathies and habits of children on the side of Christ has received a mighty impulse at this time — simultaneously from many evangelists. In this walk he has done a great work. If envy were lawful at all in the matter, I would envy him the place which he has been enabled to gain for Christ in the hearts of hundreds of children, and the place which he has himself in their hearts as the servant of the Lord.

And here we shall notice so far as proper respect for misapprehensions and the desire to know Mr. Hammond's position, by others is concerned, some of the objections made to his methods of advancing the kingdom of Christ. We cannot better introduce and discuss the unattractive subject, than by a quotation from Jonathan Edwards' "Thoughts on the Revival of Religion in New England, A. D., 1740." In this interesting and instructive volume, he devotes a large portion of the contents to answering the popular objections to the work of God; which are similar to those heard in all ages, and repeated whenever the Lord pours contempt upon human wisdom, and moves with Pentecostal power upon the people. While quackery, unavoidable in all science and every profession, may be condemned and opposed, and the reliance upon religious novelties and machinery deprecated, Edwards contends nobly for a just discrimination in the matter, and claims Christian confidence and sympathy for revivals and the actors in them, when the Spirit of God clearly puts his unerring seal upon both. We select number six of his topics, because it meets a common occasion of suspicious questioning now-a-days. It is, "The complaint of too much singing, and of religious meetings of children."

"We that are grown persons have defects in our prayers that are a thousand times worse in the sight of God, and are a greater confusion and more absurd nonsense in his eyes than their childish indiscretions. There is not so much difference before God, between children and grown persons, as we are ready to imagine; we are all poor, ignorant, foolish babes in his sight: our adult age does not bring us so much nearer to God as we are apt to think. God in his work has shown a remarkable regard to little children; he has been pleased in a wonderful manner to perfect praise out of the mouths of babes and sucklings. I have seen many happy effects of children's religious meetings; and God has seemed often remarkably to own them in their meetings, and really descended from heaven to be amongst them. All should take heed that they do not find fault with and despise the religion of children from an evil principle, lest they should be like the chief Priests and Scribes, who were sore displeased at the religious worship and praises of little children."

We think with this great man, that the danger is

not in seeking to bless and save, even if many are only moved by sympathy at the time; but in neglecting and repelling with an atmosphere of distance and doubt, the "little children," of whom the Master said, "Suffer them to come unto me, and forbid them not."

We quote from Dr. Griffin, of Newark, N. J., upon this touching theme, in the following descriptive sketch of a revival in that city:

"The appearance was as if a collection of waters, long suspended over the town, had fallen at once, and deluged the whole place. For several weeks the people would stay at the close of every evening service to hear some new exhortation; and it seemed impossible to persuade them to depart, until those on whose lips they hung had retired. At those seasons you might see a multitude weeping and trembling around their minister, and many others standing as astonished spectators of the scene, and beginning to tremble themselves. One Sabbath, after the second service, when I had catechized and dismissed the little children, they gathered around me, weeping, and inquiring what they should do. I know not but a hundred were in tears at once. The scene was as affecting as it was unexpected. Having prayed with them again, and spent some time in exhortation, I attempted to send them away, but with all my entreaties I could not prevail upon them to depart until night came on, and then I was obliged to go out with them, and literally force them from me."

This scene suggests another fact of late revival effort, often noticed with condemnation, at least distrust: The inquiry meeting at the close of service, sometimes at evening, continued till a late hour.

That the most favorable time for personal inquiry and appeal is at the very moment when truth is stirring the conscience and the heart, is apparent; and that the Spirit's operations, since the world began, have been without limitations of human origin, is equally clear. Order and rational thought are the only unchangeable laws of his working; meaning by order, the opposite of confusion and noisy demonstrations of feeling which are an affectation of zeal.

Dr. Griffin, Whitefield, and many others distinguished for success in winning souls to Christ, have left their testimony. And does any one doubt the assertion, that inspiration alone saves the reputation of Paul for sanity and prudence, when it is recorded of him, that, after preaching till midnight, and a young man falling from the upper window, came near to death, he cared for the sufferer, then resumed his discourse to the multitude till morning?

God teaches us in manifold ways his supreme regard for the soul of man, and his displeasure toward those who apologize, for neglect of it, by an appeal to propriety, and a quiet which leaves unmoved the masses of the impenitent on the margin of hell. The theory of a gradual and continual increase of converts and additions to the church, is beautifully calm, but was never realized to any extent and never will be, before the morning glory of the millennium floods the earth.

Speaking personally to the people, and using the press, in attracting public attention to the meetings, are also spoken against by even good people. The former is too plainly Apostolic and Scriptural, to need a defence, if only kind and courteous. The wondrous power of speech is monopolized by the world, and must be converted to Christ by his disciples again. And certainly the press belongs to God, and ought to be used for his glory, and not for man's ambition. If this be the motive and aim, no matter how freely the mighty means of good or evil, be employed in gaining the listening ear.

Edwards thus alludes to the subject:

"One thing more I would mention, which, if God should still carry on this work, would tend much to promote it; and that is, that *a history should be published* once a month, or once a fortnight, of the progress of it. It has been found by experience, that the tidings of remarkable effects of the power and grace of God in any place, tend greatly to awaken and engage the minds of persons in other places."

He further writes upon the peculiarities of a revival, and pointedly deals with a disposition to cavil and reject instrumentalities, because new and without precedent. They, that do so, "limit God where he has not limited himself; for whoever has well weighed the wonderful and mysterious methods of Divine wisdom in carrying on the work of new creation, or in the progress of the work of redemption, to this time, may easily observe that it has all along been God's manner to open new scenes and to bring forth to view things new and wonderful, such as eye had not seen nor ear heard, nor had entered into the heart of men or angels, to the astonishment of heaven and earth, not only in the revelation of the works of his mind and will, but also in the work of his hands."

Respecting the narration of Christian experience, which, in connection with a constant appeal to God's word, and intense earnestness, is one of the chief sources of power in the youthful Evangelist noticed in these pages ; Mr. Tracy, in his " Great Awakening," says:

"It is doubtless true, that there can be no infallibility with fallible judges ; and that the errors of enthusiasts have done much to bring the relation of experience into disrepute ; and that some religious men have been made ashamed to show any respect for the practice by the sneers of those, who, having no religious experience themselves, hate and despise all regard for it in others ; and that for such reasons the subject has received less attention than it deserves. * * * * *

The history of the " Great Awakening," is the history of this idea, (" the new birth ") making its way through some communities where it had fallen into comparative neglect, and through others where it was comparatively unknown ; overturning theories and habits and forms of organization inconsistent with it when it could prevail, and repelled by them when it could not."

We close this view of the instrumentalities used in the " times of refreshing," with letters and earnest words from eminent living preachers and pastors. The first is from the pen of Rev. John Henselwood, of Haddington, Scotland, the home of the celebrated Dr. John Brown, addressed to Mr. H.:

East U. P. Manse, Haddington, June 17th, 1861.
MY DEAR BROTHER;

" It may seem strange to you that you should be spoken against by any party, and especially by any party making professions of interest in the Redeemer's cause. But I presume you can scarcely be ignorant of the fact. Now, while I believe this enmity has its origin partly in hostility to an earnest and vital Christianity, and also in part, to feelings of envy, jealousy, and pride, yet, much of it arises also from other causes which are scarcely so bad. These causes are many and various, and not a few of them, I believe, orginate in ignorance and misunderstanding as to the character and motives, of your efforts and aims. Pure and *disinterested* love of souls is a thing so rare either in ministers or in any other class, that its existence can scarcely be credited; and rather than believe that any one, who professes to have such love, is sincere in his profession, men will believe almost anything else. Hence every act of such an individual is liable to be misconstrued, and his most disinterested performances are scrutinized with an eye to discover, if possible, how they may be stript of their disinterested character, and be brought down to the level of ordinary human actions—of which the predominating element is selfishness. What renders such attempts so successful, is the melancholy fact that the purest and most disinterested love of souls to be found on earth is, always at the best, impure and mixed with selfishness; so that there is generally enough, even in the best actions, to furnish a handle whereby they, who feel disposed to find it out and to use it, may rob you of any opportunity you might otherwise have, of exhibiting the power of true Christian love. How much need therefore, have we, who profess to have a disinterested love of souls, to be ever on our guard against all yielding to selfishness in any of its forms. How much need, in a word, that we be *really* and *wholly* devoted to Christ and filled with his spirit. Oh for a few — even if they were a few — men of such a stamp! They would be the harbingers of that golden age we are longing for, when the world shall be filled with *real, living, loving* Christians."

Rev. Dr. Carruthers, of Portland, uses the following language in a letter to a friend, which we are permitted to quote:

" My visit to So. Paris, was most interesting. It would be a grand movement if the adjoining villages of N. and P. Hill were, for a month, the scene of labor to Mr. H. Unitarianism and Universalism — the two main wings of Satan's army, are there so strongly entrenched, as to require some of those *shells* which he knows how to throw, in order to dislodge them. They are absolutely beyond the reach of the ordinary means of grace — and the gospel, as set forth in the ordinary discourses of the evangelical pulpit, has little of adaptation to these subtle and soul-ruinous forms of heresy. Their abettors, besides, seldom come where they can hear the truth, and hence the peculiar value of such an order of " evangelism," as shall draw them from their strongholds and compel them to hear the words of truth and soberness. Such labors as those of our honored brother are greatly needed throughout the State of Maine; and. I have little hope of its evangelization otherwise than by such *prayerful, persistent* and *peculiar* efforts. The dislike and opposition manifested towards these forms of Christian labor, are, in my mind, distinctly traceable to very different causes from those for which credit is desired; and I sincerely mourn the probable issue of such methods of treating the testimony and the work of the Holy Spirit. God grant that He may not be so grieved as entirely to withdraw his precious influences and leave this portion of his heritage to desolation, sterility and death! For myself, my family, my church, my parish, I am sincerely thankful that we were not left to look coldly on our devoted brother, and to refuse co-operation in a work fraught with such momentous consequences to so many souls. I have no doubt of the deep sincerity of not a few who refuse their sympathy with this great work — but *sincerity* is no adequate test of truth and duty — and careful inquiry and examination should, in every case, precede proscription. To their own master, however, they stand or fall. Let us be faithful to our own convictions — let us cherish the precious gift of the Holy Spirit and watch, and work, and wait in humble reliance on the promised presence and power of Him who is above all, and through all, and in you all."

We cannot omit a pleasant note from Rev. Mr. Bonar, the well-known and admired poet, whose lines are more frequently quoted, perhaps, than those of any living religious writer; feeling quite sure it will interest the reader, and inspire confidence in his friend :

Kelso, April.

" I have been following your footsteps with interest in many quarters ; and I now write to ask you to visit the borders. I would earnestly entreat you to come to our help here. This is the centre of a very populous district. Many of our villages have been visited with blessing. As yet Kelso has only received a few drops. We are waiting for the shower. Will you not come and help us? Do try. I need not use arguments. I commend the matter to God, and remain yours very faithfully in the bonds of Christ,

HORATIUS BONAR."

We feel assured that the reflective, Christian

reader, will feel that God our Saviour has sent forth a laborer into his vineyard, to do a work which will honor Him, the dust of whose chariot wheels, in his conquering marches, not unfrequently blinds the eyes of wondering beholders. He pauses not to consult the doubting friends, nor answer the scorn of unscrupulous enemies. Let his saints rejoice that he reigns and works; praying for wisdom to discern the signs of these threatening times; and for grace, whereby we may "serve God acceptably, with reverence and godly fear."

The voice of Providence and grace, to those whose great object it is to win souls to Christ, repeats the sentiment of one who had labored in the harvest of souls, with woman's love and zeal:

"The fields are white for harvest,
 The reapers they are here,
Armed with the Gospel sickle,
 The waving grain to clear.
With heart and hand united,
 Thus work this busy throng,
While o'er the fields resoundeth
 Their glorious harvest song.

"Ho! all ye Christian reapers,
 Go, labor while you may!
Into your Master's garner
 Oh! gather all the day.
He 'll bless the feeblest efforts,
 He 'll give to all their meed,
Who in his name go weeping,
 Go scatter precious seed."

CHAPTER III.

Revival in Gifford. Haddington — its historical interest, and the awakening. Mission to the West of England — Great open-air meeting at Huntly. The work in adjacent towns — Aberdeen, Dumfernline, Edinburgh, Tillicoultry. The mining district, Motherwell and Wishaw. The closing year's record.

Gifford, a farming town four miles from Haddington, was the next field of effort; meanwhile Rev. James Stewart, pastor of the Free Church, was laboring in Musselburgh. Nearly a week later, upon returning to his charge, Mr. S. found large numbers inquiring the way to the Cross. Meetings were held daily, till many of them were rejoicing in the hope of eternal life.

A call was extended to Mr. Hammond by the church in Musselburgh to settle over them as their pastor; but his heart was in the work of the Evangelist.

Six churches and five ministers of Haddington united in extending the invitation to commence a series of meetings there, and he at once accepted. For a week, they were held in the different churches.

The old cathedral where Dr. John Brown, the great expositor, and John Knox preached, seating fifteen hundred, was filled. The Holy Spirit was present, and a number were led to the Lamb of God, while Christians were refreshed, and rejoiced together in his saving presence.

An intelligent lady, daughter of an officer in the Bengal Army, who had been for years a member of a church, gives a clear narrative of her experience, at this time :

" You cannot think how much I value the privilege of being able to write to a Christian friend. For the first few days after I really thought I had found peace in the Lord Jesus, my whole soul seemed to be filled with joy and thankfulness, and I felt an utter distaste and hatred for all the worldly sins and pleasure which had formerly constituted my sole enjoyments. Oh! how I wish that I had continued in this happy state. And yet I have cause to thank my Saviour that, amid all the doubts and temptations which are continually distressing me, *I still love to pray*—which I never did in my life before. What should I do without prayer? I am often inclined to envy my sisters in thus going *straight to Christ* for salvation, instead of living for years as I have done, supposing myself to be a Christian, trusting to merit heaven through a close observance of all our church rites and ceremonies, instead of trusting *alone* to the finished work of Jesus Christ.

I have been talking much of late to my second sister, and have been praying especially for her that she may come at once to Jesus, if she could only be made to see her need of a Saviour, and that she "must be born again." Although so young, she has for some time past been a member of our church by her own desire, and yet she told me that she could not really say, *she loved Jesus*. May I ask you to join in praying for her ? It well becomes me to be deeply concerned for her; but a few weeks ago and I was in the same darkness, and quite unconscious that, notwithstanding all my professions, if I had died *then* I must have been *lost.* What can I do? *Time* is so uncertain, and *eternity* is for ever. I never rightly understood the value of a soul till now. Yes, Jesus is now indeed precious to me; I would not give some of the hours which I sometimes enjoy in his presence, for all the world has to bestow."

Soon after, he went to the south-east coast of England, Lowestoft, where a tremendous gale had destroyed about one hundred and sixty persons who were fishing on the Sabbath.

It was thought that the minds of many would be tender, and that they might be induced to give up their Sabbath-breaking. For four weeks he held meetings in towns along the coast nearly every night. Mr. Hammond wrote: "It was a mistake trying to combine the two things. Had I devoted my whole energies to the revival of religion and the conversion of souls, I think it would, though indirectly, have done more for the promotion of the better observance of the Sabbath."

We find a report of one of these meetings, from which we quote an extract, as possessing interest in respect to the Sabbath question itself:

"On Wednesday evening last, the 18th, a full meeting was held at the National School-room, Gorleston, for the purpose of promoting the better observance of the Lord's Day, and especially among the owners, masters, and men, of the fishing boats in that village. Rev. W. W. Blanford, Curate, presided. Among those present were J. Garnham, Esq., R. N., Capt. S. Smyth, R. N., Rev. E. P. Hammond, (from New York,) &c.

"The meeting commenced with singing. The verses from 12 to 21 of the 20th of Ezekiel were read, followed by a short prayer. The Chairman then introduced the business of the meeting, observing that two institutions only had been appointed in Paradise, Marriage and the Sabbath. Mr. Hammond was introduced and commenced by speaking of what had already been done in the adjoining towns. In Lowestoft and vicinity large public meetings had been held, attended by the most influential of the resident and by many of the boat-owners and fishermen; and pledges were now being circulated there, and had been signed by large numbers. In Southworld all of the boat-owners but two had given in their pledges against the Saturday night and Sunday fishing. In Pakefield and Kessingland there was almost a universal feeling in its favor. In Kessingland especially they were anxious for both nights' fishing being given up. The only excuse he found offered for Sunday fishing was that *others* practise it. This reminded him of having seen a flock of sheep leaping one after the other over the side of a steamer into the ocean and perishing. This he applied in a most solemn manner to those who, in spite of this dreadful judgment from heaven, were continuing to set at defiance the commands of God in desecrating His Holy Day, and who were thus treasuring up for themselves 'wrath against the day of wrath' — a more dreadful 'day' to such than that sad 28th of May, 1860.

"Mr. H. spoke of the physical argument in favor of making the Sabbath a day of *rest* after the toils of the *week*, even as the *night* is for rest after the labors of the *day*. This was the *divine* plan, and those who infringed the laws of nature, and especially of the decalogue, will sooner or later find themselves the losers.

"A Sabbath well spent
Brings a week of content,
And health for the toils of the morrow;
But a Sabbath profaned,
Whatsoe'er may be gained,
Is a sure forerunner of sorrow."

Mr. H. gave some interesting accounts of the great revival of religion, which he had witnessed in America, Ireland, and Scotland, and showed the influence of this work in producing the better observance of the Sabbath. *This, after all, was but a surface question. When men could be brought by the influence of the Spirit of the Lord, by thousands and tens of thousands, as it had been in the United States, to feel the heinous nature of all sin in the sight of a Holy God, and to look alone to Christ as the only ground of justification, then would the Sabbath become a joy and 'delight.'*"

"No such meetings as these would then have to be called. At a meeting in Lowestoft a fisherman, who had recently been converted to Christ, said, 'A bushel of guineas would not tempt me *now* to fish on the Sabbath.' He felt the great thing needed was the revival, or rather the introduction of real religion into each man's soul, that each should be born again, and made a new creature in Christ Jesus. Then they would value the Sabbath Day as a most blessed privilege as well as a *right*. The following is one of his illustrations in order to demonstrate the claims of the fishermen for the enjoyment of the Sabbath. I once stood in Castle Garden, at New York, and saw a weather-beaten ship, with mast and rudder gone, sails tattered and torn, being towed into the great dry dock, there to be refitted and made ready to battle again with the tempests and raging billows. What would you have thought if the officers of the harbor had given orders for the disabled bark to be towed out again to sea, and left to struggle in vain with the contending waves, and at last to sink to rise no more? Such inhuman conduct we should all condemn. But do we not, as boat owners, in passing sentence against these officers, condemn *ourselves?* What are those of our crew but weather-beaten mariners on the sea of life? And are we not even more guilty in refusing our fishermen the enjoyment of the privileges of the Sabbath, than those officers would have been had they denied that disabled ship the use of the harbor for repairs? Are we not thus depriving our men of one of the richest boons of heaven — even the God-given rights of the Sabbath as a day of rest for the weary body and the hungry soul? He concluded his interesting address by pressing them with earnest exhortations, mingled with striking illustrations, not to delay turning to the Lord. The Scriptures everywhere insisted upon immediate repentance and faith in the Saviour. His language uniformly was, "Now is the accepted time, now is the day of Salvation."

From Lowestoft, Mr. Hammond went to Huntly, in the north of Scotland, to speak in the open-air meetings, held for two days under the prtronage of the Duchess of Gordon, who expended $2000, it was stated, in defraying expenses of trains going to and returning from the grounds, and other demands upon her liberality. It was the inauguration of a series of similiar gatherings in the kingdom, attended with incalculable good. We take extracts respecting the grand convocation, from the British Herald:

"A great work of grace has been going on for a considerable period in different parts of some of the northern counties of Scotland, particularly in Aberdeenshire and Banffshire; and the assembling of 10,000 souls, at the Huntly open-air meetings in the end of July, gave to all doubters a demonstration of its genuineness and extent. Twelve months ago such a ' gathering ' for prayer and preaching would have been impossible in that district. We believe that a large proportion of the adults, composing the meetings of 25th and 26th July, were converted persons, and perhaps we should have found on inquiry that one half of these converts were not yet a year old. That assemblage proved, to the satisfaction of all impartial Christian visitors from distant parts of these and other lands, that the Lord had for some time been doing great things by the outpouring of his Holy Spirit, and that He was continuing to give " showers of blessing." The Rev. A. Moody Stuart, of Edinburgh, who took a leading part in conducting the services of these meetings, has evidently the same impression, for we find him writing to that effect in a published letter now before us, part of which runs thus : ' The great gathering in the Castle Park at Huntly, proves, by the mere presence of the congregated multitudes, that there still burns within the people an unquenched thirst for the water and the word of life, while its fruits indicate that the Spirit of God is still moving on the face of the deep, converting darkness into light and death unto life. All who, then ' heard of it at Ephratah, and found it in the field of the wood,' have returned with ' a banner given them, to be displayed for the truth,' and with the desire to stir themselves and their brethren throughout the land ' to be of good courage, and to play the men for our people and for the cities of our God.' If we go forth in Christ's name bearing his reproach, — if we ' put our trust in him and cry to God in the battle,' — then assuredly it will be written for us in the records of Israel, that ' there fell down many slain, because the war was of God.' The Lord is evidently going forth before the face of his people; and if we follow him, ' the earth will shake and the heavens will drop at his presence.'

"The forenoon of Wednesday was specially set apart for addresses to the young. The large concourse of people were formed into a sort of natural amphitheatre, in a suitable part of the park. General Anderson, of Edinburgh, presided on both days.

"A number of interesting addresses were delivered to the children; and, at the same time, a very important meeting was going on in the large tent (His Grace the Duke of Richmond's marquee,) at the entrance to the park — presided over by the Rev. A. Moody Stuart. The greater part of the spiritual impression experienced during the first day was realized there.'

"On Wednesday, the chief blessing appeared to accompany the services in the tent; but, on Thursday, the power of God seemed to rest more particularly on the services in the open-air, where 6,000 or 7,000 were assembled. The attention of the people became so riveted at the great meeting that, even when the awakened were requested to repair to the tent that they might be conversed with as on the previous day, comparatively few availed themselves of the opportunity, choosing rather to remain where they had been wounded, expecting, no doubt, that 'the power of the Lord,' which was so manifestly felt, would 'be present to heal them.' And we believe many were filled by the God of hope " with all joy and peace in believing."

"As regards outward decorum, there was nothing whatever to offend even those with whom the secondary precept — ' Let all things be done decently and in order ' — has passed into the first and great commandment of the law, and who so confine the ordinances between lines of iron as to render the apostolic injunction void by leaving no room for its application. Impartial witnesses, who took no part in the proceedings, willingly testified, that amongst the many thousands assembled, there had not been seen one disorderly person, and the hostile press is compelled to admit that the 'preaching passed off very decorously.'

"Surely when the harvest is so great, and the fields are so white, it is time for us to pray the Lord of the harvest to send forth laborers into his harvest; and each of us, sickle in hand, to say to that Lord : 'Here am I, send me.'"

Another graphic writer says :

"The cloudy aspect of the sky led many to expect that this would be a day of rain. These apprehensions, however, were soon dissipated. The sky, though overcast in the morning, was gradually illumined with the brilliance of the sun.

"At an early hour, the quiet of our street was broken ; and the sound of bustling feet played ceaselessly on the ear. As the large iron gateway of the Park swung open, Castle Street became one stream of quickly moving figures, dressed all neatly, some elegantly, but few flauntingly. The hour of meeting approached, and the avenue leading to Gordon Schools had become one surging concourse of men, women, and children. Every street poured its tributary bands into the heaving crowd that wound its way to the rendezvous. The sight was really one of grandeur. All moved along in dense masses or long drawn out columns : eager as crowds ever are, but serious as crowds rarely are. Then mark the centre to which all are tending — the simple declaration of a truth older than our nation, more familiar than our fireside legends, more repugnant to the unregenerate heart than any figment of the vast cycle of universal truth ; but yet, when appropriately displayed, more potent to fascinate and mould than any metaphysical principles or philosophic codes; a truth more fitted to enthral than any system of beauty or grace that can enlighten the reason, or sparkle its brilliance in the imagination of man.

"Many motives swayed the multitude. They could be read in the varied countenances as they swept onwards — the jesting leer looking out from the eye, the sportive play of fancy beaming on the face, the quiescent repose of the features, or the troubled cloud that hung on the brow. But their centre was one. It was a triumph of the unseen over the visible; a victory of the spiritual over the secular. The innate majesty of truth was divesting itself of the trappings of conventionality. The gospel was ridding itself of the incrustation of ceremony that dulls its radiance and dims its effulgent lustre. The ornate furnishing of church or chapel were for a time disused, and man worshipped his God in the temple of his own uprearing. He knelt on his velvet sward, beneath the lofty archway of the sky. Yesterday's meeting had evidently been effective. The concourse was denser — the air of anticipation was deeper. Yesterday, the gala-day aspect of the crowd was sometimes painful; to-day, it was blended with the seriousness of the Sabbath."

As a farther result of the meetings — the tide of feeling setting back into the sourrounding towns— night after night, the people in Portsoy, Banff, and adjacent places, the masses assembled, and remained for inquiry hours together. At Skeine, Aberdeen, and Perth, in the open air, immense gatherings were addressed by various c ergymen, and hundreds it is believed, were savingly touched by the power of truth wielded by the Holy Spirit. "It was a glorious sight to see so vast a multitude evidently moved by the divine influence."

In one of the large churches of Aberdeen, crowded to its utmost capacity, after an earnest appeal, the expressions of anxiety were so general and thrilling, that one of the elders standing in the porch, called Mr. H. to the door and said the congregation must be dispersed — he didn't want such excitement. But the people would not go till they were driven away, and flocked to another temple where an inquiry meeting was in progress, and enjoyed an awful, yet glorious and memorable season.

None can estimate the number of hopeful conversions during these various meetings; but many living Christians were added to the churches, and the "outlying masses," carried with them to their scattered homes, the precious seed of the kingdom.

The next call to a harvest-field, was from Dunfermline, the birth place of Charles I., in Rev. Mr. Young's church, an edifice holding 2000 people, where Ralph Erskine and George Whitefield preached a hundred years before. Here is the "Auld Cathedral" and Abby of Dunfermline, built nine hundred years since; and here rest the ashes of Robert Bruce, the Hero in the battle of Bannockburn.

Although interesting thus in historical associations, it was a field thirsting for the rain of grace. The spacious temple was soon filled, and the baptism from above fell upon the multitude. On one occasion, we notice in the Dunfermline Press, of Sept. 10th, 1860, that

"Rev. Mr. Hutchinson said he had come to the meeting merely as a listener, but as he had been called upon to speak, he would only say a very few words. Some people appeared to be of opinion that these meetings were out of the way and unnecessary, and to correct this he would just give a few reasons why he considered these periods of revival as beneficial. Many thought the effect was merely passing — in a few weeks it would wear away, but he had the best of all testimony — the testimony of experience — for saying that such was not the case. His first impressions of religion had been received at a revival meeting. Seventeen years ago, induced by the excitement caused by the meetings, he had attended one, and it was there that he was first awakened to a true sense of his condition as a lost sinner. To show them that this was not a transient emotion, he might tell them that thirty-seven young men like him had also been impressed, and had met together for prayer and religious exercise. He had lost sight of five of these, but of the remaining thirty-two he could report favorably. Not one of these had fallen away from their first hope. Some of them had died " the death of the righteous," while the others were, like himself, doing their best to live up to their profession. So much for the testimony of *experience.* But he had another cause for believing in the utility of these revival meetings, and that was founded upon *reason.* He looked on revivals as a variety in God's mode of promoting our spiritual culture. God ever works by the most varied means. Let them look at nature. There was a time in nature for the silent dew, and a time for the influence of the genial sunshine, and there was also a time for the raging storm. So it was also with regard to religion. There was a time for the ordinary preaching of the Word; a time for instruction, for meditation, and Christian action; and there were also seasons for arousing, elevating, and refreshing feeling. And his intellect convinced him that a genuine revival was such a time. It was a flood-time in our spiritual experience, which, if embraced, might contribute much to the richness and variety of our religious life. In order, however, to accomplish this end, it must be real, it must affect the whole intellectual and moral nature — filling and animating the whole soul with the glorious verities of religion."

During an inquiry meeting, as Mr. H. was passing down the aisle, a man put out his hand, and said with great earnestness, " have you any word for an anxious sinner? I have opposed the work going on, and thought the people were getting daft, (mad), and I would have nothing to do with it. But one night my little girl came home and inquired of me, ' Father, do you love Jesus? I think I love him.' That was the greatest sermon I ever heard. Though I had heard many, nothing pierced my heart like it. I have staid away three days in distress, and have come to ask what I shall do to be saved." He soon found peace in believing, and put up his domestic altar; the result, under God, of an angel daughter's ministry of sanctified affection.

Before the large edifice in which meetings were held was filled, the Evangelist went to the Cross, the central place of concourse, and addressing the people, invited them to the house of God. Rev. Mr. Young, and several theological students, followed the example. On one occasion a notorious infidel threatened violence if this were attempted near him. While Mr. Young was preaching, he was smitten down like Saul, and soon after stood up and told the story of his deliverance from the bondage of sin; a witness to the necessity and divine approval of aggressive movements by the Church of

Christ, even if they bear the stamp of novelty — the tactics of a consecrated and prayerful zeal in the salvation of men.

Subsequently Rev. Mr. Young wrote to a friend:

"You will be glad to hear that the work of the Lord is going on prosperously here. On Sabbath evening the house was filled from floor to ceiling. The numbers who remained to be spoken with, also increase, and many do seem to be seeking the way of salvation. We have many adversaries, but the Lord is with us, and we need not fear what men shall do."

Not a few earnest Christians had long been praying for the Holy Spirit's presence, and thus this ancient city received the seal of God's blessing upon that Gospel, which has made Scotland a name and praise in the earth.

In Kircalde, Montrose, Dunbar, Crieff and Brechin, very large assemblies were addressed, and sinners awakened and saved in that brief period of special effort.

Oct. 8, 1860, Mr. H. went to Edinburgh, to supply the pulpit of Richmond Place Chapel for four weeks, and addressed meetings every night during that time, with an increasing measure of the Spirit's influence. Many from all denominations flocked to Christ. Dr. Alexander, Reginald Radcliffe, Richard Weaver and others addressed the meetings. The Edinburgh Mercury says:

"On Monday evening, Richard Weaver was advertised to preach in Richmond Place Chapel at eight o'clock; but before seven o'clock the house was filled, and the services were conducted for an hour by Mr. Hammond. At eight o'clock, Messrs. Weaver and Radcliffe entered, and Mr. H. was asked by them to go outside and preach to the thousands crowding the streets before the chapel. There was such a crush, however, that the only way he could get out was the novel one of walking upon the shoulders of the stalwart men, who compelled him to do so, and who stood like a rock under him, so eager were they to let him get to preach to their less fortunate friends outside. After Mr. Weaver had preached for about half-an-hour, he preached again outside, and Mr. Radcliffe continued the service in the chapel. There were eighteen hundred crushed into the place, and hundreds remained for conversation; while the preaching was going on in the streets until past eleven o'clock. As an opportunity had been given at the morning meeting in the same chapel for any one to speak or pray, a speaker said, that a few nights before, when the invitation had been given both for those who were anxious and those who were not anxious, but who might desire conversation, to remain, there were two among the latter who embraced the opportunity. The conversation with those who professed to have no anxiety for the salvation of their souls was blessed of God in producing a deep conviction of their lost condition, and he trusted they were now striving to live for Jesus. He believed that good impressions were often lost from the want of a more cordial invitation to remain for personal conversation and special prayer. Another gentleman said, that the previous night a young lady was passing from the meeting unimpressed by the words of the minister. While passing out, she was asked kindly if she was in the 'ark,' referring to what had been the subject. That simple question was the first arrow that had ever pierced her heart, and was the instrument in awakening her to a sense of her lost condition. She found little sleep that night. Afterwards she said, 'I have been a member of a church seven years in Edinburgh, but those were the first words that ever manifested any interest about my soul.' The same speaker said that in Dundee, at the close of a large meeting, it was requested that if there were any scoffers present they would remain in a part of the house designated. A number of professed scoffers remained. The first one when asked if he was a scoffer, said, with tears in his eyes, 'I came here one, but am not so now;' and, said the speaker, every one of those professed scoffers was smitten with a deep sense of guilt.

"Such things as the following are spoken of as taking place there nightly: — A lady, on the way to the chapel, spoke to a young woman on the street and invited her to come to the meeting. She did so; and, as Mr. Hammond was describing sin with great impressiveness, the young woman began to weep very bitterly, and continued inconsolable after the meeting was closed. She had been in agony for a great part of the night; but she appeared at the next morning prayer-meeting with a beaming countenance, having found 'peace in believing.' This prayer-meeting is held from half past nine to ten o'clock every morning. It is on the model of the Fulton Street prayer-meeting, New York — an open meeting. Three addresses, one reading of the Scriptures, three singings, and five requests for prayer are read and commented on, and three or four prayers offered, all in the space of half an hour!"

Tillicoultry, a village of four or five thousand inhabitants, under the shadow of the Achil range of mountains, was the scene of a rich effusion of the quickening Spirit. We cannot omit just at this point, a quotation from a letter written to his mother by Mr. Hammond, after visiting one of these summits:

"I ascended the mountain yesterday, and a grander sight I scarcely saw in all Switzerland. No scene hardly ever made a greater and more suggestive impression on my mind. It would take pages to describe it all to you, and to speak of the thoughts suggested. I thought of you, dearest mother, and the time when I should meet you in the promised land, away from lifes sorrows. When near the middle of the mountain, a cloud of beautiful mist rested on its snow-white summit, and another cloud below us shut out the sight of the smoky village. Time seemed to be no more, and we were gazing away to the delectable mountains and to the golden city. Oh, mother, we shall meet above, and we shall see our blessed Jesus there, who was a 'man of sorrows' here on earth' and acquainted with grief.' Let us rejoice to know that even now he sympathizes with us, that He is 'touched with the feeling of our infirmities.' One hundred anxious inquirers remained for conversation here last night."

The daily services in Tillicoultry commenced Nov. 16th, under the influence of all the evangelical denominations. One of the clergymen thus writes for a Glasgow paper:

"For some months past we have met together in a union prayer-meeting, to seek a revival of grace among Christians, and a breaking forth of saving inquiry among the unconverted. All the ministers of the place have taken part, and presided in rotation at these meetings. The deadness of the spirit and prayers of the meeting for a time showed how much we needed to be revived. We at last invited Mr. Hammond, who has been laboring in revival work for some months past in our country, and who had given us a flying visit for one evening, to come and labor among us for a few nights. He came; the Lord owned his labors, and he spent a precious week with us. The meetings in the Popular Institute Hall grew in numbers to the last, and on Sabbath evening last about 1400 were present. At the close of the address each evening, there was a second meeting, called 'The Inquiry Meeting.' Toward the close of the week from 200 to 300 waited to it; numbers of them were deeply convinced of sin, and waited to be guided to the Saviour; numbers, were Christians, who waited to direct the anxious to Christ; numbers waited through mere curiosity to see what was to be done; and a few waited to mock.

" Prayer-meetings among the boys by themselves, and among the girls by themselves, have sprung spontaneously up in some of the factories. False professors of Christianity are breaking down. Unconverted communicants in churches are among the inquirers, confessing themselves yet unsaved. There is no striking down, nor any development whatever of hysteric excitement; all is deep and quiet and orderly among the awakened. The Christians are laboring in season and out of season. It is fatiguing to lose sleep, and to be exposed to numerous inconveniences, but let us not seek our own, but every man the things of others; let this self-sacrificing Spirit of the Lord be in us, who, though he was rich, yet for our sakes became poor, that we through his poverty might be made rich. Let us understand and love these lines of R. C. Trench: —

> ' The seed must *die* before the corn appears
> Out of the ground, with blade and fruitful ears.
> *Low* must these ears by sickle's edge *be lain*,
> Ere we can treasure up the golden grain.
> The grain is *crushed* before the bread is made,
> And the bread *broke* e'er life to man conveyed.
> Oh! be content to *die* and be *laid low*,
> And to be *crushed*, and to be *broken so*,
> If thou upon God's table mayest be bread,
> Life-giving food for souls an hungered.'

" It is delightful to see some of our most influential men and ladies working side by side with the humblest Christian in the inquiry meeting. It mightily shuts the mouth of prejudice, and comes to the help of the Lord."

Meetings of a similar kind were held in Linlithgow, the old residence of the Kings of Scotland; and a number were redeemed to become eternally "kings and priests unto God."

At Motherwell and Wishaw, about twenty miles from Glasgow, in the great coal region of Scotland, followed rich displays of the Holy Spirit's victorious might. Strong men bowed before his presence, and declared, in the great congregation, what God had wrought in their behalf, with tears and hearts aglow with the new life "hid with Christ in God"

The Edinburgh Mercury contained a report respecting the character of the awakening there, from which we take a few extracts:

"At a meeting held in Richmond Place Chapel, Edinburgh, on Monday night, some statements of a very interesting kind were made regarding the awakening in Wishaw and Motherwell. After a speaker, who had been there a fortnight ago, had given a statement of what he had seen in these places of the commencement of the work of revival, the Rev. William Reid was asked to address the meeting. He began by saying that he could, from his own personal knowledge, confirm all that had just been said about the wonderful awakening that was going on in the mining districts referred to. He had been at Motherwell some time ago, and had spoken to a full church on a week evening; and had seen many there who had been not only greatly reformed and rendered sober and serious, but who were hopefully converted. With regard to Wishaw, he had been there last Sabbath, and he had seldom seen anything like the intense religious anxiety manifested by the multitude, which assembled to hear the word in the evening in the public school.

They seemed to hear of the *living water* like men dying of thirst; and many of them came to Jesus and drank. The building in which they sat was filled to overflowing, long before the hour for commencing the services, and many returned home who could not get admittance, while some hundreds were contented with standing-room during the whole evening. At the close of the regular service, about three hundred remained for the inquirers meeting, and about one-half of them seemed to be awakened, and to be the subjects of spiritual anxiety. Men were dealt with in one room by themselves, and women in another room; and even when nearly three hours had elapsed the cases of awakening had not been all attended to. It was not only the poor and illiterate that had been affected, but men and women of education and superior circumstances. He had seen nothing like the religious anxieties he then witnessed, since the visit of Messrs. Radcliffe and Weaver to this city; and he could not but thank God, from the bottom of his heart, for the indefatigable labors of his brother, Mr. Hammond, through whose instrumentality this great awakening had taken place. His services are most valuable. Every man has his own gift and work; and Mr. H., he believed, was specially fitted for breaking up the fallow ground, and commencing a series of revival meetings."

A well-known physician furnished an example in his own experience, of striking conversion. For twenty years he had been a professor of religion, joining the church in accordance with a custom in Scotland, which the Rev. James Smith of the establishment, in Aberdeen, so pointedly condemns; that of receiving persons to the communion upon profession of an orthodox, instead of a saving acquaintance with Christ. Mr. S. thinks half of the cases of conversion in the revivals, were connected with the churches.

Dr. M. was at first bitterly hostile to the measures, and severely rebuked his servants for remaining to a late hour at the services. Soon after, from curiosity, he went, and was urged by a friend to remain with him to the meeting for inquiry. He refused, adding, "the place was too hot for him." But meeting Mr. H. in the street, not well, he proposed kindly to prescribe, a pretext to open the way for personal conversation.

Upon entering his parlor, the Cross was presented, but his proud heart rebelled. He was willing to send to London for books to read,— would do anything himself,— like the Assyrian when bidden to wash in Jordan. With a gentle pressure of the hand, he was urged to bow and submit to Christ at once. He yielded, and as he expressed it, "closed with Jesus that hour." A few evenings later, with his wife happy in the smiles of the Lord, he was pointing the anxious to Calvary; leaving the sanctuary at midnight, often, in his self-forgetful zeal; and afterward went abroad preaching the word.

The Glasgow Herald contained the clear, sharp answer below to criticisms upon the "religious excitement:"

"*Wishaw, April* 17, 1861.

'Sir,— Your correspondent 'Imprimatur,' in the *Herald* of to-day, expresses his astonishment that you have not raised your warning voice against the 'dangerous and immoral tendencies of so-called revival meetings.' I suppose he means those held in Glasgow. I hope, Sir, you will believe me that I am equally surprised, that you have of late opened your columns to a one-sided view of this great movement; and would not have troubled you with any remarks on the matter, had your correspondent from Inveraray yesterday, and 'Imprimatur' to-day, given the public the least hint, that they knew anything of the movement at all, its designs and results. I beg to inform them that I live in the midst of a large mining population, which was visited by Mr. Hammond five months ago. When it was announced that he was to hold revival meetings, I determined to make myself judge of the whole matter, and attended nearly all the meetings he held in this place, and fully expected to have heard terrorism in all its force evaporated from him; but, instead of this, it was completely the reverse; not a word was spoken of an alarming nature that was not quoted from the words of Jesus himself. I kept a strict watch on all I saw, and found nothing to alarm or disturb even the most fastidious. All was solemnity, and quite in unison with the circumstances of the people assembled. And now that the movement is five months old in this place, one would be led to believe, from the remarks of 'Imprimatur,' that the bad effects of these meetings would be telling upon the community, and the 'young females' in particular. I am proud to say, that no such cases have occurred in all the circle of my acquaintance with the movement; and I am apt to believe, that your correspondent resembles much those so-called Christians, who deny the right of any person to meet for prayer after sunset, but who would frankly and freely give accommodation to parties of young men and women to meet in their rooms, barns,

&c., to drink, dance, and sing *till morning*. On the contrary, I can point to men, both rich and poor, in this locality, who, previous to these meetings, were infidels, scoffers, drunkards, swearers, wife-beaters, &c., and who have now become regular church-goers — sober, industrious, and good members of the community. And, with regard to the invitations that are spoken of by your correspondent, such as 'Come to Jesus,' I must say it is better to hear a company of men and women calling upon one another in this manner, than inviting one another to the dram-shop. And, as an instance of what has occurred in this place on the pay night at some of the public works, instead of men entreating one another to go and drink their wages after they get them, they go in bands and pray together till midnight; and if these meetings have been the means of making happy one fireside, they certainly should 'Imprimatur' also. I hope that your correspondent, who assumes this name, will seriously look into the whole case, before he solicits you to warn the public from attending meetings which have no other object in view, than to make them followers of the meek and lowly Jesus, and good moral subjects of our beloved Queen.

I am, &c.,

AUDI ALTERAM PARTEM."

In Mr. H's first memorandum of the New Year, he writes : " It is safe to record, that after careful calculation, about seventeen hundred profess to have been awakened and found Jesus, within the past year. Many more have been led to ask the great question, ' What shall I do to be saved ? ' and how many of these have since found peace, the judgment day alone can determine. May the Lord ever lead me to feel my own nothingness and Christ's fullness, and to remember that it is not by might, nor by power of man, but by my Spirit, saith the Lord.'"

How true the words of Dr. Bonar,

" He liveth long who liveth well,
   All outer life is short and vain,
He liveth longest who can tell
   Of living most for heavenly gain.

Waste not thy being ; back to Him,
   Who freely gave it, freely give,
Else is that being but a dream,
   'Tis but to *be*, and not to live."

CHAPTER IV.

The work of God in Annan. Testimony for a secular paper. Rev. Mr. Gardiner of the established Church. Other statements and incidents. The work extends to Dumfries. Its progress. Stirring scenes and incidents. The Soldier. The Infidel. The means of success in winning souls.

January 13th, 1861, in Annan, a pleasant town in the south of Scotland, on Solway Firth, containing a few thousand inhabitants, but a centre of business importance, daily services were commenced. The clergy united in the holy enterprize warmly and devotedly.

The Dumfries Standard makes the following record:

"The meetings have been crowded to excess, many having been forced to go away from want of room, while three to four hundred people have remained after ten o'clock, and been occupied until midnight, in receiving spiritual assistance. Scores of persons who had never before seriously thought of death, judgment, and eternity, have, with tears in their eyes, remained at the inquiry meetings, and conversed most anxiously about the state of their souls. The aspect of the town has, in consequence of this revival, been completely changed. It is not now on matters of amusement or business that the conversation turns. Every one talks of the great religious change, and wonders now that so much scepticism about the revival in

Ulster and the West of Scotland had before prevailed among the inhabitants of Annan. Many young sailors, who had scarcely ever attended a place of worship, have been brought to a knowledge of their Saviour; many a drunkard has deserted the public-house in horror of his previous life; the artisans of the town have abandoned the corners where they lounged in the evenings, and have betaken themselves to prayer and meditation; and even 'the Arabs' of the burgh, the boys who were for ever shouting and yelling about the streets, have every evening been engaged in singing psalms and hymns. The week has also been a busy one with the ministers of the town, who, not content with the spiritual comfort they afforded to the anxious during the inquiry meetings, have been engaged during the day in calling on those who are the most distressed about their souls salvation. Many souls seem to have found 'perfect peace.' The young of both sexes have shared most largely in the blessing — though grown-up persons, and even aged men and women, and in some instances husbands and wives together, have publicly inquired after, sought, and found the Saviour. It is a season of great joy to all the Lord's people in Annan. The blending of hearts in Christian love is amazing to behold in so short a time.

"All the usual features of deep religious awakenings elsewhere are strongly marked here, with the exception of 'prostrations' and extravagances, for which praise is due to God. During the addresses, solemn earnest attention is the only feature visible on the audience, but when the public meeting is over, and the ministers and other Christian friends move among the anxious from pew to pew, the power of God's truth in convincing of sin is manifest; and, to an onlooker who has a heart to sympathize with the work of saving conversion to Christ, nothing can possibly be more solemnising, than to see throughout all the church, on ground-floor and galleries, groups in earnest close conversation on the great concerns of their soul;

and by and by the groups kneeling, or, if too crowded, their heads bowed on the book-boards, when prayer is made to God on their behalf. An avowed infidel, who came several miles to see and scoff, was convicted and converted the same night. Several young men have publicly professed their faith in Jesus, and have given an intelligent account of their change of heart. The public mind is deeply moved. A solemn awe seems to hang over the whole community. Scoffers there still are, and likely will be; but many who warmly opposed at first now more warmly approve. The prayers of God's people are asked for Annan."

Rev. Mr. Gardiner, of the United Presbyterian Church, at a meeting of Synod in May, 1861, four months later remarked:

" Having adopted the recommendation of the Liverpool Conference of the Evangelical Alliance, to hold a week of special prayer for the revival of vital godliness, the week commencing on the 6th and closing on the 13th January of the present year, they found the nightly meetings well attended, and a peculiarly solemn spirit pervading them during the entire week. The way of the Lord being thus prepared, so to speak, Edward Payson Hammond, who was previously little known to any of them, even by report, began his labors among them as an Evangelist on Sabbath, 13th January, and succeeded in inducing a goodly number to remain for conversation on the concerns of the soul after the regular service was over. At this meeting a few were found to be in a state of anxiety, while the greater proportion were present probably from motives of mere curiosity. The movement thus inaugurated gathered strength night after night, from that date, with a rapidity truly surprising, and continues in vigorous action to the present time. Crowds flocked to Annan, from ten or twelve parishes around, for spiritual benefit, and usually remained to a late hour. Many, very many, after passing through a longer or shorter period of soul-conflict, gladly received the Word, and returned to their homes as in primitive times to tell what God had done for their souls, thereby widening and deepening the interest in the work, and prompting others to utter the earnest cry, 'What must we do to be saved?' insomuch that within less than a month the awakening might be said to have embraced the whole of the south of Scotland. All classes of persons, too, were brought under the blessed influence — the young and the old, church-goers and church-neglectors, masters and men, ladies and maids — all were equally stirred to the very depths of their nature, and were to be found sitting side by side in the inquiry meetings, directing or being directed to 'The Lamb of God that taketh away the sin of the world.' A kindly Christian sympathy took possession of all hearts, rendering the people oblivious of class distinctions, and causing them to realize their common brotherhood in nature and in grace. Nor was any particular view of their state before God peculiar to any one class of the awakened. In each class some were affected by an awful consciousness of their spiritual death, others by a sense of their guilt as rebels against God, and others by a perception of the danger to which they were exposed on account of their continued unbelief of the truth; while probably the larger number were deeply penetrated with godly sorrow for their gospel-hardened insensibility to the great and unparalleled love of the Lord Jesus. The Rev. gentleman then bore testimony to the beneficial effects of the revival on the morals of the people. Total abstainers, themselves being judges, testified that no agency ever employed has effected a tithe of the good, in the direction of sobriety and temperance, that the revival has accomplished — and accomplished, too, without, or almost without, any reference to this particular sin. Of the number who have been hopefully converted to God, in and around Annan, during this season of refreshing, he could form no correct estimate; but he believed he was understating the truth when he said, that he had himself conversed with upwards of five hundred anxious inquirers, the great majority of whom professed to have 'believed with the heart unto righteousness,' and who, with a single exception, are giving evidence of a saving change, by bringing forth the fruits of the Spirit in an eminent degree. He might just be allowed to add, that all who had visited them had been pleased to bear a unanimous testimony to the thoroughness of the work in Annan."

The testimony of Rev. Mr. Gardiner, of the Established Church, is very emphatic:

" Living in that little town, which has been so conspicuously the scene of revival, himself engaged in much of that work, likewise intimately associated with those who have been (under the hand of God) the most prominent agents in the movement there, revival was to him a grand spiritual reality, an incontestible fact. Holding these convictions, and warm from the influences of this reviving religious life, he had come to Glasgow, where a similar work was positively going forward. But, when inquiring with intelligent curiosity respecting it, what was his surprise to find that, in many circles of society, it was still the subject of cavil, and denial? It was a disclosure of how tenacious we are in this country of the hereditary and traditional, and of the distrustfulness with which we regard anything approaching innovation, though that should be nothing else than the outcoming of the requirements of progress. Mr. Gardiner went on to say that in some quarters, to his great surprise, he had found it even painful defending revivals here, and that were he to accept of the exaggerated accounts which he found circulating, he would have been led to think that all who were interested in these meetings, the audiences not less than the leaders of the services, were little short of fools and madmen. Leaving these prejudices, which he believed would disappear in this city as they had done elsewhere, he could with more pleasure speak of what had taken place in Annan. There, no longer any doubt was expressed regarding the veritable work of the Spirit. The effects of its operations were so apparent, that they had an existing witness in the changed lives of many, the full churches, and the eagerness for religious instruction, and the cordiality subsisting now between class and class. For two years previous they had weekly prayer-meetings, and many other additional instrumentalities, eagerly desiring to obtain heaven's blessing upon a town which seemed so dead. All that time the heavens appeared as brass above them. One minister visited Ireland during the great revival, to bring home intelligence of the doings there. Still there was no visible change, though perhaps these recitals awakened expectation. These were the needful preparations, he believed; but true revival came to Annan with Mr. Hammond's visit there. From a chill, dreary wilderness, it was now vernal as a garden in spring. The good fellowship that now subsisted among the different bodies of Christians, the willingness to leave minor differences in abeyance, and heartily co-operate in the advancement of the chief duty of winning souls to Christ, were in themselves blessings which he hoped would long continue to mark the religious life in Annan, and were some of the means which were most likely to promote spiritual advancement. It would be well for Christians to concentrate their minds on God's work, and cease to prescribe its conditions, since we were seeing in every quarter that, irrespective of our preferences and pre-conceived notions, the work was begun and carried on, and countless souls the while redeemed from death to life. He might further state that, in many of the churches in the neighborhood, and in most instances where the ministers of these different places had taken no interest in the revival, revival had in measure reached them through the visits and the intercourse which their people had had with the awakened people of Annan."

The Rev. Mr. Young, Independent, contributed to the papers of the Congregational Union, the following :

"Of the number of conversions I can form no sort of estimate. They are of all churches, ranks, and ages. Leading men in the town have taken, and are still taking, a deep interest in the work. The young have been most abundantly blessed. Three days ago, I observed to an intelligent Christian friend, ' It really seems as if *all* the young men were converted.' He gave a cordial assent, and added that the same might be said of the young women. Of course, I am far from believing that this is literally true of either class. Doubtless there are many of the young, as well as of the old, who are unsaved still ; but I am safe in saying that the number of the saved is very large indeed. That the Lord may still enlarge it is our earnest prayer ; it is also what we anticipate.

"Requests for prayer in special cases have been very numerous. I find that I have in my possession about one hundred and twenty, and these are not nearly the whole. Most striking have been some of the answers. On one Thursday evening, a Christian husband asked us to pray for his wife and two sons. The former was then, and had been for years, an inveterate opponent. Yet only two nights after the husband could request us to give God thanks because his wife and one son had been converted! One other case I may give. A thoughtless, though amiable young man, was one evening specially prayed for. He was not at the meeting ; yet about the time that the petition was being presented, the Lord deeply convinced him of sin ; before next night he had peace in believing, and on the second night he was earnestly seeking the salvation of others ! He still goes on well. Other cases, almost as noted, have rebuked our unbelief, and have shown that if God's people will only trust him, he will do 'exceeding abundantly above all that we ask or think.'

" Very blessed has been the work among the children, and especially among such as had been under Sabbath school instruction. There is ample evidence already — and the evidence, we hope, will accumulate — that not a few of the scholars have passed from death unto life.

" As the work was in all the churches, I should be sorry to speak as if it had any peculiar connexion with one of them. It has not. Yet with deep gratitude I have to say, that our own congregation have received large blessings, that our church members have taken at the very least their full share of directing inquirers, that they have sacrificed much in order to come to the meetings, and that in blessings bestowed upon themselves and upon their families, their large sacrifices have been amply repaid. To one thing I would ask special attention. It has been where, in time or money, the largest sacrifices have been made that the largest amount of blessings have been received.

"I have said nothing of the Sabbath meetings in our own place of worship. These have been such times of refreshing as I never expected to have seen. Sermons have not been required, and would have been quite unseasonable. Thanksgiving for the general awakening, and for blessings to families and individuals — brief, pointed exhortations, obviously coming from the heart, and eliciting from other hearts an earnest response — the observance of the ordinance of the Supper with a deeper feeling of humility and thankfulness than we had ever before been able to cherish — conversation with inquirers at the close, and finding that under some brief address or during the conversation souls have been saved — much fervent prayer for the continued progress of the work — this gives only a faint idea of what our Sabbath meetings have been. Often before have we had special reasons for thanksgiving. To the praise of divine grace we acknowledge, that even in times past the Lord has given us numerous cases of conversion. But now, even in our own congregation, they are far more numerous; and we are only the more thankful as we think that, as to conversions at least, other congregations have shared still more largely in the blessing. A writer in the *Dumfries Standard*, writing of the revival here, says very truly, 'Members and adherents of the various churches, who had borne the character of virtuous and religious, among whom are not a few of the principal inhabitants of the town and neighborhood, have not been ashamed to stay for the inquiry meetings, with a view to be conversed with and prayed with. Many of the worst and hopelessly godless characters of the town, who were never known to think about or care for their souls, are in nightly attendance. Several of them have been deeply moved, and some of them, it is believed, hopefully converted. The union of Christian hearts is also very marked.'

"Since writing the above, I have spoken with a Christian brother as to the probable number of converts. He shares in my opinion that it is impossible to number them; but he is firmly persuaded that they amount to some hundreds; and the *data* which he and other brethren have supplied are such as to show that in the town and in the country the number of conversions is indeed very large. 'What hath God wrought!'"

Rev. George Gailey, of the Free Church, at the meeting of the General Assembly, in May, 1861, said:

"We did not seek in any way to get up a revival in Annan. I was greatly struck with a remark I saw in a letter in the *Witness*, that revivals never come up, that true revivals always come down. Some of the most delightful cases we have had were the result of the inquiry meeting. Some who came that night did so from mere curiosity, and one came merely to scoff. Mr. Hammond's words went as an arrow to the heart of two of those to whom I now refer, occupying a high and social position in Annan. They were brought to a knowledge of the truth, and took an important place in leading the movement from that time till this. The first persons spoken to were a husband and wife, two of my own church members. They were professing Christians, in full membership with the church, and bearing openly a religious character. Mr. Hammond's words awakened them both ; they never felt sin before ; they never had been convinced of sin before. The arrow of conviction went to their hearts. I have seen that couple, as I have seen many other couples, coming night after night, sitting together side by side, hand in hand, praying with and for each other, to be conversed with by any Christian minister or Christian brother who might direct them in the way of peace and God, ceasing not to attend, ceasing not to seek till they both became new creatures in Christ Jesus. I have seen case after case of that kind. Oh ! the blessed work we had, from pew to pew in our anxious meeting, is just the work we have to do from the pulpit ! We have no other gospel to preach, no other thing to say ; only, we come into close quarters with them, meeting this difficulty, and answering that question ; and sometimes the simplest word that a child could understand would be just the word the anxious one wants, and the eyes are opened and the soul gets its enlargement. I was going to speak of an aged man who was called on to tell what the Lord had done for him. Here was my old friend sitting under the pulpit for seven or eight years, and if I had been asked to point out one of the truly Christian members of my Church, I would have named him among them — a man who was never absent from the Lord's table. I have had conversation after conversation with him, and it was a case of being born again ; it was his first saving conversion to the Lord Jesus. And oh! he is a delightful specimen; and God has given him his whole family. One of his daughters — he is a man in humble life — carries joy on her very countenance. In passing your eye over the multitude in the gallery, you could not pass her face when you came to it, without seeing the ray of heavenly light there. I was called on unexpectedly to be present at the coffining of a child. When waiting for the coffin to come in, as usual I was speaking very personally to those present, trying to improve the event. I was pointing out as plainly as I could the way of peace with God — the A B C of peace with God. I thought the spiritual state of some required it. When I paused and looked up, the father was leaning forward, his face brightened, and he said to me — oh! how instructively — Oh, sir, I am beyond that stage. He told me that his mind had been deeply stirred before on the subject of personal religion, and that he attended the meetings, and had conversations with ministers and others — myself among them, though I did not recollect of it — and being in the field one day laboring with four companions, he turned up a sod of clay, and turned with it, a penny. He stooped down to grasp it, just, as he said, because he attached a certain value to it, though not a greater value than it was worth. The thought then immediately occurred to him — Do you set any value on Jesus and on peace with God, as you set a certain value on the various things of the world? That, Sir, he said, was the making of me for eternity; I was enabled to lay my soul on Jesus, and I have not had a day of darkness, or distrust, or distress of soul since. And what a change that makes now, he said. Had this stroke come upon me in the days of my darkness, it would have crushed me to the ground. But, oh! now, sir, I not only know that God is wise in the doing of that thing, but I feel that God is kind in the doing of it. There is just one other matter to which I refer, and that is to the general effects and results upon the public in Annan and its vicinity. I may just say in a word, that these are most marvellous. The general aspect of the town and country is morally and spiritually changed — absolutely revolutionized. We were almost proverbial for immorality. It is on the Border — and the Border is proverbial for badness. We had drunkenness, and all the kindred vices, and swearing. The voice of impiety is not now heard, and there is the most manifest arrest laid on the drunken habits of the people. The attendance in the places of worship is greatly increased. I may just illustrate that from my own congregation, which I may give as a specimen of all the others in town which took part in the movement. We had our usual communion Sabbath on the first Sabbath of February, three weeks or so after the movement began. We added then about forty members to the church, new converts, — members of a class so different from what I was wont to introduce into the church. We held, two weeks ago, a special commission to meet the desire in the congregation to come to the Lord's table again. I added then, I think, somewhere about fifty more members. Thus, in three months, we added about ninety members. I was not able to fix on one of that ninety or a hundred, who, if I had gone and said, — Now, have you been savingly blessed, do you think? — but would have answered in the affirmative, yea, and are giving evidence, all the evidence we can desire, of having been savingly blessed. We have a great hiring market in Annan, twice a year. One of them falls due in May; and oh! it has been a scene of iniquity. I remember when I first came to Annan and saw that fair, that I gave offence to some of my people, after seeing the intemperance that prevailed, by saying from the pulpit, next Sabbath — 'Oh! it is hard to think that anything good can be done here, while, by universal consent, two whole days in the year are given virtually to the devil, in this town and neighborhood.' But this month we faced that fair in a way we had never done before. We have a revival committee, and they looked out for this coming rock, and provided for it; and I think they have solved the problem of hiring markets and fairs in the land. There are some esteemed brethren present — Colonel Davidson, who kindly visited us, and also Mr. Mackenzie, Mr. Rainy, Mr. Reid, and a number of other members who came down to help us. About eight thousand people were brought into the town that day, and notwithstanding the attendance being three times the usual amount, yet, even on their own showing, the whisky-sellers did not do an average business. There were out-door services twice during the day. There was a refreshment tent, in which thirteen thousand or fourteen thousand cups of tea and coffee were sold, at a penny for each. A penny was charged for each thing — a bun, a penny; cheese, a penny; bread and butter, a penny;— for we went on the penny principle. Nineteen thousand pennies were thus taken in course of the day; the tent being opened with prayer and closed with prayer. On Friday first there is to be a meeting to take steps to erect a hall for the purpose of having it open on every future fair and market-day I believe if £1000 were required at this moment to carry on the revival work, the sum would be raised before Saturday night in the little town of Annan."

We have a strong confirmation of the reality and greatness of the blessing enjoyed in Annan, from the pen of Rev. Mr. Young, which we give. It was written as the date shows, more than a year after the revival scenes described, and addressed to a friend in America.

" I have the most lively and happy recollection of Mr. Hammond's coming to Annan. It was on Saturday, 12th January, 1861. On the same evening he called on some of the ministers, and looked in at a prayer-meeting, which was then being held.

On the Sabbath forenoon he spoke in two places of worship, speaking shortly in each. In the afternoon there was a crowded meeting in the Free Church. The four ministers who had long co-operated in holding a union prayer meeting and who continued throughout the revival to co-operate with one another and with Mr. H., were all present. The writer of this did not speak, but the other ministers spoke to good purpose, and Mr. H. gave an excellent address. That night there was an Inquiry Meeting. This was properly the first night, yet thus early the good work began. Among those with whom he conversed were two of the leading men of the town, and those two, along with others, have ever since taken a deep interest in whatever may glorify God or be of advantage to man. Of the enormously crowded meetings which followed I cannot speak in detail. The largest available place of assembly — usually the United Presbyterian Church — was filled to overflowing: not the town only, but the country for many miles around was deeply awakened; sometimes meetings were held in two churches at once, Mr. H. speaking first at one and then at the other. Each afternoon there was a delightful meeting for prayer. At night, the first meeting commenced at half-past seven, though the people came so early that the meeting really began with praise and prayer at a much earlier hour. About ten, the first meeting was closed, and from ten to one o'clock we spoke with inquirers. Never, even in my most hopeful moments, did I anticipate scenes like those which the Lord in his rich mercy then allowed me to see! The workers were, Mr. H., a young man who accompanied him, the four ministers, and a large number of earnest, Christian men, members of our churches; yet there was ample employment for all. Even when the inquiry meeting was closed, there was often reason to fear that some wishing conversation might have been overlooked. The impossibility of getting through the blessed work any sooner, was the sole reason for protracting the meetings always till one o'clock, and in one instance till after two.

"The Evangelist continued with us two weeks, and soon after he again favored us for one day with his invaluable aid. In the afternoon, a large and important meeting was held, when several persons told how they had been converted in the revival. Among these were some office-bearers in a church a short distance from Annan. In the evening, three meetings were held simultaneously. The Free Church was nearly full of children; a church belonging to the Establishment, (in which also others of the meetings had been held,) was on this evening crowded with women only; while the U. P. Church was crowded also with an audience consisting exclusively of men. Other speakers of course assisted, but on this, as on all other occasions, it was Mr. Hammond himself whom the Lord chiefly used.

"As regards the abiding results, I shall only copy the following very moderate statement, being part of a letter which I published more than three months ago in our local paper, the *Annan Observer*:—

"'I feel neither special call nor deep anxiety to vindicate the Annan Revival. It is its own best vindication. Now that, since its commencement, one year has elapsed, what are some of the good results we have witnessed?

"'First, *There have been many conversions. How many*. I have never attempted to say; but that they are very numerous, I have no sort of doubt; and speaking of all the professed converts whom I have known, I can freely state that the cases of backsliding, or even of temporary relapse, have been singularly few. With very rare exceptions, the professed converts are holding out well, trusting, as I believe, not in themselves, but in 'Him who is able to keep them from falling, and to present them faultless before the presence of His glory with exceeding joy.'

"'Second, among those who, since the revival, are taking a deep interest in religion, are a vast number of young men, many of them energetic and active, and some of them persons of influence. Among the young of both sexes, as well as among persons further advanced in life, the blessed effect of the Revival is visible and abiding. Much, indeed, still remains to be accomplished, but this is no reason why we should not acknowledge thankfully the great things which already the Lord has wrought.

"Third, *The intemperate have been reformed.* I could mention I know not how many, every one of whom now sit at the feet of Jesus, 'clothed and in his right mind.' Delightful, indeed, and unmistakeable, are cases with which I am acquainted. The temperance movement had effected much; the revival movement has effected more: there is no jarring between them — both are needed, and both are excellent, while they are mutually helpful the one to the other.

"I would only say, further, that through the revival, the children of God have had their faith greatly strengthened. Never before did they see so much of the power of prayer, or of God's readiness to answer it. They asked Him for guidance, and He gave it. They prayed Him to send laborers, and He sent them. In many cases He gave them so suddenly, that we could only think of His promises—a promise which in the people of Israel will hereafter have a still more signal fulfilment. 'It shall come to pass, that before they call I will answer; and while they are yet speaking, I will hear.'

"In speaking of Mr. Hammond, and of his peculiar qualifications for an Evangelist, I place in the foreground his humble, child-like confidence in the Lord. Believing that God has given promises, he expects Him to keep them. This expectation gives the tone to his prayers, and helps him greatly in all that he undertakes. Whenever he came among us he urged us to look for great things, and quoted oftener than once, and with excellent effect, these words of God by Jeremiah, 'Call unto me, and I will answer thee, and shew thee great and mighty things which thou knowest not.' — Jer. xxxiii. 3.

"Further, Mr. H. has a good judgment as to what should be done and what should be said. Even when he spoke but little it was the right thing, and at the proper time. He is full of zeal, but by no means too zealous for one who seeks to pluck men as brands from the burning; while there is about him a singleness of aim which I greatly admire, and which for myself I should greatly wish to possess. He was followed here by other laborers, of whom there were many who did us good service; but *it was with Mr. Hammond that the revival began, and we shall ever feel that it is to him that, under God, we are chiefly indebted.* Even yet, more than fifteen months having passed, I am finding among those who apply for church fellowship, some who speak of Mr. H. as having been the means in the Spirit's hand of leading them to Christ. I may state that since the revival began, we have — even in our little church — received about ninety new members, yet ours is only one of a number of churches in the town, with others in the country around, which this glorious revival has here filled and increased. Many of the cases of conversion are full of interest, but space does not permit me to go into detail.

"But the last among the causes of Mr. Hammond's power is his peculiar sweetness of temper or disposition. He is quite a man to be loved, for he loves every one. I have had him living with me while he labored in Annan — to have thus had the opportunity of having much intercourse with him — to have learned, as I did, how successful he had been in Dumfries and Glasgow after he left us — to have the hope, which I have, of still meeting him on earth — and especially to have the hope that through the mercy of God and the merits of the Saviour, we shall meet — as one of the beautiful hymns he taught us to sing expresses it —

> "On the other side of Jordan—
> In the sweet fields of Eden,
> Where the tree of life is blooming,"

—all this I regard as a blessed privilege for which 1 neve can sufficiently give God thanks.

"Both of Mr. Hammond, and of the Revival, I might have written much more, for where the work has been so great, and where the fruits are so abiding and visible, it is not easy to tell where to stop. The full results will appear in eternity, and will be to the honor of the ever blessed Spirit, and of that loving Saviour whom at all times and in all things it is a privilege to serve.

"I have not the pleasure of knowing the gentleman for whom 1 am writing this brief account, but regarding him as a friend of Mr. H., and as one who takes an interest in revivals, I am happy to furnish him with such an account as I have been able to give. EBENEZER YOUNG,
Pastor of the Independent or Congregational Church in Annan.

Annan, 15th May, 1862.

Dumfries, the home and burial-place of Robert Burns, the man of genius, and the mournful wreck, morally; an important Burgh, twelve miles from Annan, caught the sacred fire from the latter town, through the visit of some of its pastors. A very just estimate of sources of the principal speaker's success, under God, appeared in the Dumfries Standard, at the commencement of the daily meetings.

"Mr. Hammond never preaches essays, or deals in the elaborate or transcendental; he wants to make religion a thing of ordinary life — *the* great business of every day; and this being his desire, he presses the gospel on the acceptance of his hearers, just as a skilful trader seeks to dispose of his worldly merchandize, only that he offers 'the pearl of great price' with greater earnestness, so as to correspond with its infinitely greater value. This is, as we have already hinted, one of the secrets of his success. Many of his illustrations are brought fresh and new from the busy earth on which we tread, and have thus a strong human interest, and he has a marvellous knack of making such mundane themes the medium for conveying precious spiritual truths. And when after relating an entertaining anecdote he seeks to inculcate its lesson, the tones of his well-modulated voice thrill with a pathos and persuasiveness which are as music to the ' inner ear,' and assist materially in sending the moral home at once to the heart. He almost always manages to make a powerful impression on his audience. This, humanly speaking, is owing in a great degree to three things — first, his intense earnestness; secondly, his large-hearted benevolence; and thirdly, his simple unstilted Saxon style of discourse. While naturally courageous and self-dependent, his chief strength doubtless lies in his thorough belief that he is God's ambassador to sinful men — that he has received for each and all who come within the reach of his voice a message of love and mercy; and hence his ' holy boldness,' his unwearied devotedness in proclaiming the gospel — his oft-reiterated remonstrance, ' Why will ye die?' urged at once with amazing energy and with tearful tenderness."

Of the venerable and great man, whose name is identified with the Free Church, in connection with the services, it is said:

" Dr. Wood presided, and in a few warm, pregnant words, he thoroughly identified himself with the present Revival movement, and expressed his wonder, not that people should thus be congregating in great masses together and be anxiously inquiring ' What must we do to be saved?' but that meetings like these are so rare, and that so much deplorable apathy prevails even among professing Christians on the subject of their salvation."

We find a little work, printed in Dumfries, which has an immense circulation, from which we quote:

"The following communicated account of the movement at this early stage, appeared in the *Standard* of the 30th January:

"The work of Revival, which has been spreading in Annan with remarkable intensity and power for the last fortnight, has now extended to Dumfries with a fervor even greater than was witnessed in Annan, at the beginning of the meetings there. The large and spacious church in which the Rev. Dr. Wood ministers was, long before six o'clock on the evening of Sabbath, crowded in every part, while hundreds were pressing around the door eager to obtain an entrance, but could not. The Congregational Chapel was opened for the benefit of those who were desirous of hearing the words of life, and thus a second audience was placed under the Revival influence. At the close of his sermon, Mr. Hammond invited the anxious to remain for conversation, pressing on those who wished to be saved, and on those who hope to be saved at some future time, to remain to be conversed with on the momentous inquiry, 'What must I do to be saved?' This is the crisis of the work for the evening, to which the Christian looks with most thrilling interest. Oh! it was a spectacle which drew tears from many eyes, to see several hundreds in the lower part of the church and in the gallery, with countenances showing intense anxiety for salvation, waiting two hours in the church for conversation. Many were found suffering great mental anguish from the discovery of their sin against the God of love. The tears were flowing plentifully while they were deploring their sins and the hardness of their heart. Others had found peace to their troubled conscience in the discovery that the blood of Jesus Christ, God's Son, cleanseth us from all sin. And there were not a few, who had been unmoved under the stirring appeals, who were subdued through the power of sympathy; for, seeing others so earnest in seeking salvation, they felt it was high time for them to be earnest likewise. Many Christians gave help in the work of conversation. So far as we could learn their views, but one feeling pervaded all their minds — that the prayers which had been offered up for months past were now answered in the cloud of blessing descending on Dumfries, and that God had put his seal upon the work by the conversion of sinners.

"At six o'clock on the evening of Monday, Dr. Wood's Church was filled with the children of the Sabbath schools as it had been in the afternoon of Sabbath, and some of them gave clear proofs of conversion, and that they have found in the Saviour the salvation of their never-dying souls. At half-past seven, Dr. Wood's Church was crowded, and many who were eager to be present could not reach the door, so great was the crowd outside. Mr. Hammond preached on the leprosy of Naaman, and a very deep impression was made on the listening crowd. About the same number remained for conversation on the evening of Monday as on the Sabbath, but many who suffered greatly from the heavy load which pressed them down on the first evening, had found peace and were rejoicing in Christ the second evening. It was touching to see sitting in the same pew, the aged father, mother and daughter, agonized with the conviction of sin against the God of love, on the Sabbath; and on the Monday the daughter was mingling with the band of young converts, with a happy face and rejoicing heart, praising God. In one pew was sitting a dear boy of twelve years of age, with the tears streaming from his eyes for joy that he had found the Saviour, and on either side of him were aged men and women, groaning from the load of sin on their hearts, and in less than a quarter of an hour that load was removed, and the seat of mourning was exchanged for joy and gladness.

"The Independent Church was literally crowded on Monday night from ten till twelve — how long after, we know not; and after the inquirers, mostly males, had been individually spoken to by the Rev. Mr. Machray and others, Mr. Hammond looked in, gave a brief address, prayed, and then invited some of the converts to tell their experience to the meeting. The invitation was in the first instance responded to by a young man belonging to Dumfries, who declared that a few days ago he was a scoffer, and cared not for spiritual things. He was induced to attend one of the meetings, and was a little affected by what he heard; but he went away soon, and thought no more on the subject till on a subsequent night he went by invitation to an inquiry meeting, where he was affectionately spoken to by a young man, during whose address he had his eyes opened to see his sins. He saw that he was a poor, guilty sinner, and that, unless he was washed in the blood of Christ, he would go to hell. He went home in great trouble of mind, and tossed about sleepless in bed till three or four o'clock in the morning. Next night he got into conversation with some of the ministers, and one of them, Mr. Torrance, explained to him that he must put his trust in Jesus; and just as he was told to do that, a something came over him which he could not describe, but he did feel that he could put his trust in Christ, and this made him happy. He advised all who heard him, who were yet unconverted, to turn to Jesus as he had been enabled to do, and then they would be happy as he was; and oh, he said, let those who have found Christ tell the good news to others in the streets, that they too may obtain salvation and get rid of all their tears.

"Another man, approaching middle age, belonging to the neighborhood, we believe, next stept forward and told how about fourteen months ago he had been first aroused to a sense of his true condition as a sinner in the sight of God, but that the impression wore off. That night week, when at the Revival meeting, the impression was renewed and deepened, never, he hoped, to be effaced. In returning home he offered up a heart-felt prayer, and, the next moment, experienced a joy such as he was unable to express.

"With the view of affording more accommodation for the increasing crowds which flock nightly to the Free Church, several seats were on Monday removed from the area, thus leaving standing room for nearly two hundred persons, instead of merely sitting room for fifty-eight. But if the church could, by any possibility, have been enlarged to twice its former size, it in that case would still be filled to overflowing, so attractive are the Revival sermons, and so unprecedently intense and wide-spread is the interest felt in them, not only in Dumfries, but in all the country around. Not fewer than one thousand seven hundred and fifty persons were within the walls of the church on Monday night, many of them closely wedged together; and last night the attendance was if anything greater; while on each occasion there were hundreds at the doors, unable to obtain an entrance.

"The services on Tuesday night by the singing of hymns — 'grave sweet melody' — ensued till the arrival of Dr. Wood, who presided over the meeting. He was followed by the Rev. Mr. Greig, parish minister of Kirkpatrick-Durham, who addressed the audience at considerable length. His closing remarks told powerfully, the audience listening with rapt attention to the important statement made by the preacher when recounting his experience as such for a period of thirty years. During a large portion of that time, he now knew, he had never experienced a saving change of heart. While preaching sound doctrine to his people, he was as great a stranger to the power of the gospel as a Hindoo or a Mohammedan; and it was not till within a comparatively recent period that he realized his true condition in the sight of God, and found the Saviour for himself. He could not state the precise period when his eyes were opened; 'but this,' said Mr. Greig, 'I know, that whereas once I was blind, now I see.'

"Mr. Hammond referred to the cases of Dr. Chalmers and other ministers as parallel to that of Mr. Greig; and expressed his gratification at the address made by him. God, who had made their dear brother bold to speak the truth, would bless his statement, and continue to uphold him to the end. He then noticed the case of another minister, who had recently experienced a similar change at a Revival meeting, and whose public acknowledgment of it had been greatly blessed by God to the awakening of other souls that were in danger of sleeping the sleep of death.

"An infidel young man, a draper in Dumfries, was then introduced by Mr. Hammond, and proceeded to speak with much readiness, and at times rose to a pitch of what may truly be called spontaneous and unpremeditated eloquence, as he described the way in which he had been led from the darkness and desolateness of scepticism to the light and happiness of saving faith. He told how a companion of his, laboring under deep conviction, last week had conversed with him on the danger which those incur who put off the day of their merciful visitation. He was thus led to think seriously and solemnly on the subject. He felt as if the arrow of conviction had found its way to his heart, and on going home, told his mother he was very unhappy. He went up-stairs still tormented by doubts and fears; and prayed earnestly that God would give him peace. He turned to his Bible, and there read, in the First Epistle of John, fourth chapter, first verse, that 'many false prophets are gone out into the world.' He felt that this was true — that he had been led away by false prophets, and had been on the road to everlasting ruin. Still laboring under a sense of unpardoned sin, he found his way on Saturday night to an inquiry meeting, and there received some comfort from a conversation which he had with one of the ministers. That minister asked if he would come to Jesus; and they prayed together: and he felt comparatively happy. On Sabbath he went to a prayer meeting, and afterwards heard Mr. Symington preach from a passage in Isaiah, in Mr. Scott's Church; and from the remarks then made he obtained much relief. His faith was confirmed, and his peace with God through Christ was sealed, as during the same evening at an inquiry meeting he mixed with those who were anxious for their souls, and endeavored to lead them to the Saviour, whom he had himself, after many wanderings, found. Now his faith in the all-prevailing atonement was unwavering; and he experienced a happiness which till that night he had never known.

"Mr. Hammond, kneeling down on the platform, offered up prayer — the tones of his voice, and his eyes streaming with tears, betraying his overpowering emotion as he returned thanks for the marvellous doings of the Lord as manifested to them in the cases just related, and many other marks of the Divine favor which had been experienced during that day and night. The young man then knelt down, and offered up a short prayer — the scene deeply affecting the audience. Mr. Hammond then, addressing the audience, put the question, How shall ye escape, if ye neglect so great salvation? That question he could not answer — the devils could not answer it, the angels could not answer it, God himself could not answer it. Escape? there was no possible way of escape if they despised and neglected the great salvation.

"Dr. Wood added a few closing words, in which he solemnly and affectionately urged each individual of the vast multitude present who still halted for serving two masters, to decide for Christ. The meeting closed by singing the following verse and chorus:

> "'Tis done — the great transaction's done;
> I am my Lord's, and he is mine;
> He drew me, and I followed on,
>   Charmed to confess the voice divine.
>   Happy day! happy day!
>   When Jesus washed my sins away;

He taught me how to watch and pray,
And live rejoicing every day.
Happy day ! happy day !
When Jesus washed my sins away.

"At the protracted meeting for inquiry on Tuesday night, from a hundred to a hundred and fifty were present in the Reformed Presbyterian Church ; upwards of two hundred in the Independent Church ; and the females in the Free Church were fully as numerous as on any former occasion. One case is reported to us as having occurred in the Reformed Presbyterian Church, of peculiar interest — that of a man from the country who had been in a state of great distress, a prey to doubts and misconception, but who was at length, after a torturing ordeal of a fortnight's duration, enabled to place his trust in the Redeemer and find in Him peace and rest. In the course of the proceedings in the Independent Church, Mr. Machray made the gratifying announcement, that, at the small village of Locharbriggs in the neighborhood, a crowded Revival meeting had been held that evening, and about seventy anxious inquirers had remained to be conversed with — results which, he said, were in answer to prayers offered up for the people of the village, at the meeting which had been held in that church during the day. Several ministers, in addition to those already mentioned by us, have given assistance at the protracted meetings, and, as formerly, ladies and laymen in considerable numbers are taking part in the work.

"Among the cases which occurred on the same night in the Free Church, the following one excited an extraordinary amount of attention : — Robert Milligan, aged forty-nine, a native of Kirkcudbright, and for twenty-seven years a soldier in the 1st Regiment of Life Guards, was present at the general meeting, and he was observed to be much affected by the various addresses that were delivered. He was, it appears, especially struck with the statements made by the Rev. Mr. Greig, and thought within his own mind it was high time he was beginning to examine himself, when a minister like Mr. Greig had confessed that he had been long personally ignorant of the gospel. Towards the close of the meeting Mr. W. Milligan, junior, conversed with him, and they went together for a little to the house of the former, and after conversing and praying there they returned to the church, he expressing a strong wish to see Mr. Hammond, who was busily engaged at the time with other anxious inquirers.

"The scene which ensued was highly affecting. Mr. Milligan is a tall, well-made man, barely past the meridian of life, and his buirdly figure was very prominent as he hurried up the area, and seizing Mr. Hammond by the hand, said loud enough to be heard over a great part of the church, 'Sir, I am a soldier: I have been in many a battle, and received many a wound, but never such a one as I received to-night. The arrow sent by that Rev. gentleman (pointing to Mr. Greig,) went through and through my very heart.' Mr. Hammond asked, 'Are you now then resolved to be a soldier of the Cross — enrolled in the blood-redeemed army of Jesus?' 'Yes,' was the answer, 'I have too long earned the wages of sin, and will henceforth devote myself to the service of the Saviour.' Mr. Hammond offered up a few appropriate words of prayer; and the soldier, then holding up both hands beseechingly, prayed with great fluency and unction. After which he instinctively flourished his bonnet, as he said with modest confidence, 'I am not ashamed to own my Lord.' This truly impressive and touching episode had a most thrilling effect upon the onlookers, many of whom sobbed aloud, while others gave expression to a feeling of exulting joy. Soon after, it appears, Mr. Milligan told what had happened to his wife, and appeared in company with her at the meeting, where she formed one among the many inquirers after salvation, and is now like himself, it is said, happy in believing.

"A respected leader of the Free Church, Dumfries, remarked the other night that the scenes he had witnessed during the ten days and nights preceding were so extraordinary, that he felt himself at times overcome with amazement, and almost tempted to question their reality. And yet, he added, they are not dreams, delusions, but substantial realities, as veritable as they are wonderful and solemn. The same ideas, we doubt not, have passed through the minds of many who have been present at the Revival meetings, and especially at those held for inquiry, when, in the dead of night, numbers have to all appearance been made spiritually alive. The protracted meetings are marvellous, on account of the hundreds who take part in them for the purpose of receiving religious instruction and comfort, and still more so because of the considerable proportion of those who declare to their advisers, that they have found what they were in search of — whose language, once that of doubt or despair, is now, 'I do believe, I now believe that Jesus died for me.'

"The inquiry meetings are also remarkable for the cordiality with which people of all denominations and ranks mix with each other, forming, so to speak, one large family, equal in the sight of the same heavenly Father, and knowing, or at least showing none of the distinctions which are so pertinaciously clung to and so reluctantly parted with in the ordinary world of life. Too often the poor are made to feel bitterly their inferiority of station, but here Dives comes not — at least does not venture to appear in the purple and fine linen of his pride — and those who are literally in the condition of Lazarus, are recognized to be brothers and sisters by men of high position, and by those who are gentlewomen in every sense of the word. Mill-girls and fine ladies talk lovingly together on topics of transcendent interest to both. Women who have fallen — poor Magdalenes — panting for heart's ease, if not sighing penitentially, form units in the throng; and so far from being shunned as something vile, are welcomed with the feeling which made the father in the parable kill the fatted calf for his son. The unprecedented religious awakening now experienced in Dumfries may subside, and no one expects that the excitement can continue long unabated — in the nature of things it must decrease; but the memory of these inquiry meetings will have a continued fragrance — they will be remembered as affording in some respects a foretaste of millennial times; and viewing them even in the subsidiary temporal sense, without reference to the spiritual benefits there originated, they will, we think, tend to strengthen the bonds of social existence amongst us. Those who experience the luxury of doing good to the poor, know that the latter are grateful for kind words as well as for charitable benefactions, that they sigh for sympathy, and gratefully appreciate any evidence shown to them that they are cared for, body and soul, by the rich. The coldness and superciliousness shown towards those in humble life, and that often too by professing Christians, are at the bottom of much of the heart-burnings and neglect of religious ordinances which prevail in the lower strata of society. Treatment of a contrary kind not only promotes social peace, but is a step towards the reduction of practical heathenism. Hence, if for nothing else, we attach great value to these inquiry meetings; and we trust that the spirit which prevades them will be manifested out of doors. It must not be allowed to languish, far less to die out, after these delightful reunions have drawn to a close, but be brought to bear upon the outcast and destitute of our population.

" The Wednesday evening meeting in the Free Church was for males alone. The place was crowded by men and boys, many of them from the neighborhood; and as a proof of the anxiety felt to gain admission we may state that two or three hundred of the country people having had to go away early, their places were no sooner emptied than occupied by persons from the town. As the meeting proceeded, it was gratifying to see laboring men in various parts of the church with serious faces and Testament — evidently new — in hand, carefully turning up passages of Scripture as referred to by the different speakers. Altogether the assemblage was an extraordinary one, comprising, as it did, much of the bone and sinew which constitute the main strength of the country and the chief defence of the State. The Rev. Mr. Torrance made a few remarks; the Rev. Mr. Millar, of Carlisle, followed, and then the Rev. Mr. Symington. Mr. Fraser, of Colvend, was the next speaker. He stated that when he first heard of these Revivals, he had some misgivings respecting them; but he resolved, for the sake of his parishioners and himself, to inquire into the subject personally. For that purpose he had come to Dumfries; and what he had seen and now saw satisfied him that the Awakening here was the work of God. He would return home with the resolution, to be more zealous than ever in urging his people to seek the way of salvation. Mr. Fraser further expressed himself as highly pleased with all the proceedings; every minister, he thought, should make inquiry for himself into the matter, and not decide upon it from mere hearsay. Those who did not see their way as yet to give the movement their active support, should be cautious how they derided it or in other respects opposed it; and he was clearly of opinion that those who carefully examined the subject for themselves, would come to a satisfactory conclusion regarding it.

"Mr. Hammond introduced a working-man of middle age, who proceeded to address the audience. We give his statement as near as may be verbatim: 'This is the first time,' he said, 'in my life that I ever rose to address a meeting on any subject one or other. I see many faces here that ken me weel, as I belong to the place. They ken who I am, but they dinna ken what I was inwardly. Before these meetings took place I was a stranger to God. I professed Him outwardly; but inwardly I was a subject of the devil. I was an infidel in principle, though still professing to be a Christian. My chief occupation on the Sabbath day was to gang amang the fields and woods, for the purpose of studying nature as we termed it; and there are men here I ken, and who I love weel, who used to go there for that object. But oh, if it had been God's pleasure to take me away a fortnight since, I must have been hurled into eternal misery. I noo ken and feel that at that time I was without God and going fast to destruction. I aye heard folk talking about sudden conversions and such like, but I thought it was nonsense; and before this night week I kent naething about it, and did not feel Christ in my soul. There are men in this meeting who hae seen me struggling and striving for Christ, and at last I have found Him. Some said to me that as long as there was life there was hope; but my answer was, If I'm saved at a', it will be by fire. In Mr. Symington's church this night week I was urged to come to Christ and be saved; but I resisted the invitation. I was in great trouble, and a man I met with there tried to comfort me; but my soul was overwhelmed. He said, 'Will I pray for ye?' and with that he leaned down and poured out his soul to God for me, a guilty and miserable sinner. He saw that, though some little relieved, I was still in great anxiety and distress, and he said, ' Just gang away hame, and dinna weary yoursel sitting here, but gang to yer ain house, and pray to God for grace.' I rose, and gaed away hame, and there, by mysel, sat down on my knees for the first time in my life. I had no words to express my feelings, but I sat down on my knees till I found Jesus come to my very soul. [This statement produced a marked sensation in the meeting.] I was telling some men in this house last nicht (continued the speaker) how I found Christ in prayer, and I now tell them, and a' here that are unconverted, to gang hame to their closets as I did, and importune God to pour peace into their hearts; and if they ask Him, faithfully believing on His name, the blessing will be theirs. O heavenly Father, look down on these poor deluded sinners; may they be led to look to Christ for salvation. O God, hear this imperfect prayer. Guide them in the narrow way that leads unto life eternal, for Christ's sake. Amen.' This prayer, with which the speaker closed his striking narrative, was broken by emotion, his feelings seemingly being too strong for utterance.

"Mr. Hammond proceeded to say, that he had been showing how God was able to turn sinners to himself, and here was a witness that the statement was true. God called on all unconverted men to turn from their evil ways. There were some of God's servants who did not hold the whole truth in regard to this matter, and preached sinners down to hell. In Scripture, three agencies were represented as being at work in turning or converting sinners, as described in the following different passages: 'He which converteth the sinner from the error of his ways, shall save a soul from death.' 'They that turn many to righteousness, shall shine as the stars for ever and ever.' These passages pointed out the agency of man; while others, such as John vi. 44, represented God as the agent. 'No man can come to me, except the Father which hath sent me draw him.' Then in the text from which he was speaking, the sinner himself was urged to turn. These passages appeared to clash with each other, but it was only in appearance. In corroboration of this remark, Mr. Hammond supposed the case of a man walking in a reverie on the brink of Niagara Falls, and about to drop into destruction. In this perilous position he is seen by another individual, who cries out, 'Stop, turn, or you will perish!' and the man turns and is saved That man acknowledges with gratitude the service rendered to him by the person who called upon him to turn; he speaks, too, of himself as being turned from the yawning gulf; and he also returns thanks to God for

His providential interposition, by which he was led to turn and escape. Did the man contradict himself when he thus spoke of three agencies operating to save him? not a bit; and in the same way there was no contradiction in Scripture when three agencies were shown to be at work in converting the sinner — three agents (not three instruments) — God, the sinner, and God's servants — truth being the instrument.

"We have adduced a number of cases of alleged conversion; but the awakening of those who were, in the eyes of their neighbors, consistent professors of Christianity has been another great result of the Revival in Dumfries. One case is described to us as a specimen among many: A young lady who was a communicant attended the first meeting addressed by Mr. Hammond here in the Free Church, and though impressed to a slight degree, thought but little of the service generally. She went a second time, on the following Tuesday night, and felt her heart thrilled when the following words were sung:

'Just as I am, without one plea,
But that Thy blood was shed for me,
And that Thou bidst me come to Thee,
O Lamb of God, I come!'

'Why not me?' was the lady's mental ejaculation; and while in the upper vestry among other inquirers, her attention was attracted to a female of humble rank prostrate on the floor, as if overwhelmed by a sense of sin. Mr. Hammond was endeavoring to comfort her by pleading that Jesus was a kind and gracious Saviour; and he closed his kindly exhortation by requesting the other females present to pray to Christ on behalf of their suffering sister. The lady did so in company with others, and while pleading for the poor woman, she felt as if the burden of her own guilt was that moment rolled away, and she rose from her knees with a full realization of pardon and peace, and a happiness such as she never before experienced.

"Colonel Davidson, from Edinburgh, who has visited Dumfries for the sole purpose of witnessing and taking part in the Revival movement, proceeded at considerable length, and with great effect, to address the meeting. He stated that he had gone out to India at sixteen years of age. Whilst in this country, he attended worship regularly, sometimes three times a day; but for the first seven years after going to India he did not hear as many sermons, so destitute was the station of the ordinances of grace. One day, when riding a spirited horse alone, the animal became restive, and the thought struck him, 'Were I to die just now, would not my soul be lost?' and of this feeling he could not divest himself. On the same evening he dined with the commanding officer, and in the course of conversation the illness of a brother-officer was mentioned, with the remark that ' it would go hard with him '—which remark deepened the feeling of concern in his own mind. He spent several weeks afterwards in great mental distress; but knowing that one of the officers was a decided Christian, he ventured, though in much diffidence, to break the matter to him. The words, 'Justified by God's free grace,' were, he told his brother-officer, what he could not comprehend. On parting, the officer gave him Booth's *Reign of Grace*, with an Introductory Essay by Dr. Chalmers, and told him to read the Essay. He took the book home with him, and while reading the Essay as desired, the light broke in upon him — the gospel scheme flashed vividly upon his mind. That was on the 15th of April, 1835 — a day ever memorable to him — it was the day of his second birth; and he kept its anniversary regularly as it came round. Dr. Chalmers he considered as his spiritual father. Colonel Davidson proceeded to relate some of his experiences in India after his conversion, and in this country after returning home to it. His address was exceedingly interesting, and obviously made a deep impression upon the audience. After a few observations from Dr. Wood, devotional exercises were engaged in, and the meeting terminated.

"Colonel Davidson was present at the inquiry meeting which ensued, and took an active part in the duty of ministering to the spiritual wants of the anxious.

"Much interest was felt in a remarkable statement made at this meeting by a young gentleman from a distance — a commercial traveller we believe — who had been induced to appear on the platform and say a few words regarding his own case. He had, it appears, by what is sometimes called accident, but which he attributed to the design of Providence, come to Dumfries at this season of awakening, and attended some of the meetings without being much impressed. Still he could not stay away from them, and on Thursday, while standing near the door of the Free Church, the words of Mr. Hammond, as he cried, 'You sinner at the door there, what do you think of Christ?' rung in his ears, and pierced his very soul. He said to himself 'I am a sinner, and that appeal is made to me.' Then Dr. Wood solemnly asked the audience to choose on which side they would range themselves; and the reflection passed through his mind, 'I am, I fear, not on the Lord's side.' He went home, and prayed that he might find the Saviour, but found Him not, because he was always thinking what he could do for himself. This state of mind continued, but on Friday night he still wrestled and prayed. He spent that night in deep and bitter anguish; but, said the speaker, in continuation, raising his voice to a high pitch, while tears streamed down his face,' I rejoice in that night, for my mourning is now turned into joy. Mr. Hammond, on Saturday evening, invited inquirers to meet with him in Dr. Wood's parlor at the close of the service. Well, I thought, he is a young man, and knows the trials to which youth is exposed; I will go in and take his advice. I did so, and he prayed with and for me; I prayed, and wrestled with the Evil One, who clung to me as if he would not let me go. These prayers on Saturday morning gave me some relief, but I could not say ' Peace, peace, when there is no peace.' Mr. Hammond, at our interview, told me to pray. Pray! and that before a stranger! I believe my poor mother taught me how to pray; and I did fall down on my knees and pray there in Dr. Wood's parlor. I experienced a sudden change; I felt wonderfully relieved; my legs trembled; a feeling came over me that is inexpressible. I felt a glow of joy that is unspeakable. Three young persons came in, and Mr. Hammond said, ' Pray for these poor souls;' and I, after being just delivered myself, prayed that they too might be freed from the bondage of sin and Satan. O sinners — those in this assembly who have not yet come to the Saviour — do not think that this happiness of mine is mere excitement. I call upon you to repent, and experience with me the solid joy which the believer feels who brings the burden of his guilt to Christ, and gets it taken all away. I felt a diffidence at first in addressing you, but I thank God who has enabled me to bear this testimony to what has been done for my soul. Were any of my friends to enter this meeting and see me here speaking to you, they would be astonished; and if any of them really are here, if they would just come forward, I would try to comfort them if they are in distress.' The gentleman closed his address by earnestly exhorting all to come and adopt the language of the hymn:

> ' Just as I am — without one plea,
> But that Thy blood was shed for me,
> And that Thou bidst me come to Thee,
> O Lamb of God, I come!'

" A correspondent has kindly favored us with the following statement: 'The work of conversion is advancing in Dumfries with unabated intensity. Last Sabbath, all the churches in which the Revival is advancing were crowded beyond anything ever before witnessed by their respective ministers. The number of the awakened was greater than on any previous day.

Large numbers were drawn to the town from all the surrounding country to the extent of twenty miles — some already enjoying peace with God, that they might have a time of refreshing; and others convinced of their sin, that they might have, under the shower of the divine blessing descending here, the cleansing away their guilt and the privilege of enjoying God as their Father.

"Many will have to bless God for ever that Sabbath, the 10th inst., was the day of their spiritual birth, that the eyes of their understanding were opened, and that they were translated from the kingdom of darkness into the kingdom of light. There have been among the converts many cases of intense anguish, protracted for several days, and arising from their eagerness to see the grand moral change passing over their heart; thus withdrawing their thoughts from the great propitiation to their own hearts full of all sin. Thus their anguish has been increased, and expressed in their piteous sobs and cryings, till some one skilled in the art of leading their thoughts to their Redeemer, has pointed out their mistake, explained the actual work of the Saviour finished on the cross, and exhorted them to trust in his all-sufficient and boundless sacrifice; and then in numerous instances have they almost instantaneously exchanged the agony of conscious guilt for the joys of pardon and the hopes of everlasting life. There is a great diversity in the degree in which the converts have been convinced of sin. A large class have experienced little distress of mind, and have seen the greatness of their guilt only after they have discovered that the blood of Jesus Christ has washed it away. When they have realized the truth of God's infinite love to them, in blotting out their transgressions through the death of his own Son, it is then that they see the depth of the ruin from which they have been rescued. Hence their sorrow for past sin mingles with their joy for present pardon.

"We are now at the stage of this religious movement when

we are qualified to estimate the causes by which it has been produced, and to see the means by which it may be continued and enlarged till the whole county of Dumfries may be brought under its saving power.

" And first of all, in point of importance, is prayer for the influence of the Spirit to open the heart to the gospel. The prayer of faith brings the blessing just as certainly as the apostles wrought miracles on the bodies of men in the first age of Christianity. During the last three weeks the minds of scoffers, and infidels, and profane swearers have undergone a radical change, just when a few earnest and believing men were praying especially for them. The tidings of God's infinite love to them have been embraced, and in a few moments their hearts of stone have become like the hearts of little children. Mr. Hammond is pre-eminently a man of strong faith, assured that, when he asks the Holy Spirit, God is willing to bestow Him. At our forenoon meeting, he exposed the unbelief of Christians in their prayers, when they ask if God be willing to give His blessing, He would grant it. That *if* shows the unbelief which remains in their heart, which renders the prayer an abomination to our Father, who has sworn that He has no pleasure in the death of a sinner.

" Some have expressed surprise that Mr. Hammond's preaching should have been followed with such amazing results in the awakening and conversion of sinners. This surprise is in a great measure the fruit of ignorance. Never was there so much prayer for the Divine blessing in Dumfries as now, and never were there so many faithful and pointed appeals to the consciences as now ; and the rich harvest is the fruit of the abundant seed. Mr. Hammond faithfully urges on the sinner his duty of turning to God, and of trusting in Christ. He shows the condition with which the sinner must comply to enter into the enjoyment of salvation. While praying to God for his help, he appeals to the sinner to do his part, to comply with the invitation, 'Come to Me, I will give you rest.' The truth which saves the soul is plainly set forth, difficulties are removed, objections answered, prejudices exposed, and the sinner is at length compelled to come in.

"Mr. Hammond is equally explicit in teaching that the believer is an agent in the work of converting sinners — not a mere instrument in the hand of the Spirit. The gospel is the instrument or hammer which breaks the heart of stone, and the believer is an agent when he uses it. So is the mason. The first stroke does not break a hard stone — it may require a second, and a third, but each stroke is separating, although invisibly, the particles of the stone, and it may be that the tenth stroke rends them assunder. Thus the mason is an agent, and so is the Christian. In prayer, God is recognized as the great agent. But it has paralyzed the Christian when he has thought of himself only as an instrument. He has lived years without once aiming to convert a sinner from the error of his ways, but when he sees himself an agent, he is constrained to work as well as to pray, and then the blessing descends on his labors. It is seen in the early church when the disciples were scattered abroad, and went everywhere preaching the Word; and in the young converts going to the towns and villages around, and making known the tidings of the Redeemer's love.

"The more that sinners feel their responsibility, and the more that believers regard themselves as agents accountable to God for working to convert sinners, the more the work of Revival will spread. Prayer and working on the part of believers are necessary to the continuance of the Revival, and in the measure in which these are given will the Revival flourish and spread."

At the close of the special services, the seven pastors of Dumfries, united in the following voluntary testimony published at the time.

"We believe the religious Awakening in Dumfries and neighborhood, to which they refer, to be a real work of the grace and Spirit of God. Mere natural feeling and human imperfection are, no doubt, mingled with it. But having been in the midst of it, and incessantly occupied with it for the last three weeks, and having seen it in all its aspects, we unhesitatingly express our conviction that it is a very wonderful and most blessed work, by which many souls have been brought to Christ, and many of God's people have received a fresh baptism of the Spirit."

The statements of the venerable Dr. Wood, are very forcible and convincing. Referring to the labors of the Evangelist, he goes on to remark:

"I happened to be detained in Edinburgh from indisposition during the first week of his visit, and on coming home found him in my church, surrounded by a most eager, convinced multitude of perishing sinners. It was a thing such as I had never seen before, and I saw my way at once to take part in it. I joined with the managers of the church in working along with Mr. Hammond, strengthening his hands and encouraging him in his work; and we found that the Lord was blessing his work — using Mr. Hammond as an eminent instrument in awakening sinners, and bringing them to the Lord Jesus Christ. When I was here before, my object in the address delivered by me in Hope Street Gaelic Church was to show, if possible, that this was no wild excitement produced by Mr. Hammond, but the real work of the Spirit of God. I think I succeeded in showing it was no mere work of man, but of God; and I repeat the statement. I find that it is not unneeded, and that persons still refuse to believe that it is the work of the Spirit of God, maintaining that it is a movement guided by Mr. Hammond and the ministers. I find numbers of those persons in and around

Dumfries, and there may be not a few such in Glasgow; but the more conversant I am with this work, the more thoroughly I am persuaded that it is a genuine work of the grace and Spirit of God. The great stir which it at first produced is now abated, and I am coming in contact with my own people more frequently, while our meetings are better attended. I have had occasion to come in contact with them preparatory to the communion, and I feel now as I never felt before in my ministry. I have found people greatly changed, of whose sincerity I cannot entertain a doubt, and am ready to hold up my hands with surprise when I meet with men who persist in calling it all a delusion, and denounce Mr. Hammond and others for getting up an 'excitement.' It is quite true that these men have looked on at a distance, and have never come in contact with the work itself; for I am persuaded that hardly any honest man can come in contact with this work, and deal with it in a faithful, honest way, without being convinced that there is something in it far above man. Mr. Hammond continued with us two weeks, laboring, I may say, day and night, and we all rejoiced in his labors. We had people coming from all places round about Dumfries at that time. One invitation after another came to Mr. Hammond from country places, three or four of which he visited for a day, or part of one. The same results attended the meetings there, which followed his labor in Dumfries. He gathered the people about him and the ministers who labored with him; and the cry was, 'What must I do to be saved?'

"This awakening was by no means confined to the town of Dumfries and Annan — it is extending through all the country round about for twenty miles, at least; and I do not believe there is a single village or hamlet within that area which has not in some measure partaken of the awakening. At his first meeting the church was filled — a very unusual occurrence — and the awakening began that night Then there were meetings at Penpont, about fifteen miles from Dumfries, and the Free Church was crowded. An awakening took place, and now, I believe, meetings are frequently held alternately in the U. P. Church at Thornhill, the Free Church at Penpont, and the U. P. Church at Burnhead. Large meetings are held there night after night, and I believe a most blessed work is going on in the district. Mr. Hammond paid a visit for one night to Penpont, and had a forenoon meeting in Glencairn. Just as if to show how little it depends upon any human agency, before he had opened his mouth a number of persons were removed from the church in deep distress about the concerns of their souls."

We have read with pleasure a further report of Dr. Wood before the General Assembly, a year and a half since the revival scenes, comprising all that he had previously stated; and in which he compared the subsidence of the excitement, to the disappearance of the waters of the Nile from the banks, leaving the richness and fertility of the fields in the wake of their withdrawal. Such was the apostolic refreshing in this favored city, which, whatever of human weakness appeared, was Pentecost in these latter days.

CHAPTER V.

Glasgow. The awakening. Mr. Hammond's method of conducting the religious services and style of preaching. The progress of the work. Children's meeting. Letters of converts. Meeting for women. Summary. Glasgow, on the banks of the Clyde, is one of the oldest and largest cities of Scotland; nearly opposite to Edinburgh.

Mr. Hammond commenced his labors in Dr. Buchanan's beautiful church, whose congregation represent much of the wealth and culture of the city. He afterward preached for a number of evenings in Hope St. Church. The awakening spread through the town with great power.

We have in a small volume published by the friends of revivals in Glasgow, a full report of Mr. Hammond's method of conducting services, containing an outline of a sermon, which we give in connection with the awakening in that city, to gratify the natural curiosity which may be felt on this point, and on account of interesting thoughts and facts in the passage.

The editor of the Examiner, Dr. Smith, says:

"On Sabbath, 24th February, according to announcement, this well-known evangelist preached in the Free College Church. At the announced hour, eleven o'clock, he ascended the pulpit.

He gave out the first four verses of the 46th Psalm, which was sung by the congregation. He then rose and said—' We are going to pray. Some here may have never prayed, and many never pray till too late.' He told a story of a Christian and infidel who were in a boat on the Niagara river, who, as they reasoned, approached the falls of that river. When the infidel became aware of his peril his courage failed, and he began to cry to God for mercy. His Christian friend, who was prepared for death, took the oars and wrought the boat ashore, when the infidel was paralyzed with terror. So many pray only when in view of danger and death. Of Paul it was said, 'Behold he prayeth.' He had often been seen standing at the corner of the streets thanking God that he was not like other men ; but that was not prayer. But now he prays as a sinner, and seeks mercy. After a few more remarks he commenced to pray. His prayer was rather brief and peculiar. He prayed for the city — for the West-end especially — for the Magistrates of the city, that they might not, like the rich man, lift up their eyes in hell. He prayed for the congregation and for its pastor, that the seed he scattered might bear fruit. He then gave out to be read the 6th chapter of Matthew's gospel, but only read the first six verses, which refer to the hypocritical and ostentatious prayer of the Pharisee, &c. He then gave out to be sung the first four verses of the 116th Psalm. Before it was sung he said that this Psalm had been properly called the new convert's Psalm, because it so well expressed his agony and relief when he found peace. After the words were sung he gave out for the text, Job. 22d chap. and 21st and 22d verses — · Acquaint now thyself with Him and be at peace, thereby good will come to thee. Receive, I pray thee, the law from His mouth and lay up His words in thine heart.' He said we are here exhorted to acquaint ourselves with God. Last summer, when travelling to France by way of Calais, there was a young man on board the steamer, who landed with others at

Calais. He left the steamer as light of heart as any, to prosecute his journey, till an officer touched him on the shoulder and demanded his passport. He said he had no passport. He was conducted back to the vessel, and had to return to England for his passport. Had I seen that young man in the streets of London before he left, I might have told him to secure a passport, and he might not have heeded me. I might have told him that Napoleon was not beloved by his subjects as our Queen was, and assumed that every one who visited France might be an assassin. I might have advised him to acquaint himself with Napoleon and his Government before he went there, and I might have secured his gratitude for inducing him to make the necessary preparations. I am here to-day to do a similar duty — to bid you acquaint yourselves with God — to urge on you the lesson of the text. The text includes *a what, a who, a why*, and *a when*. First, *we are told what to do; a what —* The text bids us acquaint ourselves with God. The advice was first given to Job, who already knew much of God. He was like many in Scotland, which is the land of Bibles and speculative knowledge, and sound theology, for all of which God should be thanked. "Many know much *about* God who don't know God — who don't know Jesus Christ. In America we, at meetings, go round among the people and say, ' Do you *know* God? not *about* God; but do you know Him.' I have seen in Switzerland the mountain glaciers glistening in the sunlight. But these glaciers in winter are bleak and cold — send down no refreshing streams to the bare pastures. It is only when the sun shines on them that they send down fertilizing streams to refresh the pastures and make the flocks rejoice. So is it with systematic theology — magnificent it is, but cold and cheerless till the sun shines on it. The head may be all right and the heart all wrong. The Pharisees were in this way. They had head knowledge, but it left the heart untouched. The text says we are to know God — not to know about him. Job says,

'I have heard of Thee, but now mine eyes see Thee.' That is knowing God, and the effect was that Job abhorred himself, and repented in dust and ashes. Have you thus seen God as a holy God ? — one that will not clear the finally impenitent — as a God that will bring every work into judgment with every secret thing.' Job was highly esteemed, and had he lived in our time he would have been an elder. Nicodemus was of the same respectable class. How many looked up to him as he passed along the streets making broad his phylacteries on that memorable evening that he met with the Saviour. As he went along they saw the texts of Scripture on his garments, and they thought him a very holy man ; but Jesus told him very plainly that he must be born again. Better to be convinced of sin now than when too late — better know now whether you have on the wedding garment. Many will go forward to the judgment under a mistake, and say have we not eaten and drunken in Thy presence, and Thou hast taught in our streets? They have been only *boarders* in the family of Christ. How many such professors there are? To whom Christ will say, ' I never knew you — you have no passport — you are not clothed in the righteousness of Christ.' Better far to be convinced of sin to-day than at the judgment-seat. Better to be bowed down under a sense of sin now than to be bound hand and foot at last and cast out. All here know about the Queen, but all do'nt know her — all do not correspond with her or dine with her. There is a great difference between knowing about one, and knowing one : Christians know God. This morning not a few of you have been saying — Oh that thou wouldest rend the heavens and come down to-day — that the mountains — mountains of sin and infidelity — might flow at thy presence. Where go the Christians every morning — returning with their countenances beaming like that of Moses ? They go to a friend, to hold converse with God ; they have a friend that poor sinners have not. I have seen a godly mother stealing away to her apartment, and I have crept after that holy mother to ascertain with whom she was speaking, but I could see no one. She was speaking with one with whom I was not acquainted, and often singing these sweet verses : —

> ' Sweet the moments, rich in blessing,
> Which before the cross I spend,
> Life, and health, and peace possessing,
> From the sinner's dying friend.
> Here I'll sit for ever viewing
> Mercy streaming in his blood ;
> Precious drops ! my soul bedewing,
> Plead and claim my peace with God.'

The Christian has a friend that will never leave, and never forsake — not in the Valley of Death, for there his rod and staff will support him. But we come, secondly, to the *how* of the text. *How are we to know God ?* By ' receiving the law from His mouth, and laying up His words in our heart.' Many complain of the terrors of the law. They say, tell us of the love of God, but not of hell-fire. The Unitarians in America, and Socinians in this country, do not like the law, but till we know God's justice we will not appreciate His mercy. No doubt some are drawn gently to Christ, but others are driven with terror. A man in the upper floor of a house in London is busy reading a book. A man with a fire escape salutes him, and tells him to come down ; but he never hears the man. He will not stir till a door is thrown open, and he sees the building is on fire, and then he leaves his book and is thankful to go with the man with the fire-escape. So it is with sinners. We may tell them all about Jesus, but men listen as if they listened to a schoolboy's oration. When urged to come to Jesus they heed not ; but when the law comes — that law which is a schoolmaster, or a servant, to lead us to Christ — comes with its curse, Jesus is prized as redeeming from that curse. Many of you are living in carnal security and will not come. That man in London would not stir till he saw the house on fire; and so you will not come till you see your danger — till the enmity of the natural heart is slain. God will not take you into his house while you are an enemy. At Dumfries, an elder got the law into his heart, and he could not eat, and could not sleep. He confessed before the great congregation that he had not till then known God. And there, too, a minister said, that for thirty years he had been a preacher, while he was as ignorant of Christ as if he had been a Hindoo or a Mahomedan. Dr. Chalmers, like Dr. Thomas Scott, for twelve long years preached a dead morality before he was savingly acquainted with God in Christ reconciled. What a contrast between the audiences before and after his conversion. Look in upon that crowd of listeners in the church of Kilmany. The full rounded periods and musical cadences of the speaker fall with pleasure on their ears. His matchless strains of eloquence transport their minds to the blissful regions of his rich imagination, but alas, while his words delight and gain ascent they are impotent to change the will and influence the life. But a change comes over the speaker. See him again in the Tron Church of Glasgow. He no longer possesses that eloquence whose object is to please, nor that higher kind which pleases and instructs, but he now possesses that which is far above these, and is the object of all real eloquence — the power of persuasion. He now speaks with winning eloquence from the depths of his own experience. The appearance of the *audience*, too, is no less changed. The tearful eye, and the compressed lip betoken the sorrowing heart and firm resolve. While on the countenance of some, despair is depicted. showing the deep work of the Spirit in convincing of sin, the faces of others are radiant with new found hopes. The speaker has received the ' *law* into his heart, and *Christ*, as the end of the law for righteousness.' When the law comes, men then listen as for their lives — not to the soft cadences or rounded periods of the preacher, but to know how they can be saved. A deacon that had heard of revivals in other towns thought he would like a revival in his own town. So he arranged with others for a meeting, and attended it, and was delighted as the speaker went on, and said to himself— 'That's a hit for so and so.' He was a deacon, and was requested to stay to the inquirer's meeting He knew not what to say to weeping souls. Not knowing him I said to him, 'Are you a friend of Jesus?' He went away without saying a word and was in great agony, and like Saul he was three days without sleeping or eating, and then found peace; and I have a letter from him in which he tells me all about it, which I would read to you if I had time. How unlike this to an elder in a town in the north of Scotland, who objected to our late meeting. He said, We don't want those things here, and our minister would not like it if he were at home. Some go away angry, and I would rather that men would go away displeased, than merely saying it was all very well. He referred to a lady at Huntly, who was a scoffer, for there are scoffers in all classes. She laughed at the idea of filling a large tent with listeners to a revivalist, and yet the preacher met the lady changed and converted by these meetings. Nor will you ever seek Jesus till you are convinced of your lost state. He told a story of an American gay painter who was so disgusted with reports of revivals in Bennet's *New York Herald*, that he sent notice to stop his paper. He tried the *Tribune*, and it was also full of revivals. He tried the *Times*, and it was worse. He began to think there must be something in these revivals, and he went to a meeting. Night after night he attended, became interested, and at last rose up in the meeting and said — " I am a lost sinner; pray for me " — and he found peace in believing. It is when we see Jesus providing a righteousness for us, wounded for our transgressions, and bruised for our iniquities, that we find peace. But, thirdly, *why are we to ac-*

quaint ourselves with God? That we may have peace. Peace. Peace is a fruit of the Spirit. Love, joy. Religion is not the gloomy thing many think it. Yes, it brings peace. I have seen magistrates standing up in the crowded meeting and saying that till now they never knew real peace. Happy now, for their sin was washed away. Know you this peace? It is a delusion to assume that you cannot know whether you have this peace. A whole epistle has been written that you may know that 'you have eternal life.' Not that you may *hope* or *trust* you have it; but that you may *know* you have it. Have you a love for Christ, for the Bible, for Christians, for holiness? Don't take it for granted. Don't leave this house till you find peace. But, fourthly, *when* are you to acquaint yourselves with God? The text says now — now is the appointed time. Christ says — 'Look and be saved.' The devil is here to-day, and he says not now. Did Peter at Pentecost say to the thousands, go and pray for six weeks? No; he said repent now.

"The discourse, of which the preceding is a pretty full outline, occupied an hour and a half in delivery. After a few words of prayer, and singing two verses of the 26th Paraphrase, he pronounced the benediction, and the crowded congregation was dismissed at a quarter-past one o'clock—Saturday, March 2.

" Appended to this report is the following remark : ' We hope the visit of this young American to our city will do good. There are in Glasgow, one hundred thousand persons who go to no church."

The subjoined account of a "children's meeting," will afford interest.

"A meeting of the most interesting kind took place on Saturday morning last, in the Hall of the College. There have been of late so many services exclusively for children, and the benefits have been so very conspicuous, that it became desirable to secure the same advantages for the children of the better classes resident in the West-end. Through the exertions of two or three ladies resident in that quarter this was secured, and Saturday morning was the initiative of these gatherings. So cordial was the response to the invitations given, that the hall was entirely full, mothers bringing their dear little children, some of them not much more than five years of age, and all of them seeming glad to be present. It was a fine sight. Parents and children all there, and all to worship God, with gentlemen in the ministry. It was the complete representation as the Spirit describes it, of the Church — the 'whole family of God on earth.' Dr. Hetherington presided, the Rev. Mr. Arnot and Mr. Hammond on either side. On the platform there were also Rev. Messrs. Muir and Alexander; Robert M'Cowan, Esq.; Mr. Gall, from Edinburgh, and others.

"After singing Psalm 23d, which is regarded by many as the child's psalm, and a short prayer by Dr. Hetherington, Mr. Arnot made some interesting remarks, clustering them round the lovely idea of 'Ministering children.' Religion had first pointed her finger to them that she might draw attention to their importance, their influence, and their value. But the eye had grown dull, and had failed to look and discern what religion would have us to see. Of late, literature had been pointing in the same direction, but he hoped that religion was again to obtain the supremacy. He thought there were many indications of that. One such had come under his own notice the other day. An elderly man had called on him in great distress of mind. He had been at the revival meeting in St. Peter's, on Thursday last, and had left it unmoved, but sauntering along the street, a group of very young children were singing,

> ' I love Jesus, Hallelujah,
> I love Jesus, yes I do ;
> I love Jesus, He's my Saviour ;
> Jesus smiles and loves me too.'

"The man of fifty summers found that *he* had no song wherewith he could glorify his Lord and Saviour. He had made a discovery of his poverty, and that the lisping child was richer than him. The melody of these young voices had done what the stirring sermon of the preacher had failed to do — melted the frozen heart.

"On the conclusion of these remarks, there was sung the appropriate hymn of

> ' Come to Jesus, come to Jesus ;
> Come to Jesus just now.'

"Mr. G. Ross gave an account of the conversion of a little boy at a child's prayer meeting, and the difficulties thrown in his way by his mother and uncle to keep him back. On returning from the second prayer meeting he caught a contagious disease, and Mr. Ross spoke touchingly of how this child witnessed for Jesus while dying.

> ' Ere sin could blight or sorrow fade,
> Death came, with friendly care;
> The opening bud to Heaven conveyed,
> And bade it blossom there.'

"Many a little heart seemed touched at this mournful recital, and we all rose and sang —

> ' We're travelling home to Heaven above,
> To sing the Saviour's dying love;
> Will you go? Will you go?'

"The Rev. Mr. Muir directed the attention of another part of the audience to the testimony of the Scriptures concerning such meetings as the present — that while there was no explicit injunction to grown-up people to come to Jesus, there was for children, and couched in language that almost warned against hindrances being thrown in their way — 'Suffer little children to come unto me, and forbid them not.'

> 'Come to Jesus, come to Jesus,
> Come to Jesus just now;
> He will save you just now;
> He is willing just now.'

"The exercises closed with singing, which filled the hall and thrilled every heart. At the close of such service, the inquiry meeting is usually a season of subduing tenderness. Familiar conversation and prayer with them often continuing for another hour, while smile and tears are seen on many faces. Though much of feeling may be mere sympathy, this cannot injure the weepers, and numbers are converted."

The classification of individuals, and the direct appeal thus received was no insignificant element of power in all these special efforts — or rather apostolic, means of reaching the multitude. The men, women and children, were each addressed. To get at people, was the great aim. As an illustration, we take from a report, the sketch of an immense gathering of females alone — with an allusion to another for men.

"We give the following summary of the address which Mr. Hammond delivered on Friday evening, at the crowded meeting of females, held in Free St. Mark's Church, his remarks being founded on the words in Luke x. 42 — "Mary hath chosen that good part which shall not be taken away from her:" —

"How small and trivial, as measured by the world's opinions, are many of the materials that are found in Scripture. Such things as we pass by every day as common-place — scarce worth a thought — find their counterpart in holy writ, and there receive a stamp and character which reveals their significance. All that is what could not fail to be, since the Testaments are a disclosure of human life as it is in itself, not as we think it to be ; and of the deep import it derives from its relation to the uncreated God, and all the high and holy spiritualities of heaven on one side, and all the malignant powers of darkness on the other. And here, in these words, what have we? The register of a woman's choice — not a very important thing, we would say ; yet the Holy Ghost judges differently, and has inserted the transaction as an integral part of the Scriptures, to continue through all time. Here is a woman, a young woman, we may believe, who has made a choice, given a deliberate preference — a preference which with her was all-absorbing—to a certain thing, and the object of her choice is called ' that good part.' Now, what is that good part which Mary chose? One came to Jesus while he was on earth, and called him ' Good Master.' ' Why call ye me good? none is good but God,' was the reply. All, then, that is truly good, enduringly good, must come from God ; and, as he is a Spirit, all that proceeds from him, all that he bestows, must be of his nature — spiritual. The true good is a spiritual thing, and is God's own gift. Mary's choice fell upon a spiritual good, and because she chose it, she got it — got it to keep for ever ; ' it was never to be taken away from her.' And was this a chimerical choice of Mary's — a dim, intangible thing — a sort of vagaery? We are not left in any doubt about it; we learn precisely what it was. It was no mere notion, no fine poetical idea, no phantasm of the imagination ; but that good part was a high and holy love for the highest and holiest Person — even the Saviour. And this is the true character of love, that it always goes out upon a living person, and is, besides, essentially elective. We cannot love a mere idea ; and we cannot love every one. Love always chooses ; and Mary had chosen. Herein lay the hidden reality, and it had the power to move her whole being. See her, after a time, mourning for her brother. While Martha, in her business kind of way, 'went and met' the Lord in the neighborhood, and held a long conversation with Him, Mary 'sat still,' heedless of the proffered words of comfort which were addressed to her; but 'as soon as she heard that' 'the Master' called her, 'she arose quickly and came unto Him.' Her love for her dead brother was engulphed in her deeper love for her 'Master.' Such spiritual love is the strongest motive power that can occupy angels or men. This was Mary's 'good part' — her portion — God, her 'portion for ever.'

"Now, it is this spiritual love, this 'good part,' which Mary chose, that we want you, dear friends about me, to choose also. There are a great many Marthas here to-night, and if they go on as they are doing, engrossed with the 'cares of this life,' they'll be reproved one day by the Master. You are cumbered with many things; you find your burden heavy; fling it from you; it will weigh you down to earth; it will make you earthy, and at last sink you to hell. Yes; Just the 'cares of this life' will do that.

"Temporally, you will find it best to serve the Lord. Rising up early, and sitting up late, and eating the bread of carefulness, makes life one unbroken drudgery; it is not the work, but the anxiety, the carefulness that does it. But the Lord says, 'He giveth His beloved sleep.' And in place of all that cankering care which eats out the life of the Marthas, the Marys, who never forget that they must do with all their might whatsoever their hand findeth to do, have yet this repose pointed at in these words, 'I will both lay me down in peace, and sleep; for thou, Lord, only makest me dwell in safety.' And you, fashionable young ladies, what are you doing? Do you ever think, when you are decking your person in order to obtain notice, and assuming those manners and modes of conversation to suit time and place, how much you are injuring your very best nature? Do you ever think how shallow, how superficial and artificial, all that makes you?— how it keeps you back from ever knowing what integrity of sentiment really is? And when you are talking with gay and flippant young men, and accommodating yourselves to their perverted tastes and crude talk, do you ever think how far you are departing from that fine womanly independence — not haughty independence, but womanly independence — which gives such unspeakable worth to womankind? You wish to be admired, and all right that you should; but have — *have* the qualities which are capable of awakening admiration in a high-toned mind, and there will be no need to pander; and whoever are not capable of discerning those qualities, but relish something inferior, their admiration is not worth having. Going to promiscuous parties has perverted more young hearts, and wasted more talented young minds, than any other thing. Such visiting is a great evil. It is there that many a fine young girl loses that freshness which has such a charm — which is to her what the aroma is to the grape, and the down upon the peach; but which, once lost, can never be restored. And what follows upon this? Mannerisms and pruderies; and these are shallow things, and easily seen through, and, like all counterfeits, they are always awkward at some point or other — but

' True modesty is a discerning grace,
And only blushes at the right time and place.'

" Wherever genuine womanly modesty exists — let whatsoever arise to her, let whatsoever approach her, clean or unclean, it matters not — this quality is never found wanting; it is never absent without leave; it is never slumbering or sleeping, but is always at its post — the most vigilant and untiring of all the warders of the citadel of her being, that walk patrol by day, or call aloud the watches of the night. But parents are as much to blame, as their daughters and many times more so. They rear their children — in the nurture and fear of the Lord? No; but, worldly, time-serving themselves, they bring up their children to be as much like themselves as possible. Their education is on a false principle. Instead of bringing up their daughters to fit them for the lovely and lofty duties of life, to have those principles which fit them for meeting the dangers, and sorrows, and vicissitudes which life brings to most, with patience, self-denial, and hope, the influence of many a home is to dispose the young female mind to think only of getting married — making an eligible settlement. True, the ordinary destiny of women is to be married; but there are higher destinies than that, to which they may attain; and it is a pitiable thing to have always one thought and project before one's mind. But, besides, worldly men don't care for worldly women. There is many a man who cares nothing for Christianity for himself, but he believes it to be a good thing, and he seeks to find it in the woman to whom he would ally himself. Oh! dear friends, there is no such hard, selfish thing as the heart of an unregenerated man. Though he is quite incapable of honoring the life that dwells in a Christian woman, yet he knows that his honor is safe with her and he likes it to be safe.

"Now, as an instance of how much parents are to blame in educating their daughters for the world and not for God, I may tell you of one young lady in New York. The Spirit of God had been strivng with her, and she became greatly concerned about her soul. Now, if she had gone on at this time, she would have really entered the kingdom, and been a child of God. But her father thought — a fine young girl like that, moping and talking about religion! It made him uneasy; and, as his daughter was very pretty, he thought to get her married to some rich man. That man was trading upon his child's good looks just as many another father does. He said to his daughter, she must go into society, must be gay and fascinating, just as she had been before what he called a serious fit came on. There was a fine fashionable assembly in the city, which the father wished his daughter to attend; he promised her a rich dress and valuable jewels, if she would do so; she, with reluctance, consented. Grieved the Holy Spirit and lost all conviction, and from that moment was '*past feeling*.' She caught cold, and in two weeks was close upon death. She tried to think of her soul, but she could not. She had her rich dress spread out upon a table, and the costly jewels placed beside it, and, sending for her father, pointed with her fevered hand, and said these dreadful words, 'There is the price of my soul. I see plainly that what I 've often heard is true. I have grieved the Holy Spirit, and he hast left me.' And in darkness that young creature sunk into eternity, the victim of her father's worldliness. Ah! 'godliness is profitable unto all things, having promise of the life that now is, and of that which is to come.'

" And you, young Christian women here, are you going to ally yourselves with worldly men, unregenerate men? Will you come down from the lofty place your heavenly Father has given you, and be yoked with the children of the Evil One? How can you? Will you in this momentous thing disobey the word of your Father in heaven? Has He not said, ' Be ye not unequally yoked together with unbelievers : for what fellowship hath righteousness with unrighteousness? and what communion hath light with darkness?' Fear not, fear not, commit all things to Him who 'careth for you.' Believe, there is not a feeling lovely and pure in itself that he has implanted in the human heart that He disregards. He will undertake to satisfy all — all. But let Him. Emotions, desires that may pervade the whole being, but for which words are too clumsy, He will discern. Come before Him; come near to Him, as a child to a father. He knows you far better than you do yourselves. He hears the prayer of the heart, though never spoken.

" Yet all these are poor and paltry motives which I have

been urging upon you, to turn and give yourselves to Christ; but they may show you that 'godliness is profitable' for this life.

> 'They vainly struggle to preserve a part
> Who have not courage to contend for all.'

"The Christian, who is casting side glances to the world, has yet hankerings after the world. Ah! we must and should all live to God first-hand. All of us have hindrances and difficulties, arising out of early habits, education, or position, which we have to contend with; but we will resort to expedients to surmount these disadvantages, if we have Christian wisdom. And the surest way of complete conquest is entire, unreserved dedication of all our powers and self to God and the Lord our Saviour. Constantly straining upwards, never looking back, never looking down, but ever forwards and upwards—

> 'Not backward are our glances bent,
> But onwards to our Father's home'—

inhaling the Spirit, and reflecting the loveliness and holiness, that communicable attribute of the great Jehovah. Ah! dear Christians, seek to adorn your life—to saturate the world with heaven, and life with God, for that is the genius of true Christianity. Can you forsake all for Christ? Can you enter upon the high destiny which God has ensured for you! Can you say—

> 'Jesus, I my cross have taken,
> All to leave and follow Thee!
> Naked, poor, despised, forsaken,
> Thou, from hence, my all shalt be.
>
> 'Perish every fond ambition—
> All I've sought, or hoped, or known;
> Yet how rich is my condition!
> God and heaven are still my own.

'Soul, then know thy full salvation;
　Rise o'er sin, and fear, and care;
　Joy to find, in every station,
　　Something still to do or bear.

' Think what Spirit dwells within thee;
　Think what Father's smiles are thine;
　Think that Jesus died to win thee:
　　Child of heaven, can'st thou repine?'

"These lines are the utterances of a young lady, who, though persecuted by rich Christian parents, yet, like Mary, had made her choice — chosen the good part — not taken up a professsion, but become united to her living Saviour; and her choice is registered in heaven, as Mary's was — written in the Lamb's Book of Life, the heart of the Saviour. And, as she sped on from grace to glory, when the pearly gates were opening upon her, she could softly murmur —

' One sweetly solemn thought
　Comes to me o'er and o'er —
I'm nearer home to-day
　Than I've ever been before.
Nearer my Father's house,
　Where the many mansions be;
Nearer the great white throne,
　Nearer the jasper sea;
Nearer the bounds of life,
　Where I lay my armor down;
Nearer leaving the Cross,
　Nearer wearing the Crown.'

Oh, yes! for her to live was Christ, and to die was gain. Shall this be your portion, all here — Christ your all in all? Shall it be —

' 'Tis done — the great transction's done—
　I am my Lord's, and He is mine!'

Then have you that hope which maketh not ashamed? The hope of standing at the great white throne before the 'sea of glass,' striking your harp, and casting your golden crown, singing, 'Worthy is the Lamb that was slain, to receive all power, and riches, and wisdom, and strength, and honor, and glory and blessing?'

"We have tried to give the scope of the address which Mr. Hammond made on Friday evening last. The audience was composed exclusively of females, and they were of all classes and of all ages. This kind of gathering had been considered by some as novel; and novel it was, certainly. But why not special provision for special ends? It was feared it would be a failure, and we heard that it had even been proposed that Mr. Hammond should alter its character. Such meetings had been blessed in other places; and, as the undeniable aim of Mr. Hammond is to win souls, he believed God would bless the same means in Glasgow as elswhere. 'The just shall live by faith.' The church was crowded, and scores had to go away. The presence of God's Spirit was conspicuous; and that evening we think scarcely a tithe left after the close of the services, but remained for private conversation with the clergymen and Christian gentlemen who came at the close for the inquiry meeting.

"On the Saturday following, Mr. Hammond gave a service exclusively to men. From one of the leading journals we take the following short notice:—'The spacious church, holding about two thousand, was crowded to excess, and we are happy to add that good evidence appeared that his address on that occasion produced very satisfactory results—some young men abandoning their evil habits, and confessing their obligation to the speaker even before leaving the church.'

"During these few weeks past, an interest in this work of revival has been growing among those classes who are engaged in business, both as principles and subordinates, and the column of 'Revival Intelligence' is now looked for and read by many of those in the counting-house, the bank, and the warehouse. To meet this growing interest, we would give a rapid sketch of the proceedings of that evening, which may be taken as a sample of revival meetings.

"The Rev. Mr. Arnot opened the services with praise and prayer, and Mr. Hammond was then introduced. He remarked that he was aware there had been revivals of religion ever since the time of Christ, though the Spirit had been poured out more abundantly at some times than others; and it was especially apparent in the present times, that men were realizing the necessity of knowing whether they were in the sheepfold or out of it — in the city of refuge, or on the way to it; or were carelessly sleeping, while the Avenger was hard by, ready to destroy them. The Lord, in His sovereign mercy, was using largely the experiences of those who had been savingly converted, for the good of others not yet able to say, 'The Lord is my Shepherd.' Their pastor had kindly consented to allow two of those converts to relate the manner in which, in their cases, the great change had been effected.

"The gentlemen gladly availed themselves of the occasion to tell of their conversion.

"A stout elderly man, we should suppose of sixty years of age, stood forward, but at the request of Mr. Arnot went into the pulpit, that all might see and hear him. In a very unsophisticated way, he stated what is so usual — the long, careless, self-satisfied life — at last induced to go to one of the meetings in St. Mark's — felt there was something wrong — began to be troubled — went a second time — was wishful that some godly persons would speak with him, but they all seemed to pass him by. He had a strong desire to find Christ in his own bedroom; it would have been more agreeable to his own feelings. For a fortnight he walked the streets, groaning within himself; felt now what he had so often heard, that sin was a burden; at last determined to go to another meeting, and there either die or be saved. And he believed that God made his salvation hinge upon his obedience, in giving up his own likings of being saved in his own closet, and taking salvation where the Spirit was dealing it out. He stayed to the inquiry meeting, and that night found the living Saviour. He further stated that, though he knew it not, his conversion was in answer to prayer. His son had been converted sixteen months ago, also a daughter living at Dunbarton, both of whom had been sending in petitions at the various meetings."

On Sabbath forenoon, in Blackfriars Baptist Chapel, Mr. Hammond addressed the congregation from Acts xii. 7, "Arise up quickly." A large number remained to the inquiry meeting which followed. In the course of his address, Mr. Hammond read the following letter, from an office-bearer in the church:

"*My dear Friend*,—When I attended your first sermon I felt in noways different than I had ofttimes, in listening to sermons. I was not void of religious feelings, and was most strict in observing all religious ordinances, and had a pleasure in waiting upon the exercises of the house of God. I heard you on the following evening, and, though I cannot say I was unmoved, yet no deep impression was made. I however thought all was not right with me; with all my regularity and attention to divine things, I had not the Witness that all was well with my soul, and I that night resolved upon seeing you in regard to my state. I was prevented from doing this, or from hearing you again for a week, from a dangerous illness intervening, and any impression I may have had during that period had subsided, or altogether gone. I was able to hear you again on the second Monday evening, and I was then brought under strong convictions that I was yet without Christ, at enmity with God, without a saving interest in Jesus Christ, and without love for the

Saviour, who had done so much for me; that I had been dishonoring God in going on in this way so long, and not yielding him a reasonable service of soul and body. In the inquiry meeting, my feelings were intensified by the question from a friend, 'Have you found Christ?' and for the first time I had honestly met that question, and resolved to face it; and I had to confess, I could not answer, 'yes.' This was a momentous question, and I then realized its full meaning for the first time, and I was then brought into an agony of mind not easily described. I was unable to lay hold upon any consolation that night, and went home sorrowful of heart; all my church-going regularity, my exemplary moral character and behavior, what were they to rest upon at such a juncture? I found nothing less than a believing apprehension and application of the blood of Jesus to my guilty soul could satisfy me, and the difficulty arose, how am I to attain to this. I poured out my heart to God in prayer in earnestness, that He would give me His holy Spirit to direct and enlighten my darkened understanding, that he would reveal the way of salvation to me. I remained in deep concern all that night and next day. During your address, the truth did flash into my soul, and I was enabled to rely upon Jesus solely for a full and free salvation, and to give myself, body and soul, to Jesus, and rest upon Him to be a hiding place from the storm, and a covert from the tempest. What an inexpressible feeling of delight, when I was able from the heart to say, 'I know that my Redeemer liveth,' and that what I have committed to His charge, He will keep against that great day. On this occasion, long to be remembered by me individually, as well as in connection with the great work of the Spirit, a night signally blessed of God to many souls, when the very presence of Him, who ruleth over all, was, as it were, felt and seen among us, you came to me, and I was then enabled to say that I had decided for Jesus; and I was that night able to speak of Jesus and his love to anxious souls, whose position I had so lately, by the grace and mercy of God, been enabled to exchange.

"A few thoughts have occurred to me in reviewing the Lord's dealings with me, which I hope you will pardon me for stating here:— What would have been my fate this day, had the Lord, in his infinite justice, cut me off from the land of the living and place of hope, during my severe illness, to which I was subjected, after hearing you twice? Oh, the thought is appalling! but thanks be to God for having spared me, and given me the victory over death! I would also say what a fallacy it is to defer consideration of the interests of the soul, and the preparation for death and eternity, to a season of affliction, which, much to be feared, is too common. Oh, there never was a more dangerous expedient!— one of the devil's allurements — to deceive and ruin the soul. 'Now is the accepted time; now is the day of salvation!' not when the poor body is racked with pain, and when all the thoughts are necessary for the poor body in such circumstances. I can testify to this, and most certainly such is the case with the ungodly; in such a case, I can fancy the tumult within, when the summons come to an unprepared one, 'Prepare to meet thy God,' and the feeling must then be as it really is, that to be saved must be as by fire.

"I rejoice, dear brother, in being able to write you such a letter, and I thank the Lord for it.

Dumfries, 3d April, 1861.

The letter which follows, was written by an educated and refined young lady, and read in one of the meetings at Hope St. Free Church:

"*My Dear Mr. Hammond.*—I was present when you addressed the meeting on Monday evening, and, although solemnized by the earnestness and truthfulness of your appeal to sinners, I did not feel the applicability of it to my own case. I was a professing Christian, had been a communicant for three years, and had occasionally been in great grief and anxiety about my soul's welfare. While you were speaking, I felt conscious that I did not love Jesus as I ought, and I resolved to begin again a reformation, by playing oftener, and reading the Bible more. While waiting for the crowd to pass out, you came to me and said, 'Have you found Jesus?' It thrilled me to the heart; it seemed as if God himself had put that question to me. Its importance, and the singularity of its being put to me so personally, made me almost incapable of replying. At last I said, 'I am afraid not.' You said something about the 'Love of Jesus,' and 'inquiry meeting;' but I could think only of that question. I went home, and it was ever with me. I was at the next three meetings, and was intensely miserable, for I then knew and felt myself to be a great sinner. I spent half the nights in prayers and tears, and yet I shrunk from remaining to the inquiry meeting, for, being naturally extremely sensitive, I dreaded the taunts and jeers of my companions. I had been asking myself what I must give up, in order to be Christ's; and I felt I wished to make a reservation with regard to dancing and parties. Being passionately fond of music as well as dancing, I concluded that if I went only to small parties of ten or twelve and played for them, but abstained from dancing myself, that that would be enough. This will appear trivial to you, but I know many of my friends stumble at the same thing. On Thursday evening you said something about false communicants which pierced my heart. All my pride gave way; all dislike to the inquiry meeting; and the idea that I was the only one in my own circle who would be present at it affected me nothing then. I stayed, but could find no opportunity of speaking to you, and left more wretched than ever. I wrote to you the next morning entreating your prayers, and requesting to see you in the evening. You read my letter from the platform to the meeting, and some of your remarks absolutely terrified me. Your strongest denunciations against sinners seemed tame compared with those used in regard to me. I saw and realized my guilt and danger then as I had never done before. After you had so kindly spoken to me and prayed for me, you startled me very much by asking me to tell you what was the sin which kept me from Jesus. I was sincere when I said, I knew of none, and that I was willing to give up all for Jesus. I felt I could trust Him for salvation. That feeling remained for half an hour, and then all my despair and wretchedness returned. I never can describe the agony I suffered during that night, and the two terrible weeks which followed. I did not doubt God's willingness to save me, — my anguish arose from the thoughts, that I did not really understand what 'coming to Jesus' meant, that there was some mysterious feeling connected with faith of which I was ignorant, and some sin still hidden, which kept me from God. I besought Him to show it to me, and tear it away. I was almost heart-broken when the thought came to me, that my love for my mother, which approaches to idolatry, was the 'right hand' or 'eye' which stood betwixt me and the Saviour. God alone knows the struggle I had before I could bring myself to say to Him in truth to take her from me by death, rather than lose Jesus. I wrote a solemn covenant, dedicating myself unreservedly to God and his service, trusting quietly but with perfect faith in his goodness, and in Jesus' atonement. Two passages in the Bible were especially blessed to me — Isaiah l. 10, 'Who is among you that feareth the Lord, that obeyeth the voice of his servant, that walketh in darkness, and hath no light? let him trust in the name of the Lord, and stay upon his God.' Lam. iii. 25, 26, 'The Lord is good unto them that wait for him, to the soul that seeketh him. It is good that a man should both hope and quietly wait for the salvation of the Lord.' Since then I have never doubted my safety, but I have been well nigh crushed to the earth with a sense of sin and unworthiness; indeed, I have realized myself to be infinitely more weak, erring, and guilty than I did before. My struggle with sin has been such, that I feel and look as if I had been prostrated by some terrible illness. Now that I have found the 'pearl of great price,' how small and contemptible do all former joys and pleasures appear to me, when compared with the peace which, indeed, passeth understanding. I have no words, my dear Sir, with which to express the intense delight I have felt ever since. You spoke about God's love to us in Jesus Christ. I never felt so near to God as I did then. That one idea, 'The love of God,' has filled me with the most exquisite joy. I feel I could write pages, and yet be unable to describe my delight. The thought that I am no longer alone in the world, and that I have a brother and friend in Jesus the King of kings, is inexpressibly sweet to me.

"I tremble to think what would have become of me if I had not been present that evening when you first spoke to me. I must tell you about that night. Miss —— is my dearest friend, and on my asking her to go with me, her brother objected, and said he would go to take care of me, as I was doing wrong to go. He tired, and left before your address was finished. How I bless God that I did not go with him. Miss —— went one evening, and was present when you read and commented on my first letter. She called for me next morning, and on asking what was wrong, I told her how wretched I was, and urged her to think about her soul. She alluded to the letter you read, and said, that had made her think. I can never forget her astonishment, when I told her I wrote it. She burst into tears, and said, 'Oh, if you are so wicked, what am I?' She promised to wait for the inquiry meeting. I asked your prayers for her, and she is now, along with her *brother*, rejoicing in Jesus."

In the progress of the work a "special service for cabmen" was held, which a writer thus describes:

"On Sunday last a special service was given in the City Hall, at mid-day, for cabmen and drivers. It had been in contemplation for a week or two previous, but the many hindrances that encircle that large community of men, made it somewhat difficult to arrange. It had been known among the men that a service was to be given, so that, during the delay, expectation had grown ripe, and at last, when it was finally settled for the 24th, the needed arrangements were so speedily completed, that in one day one thousand tickets were circulated, and bills posted throughout the city and suburbs. How the cabmen responded to this invitation the appearance of the hall made known.

"We have often seen the City Hall full, crowded, crammed, but never before did we see it so densely packed — every inch of the platform and stair occupied; for after ensuring admission to the cabmen, all others were free to enter. There could scarcely be fewer than five thousand people within the walls — women in mutches, scores of factory girls with bare heads, men in fustian, besides the trimly dressed cabmen, and hundreds of the well-to-do.

"This was a great day. This meeting for cabmen had been desired with a great desire. But all the anxieties, the prayers, and preparations, how infinitesimal were they compared to the royal munificence with which they were crowned, heaped up and running over. To Him who ruleth the small things as well as the great, be all the praise and the thanksgiving, 'for He hath done excellent things.'"

Upon a Sabbath evening, at Cowcaddens, a district of Glasgow, the people so thronged to the places of appointed worship, that when the time arrived, five churches were filled by the overflowing masses. The meeting is well described by an eye-witness:

"Dr. Eadie had invited Mr. Hammond to conduct the evening services in his church. The place was so densely filled before the hour of service, that it was with much difficulty he could reach the pulpit. The hall below was immediately filled, but the crowd outside seemed in no way diminished. Milton Free Church, a few yards off, was opened, and very soon filled, till the people were swarming round the doors. Large parties that had come from the Crescents and the Terraces on the Western Road, no doubt drawn there from curiosity, but also moved by higher motives, sought out another church where they might worship God. Mr. Perrot very courteously put his pulpit at the disposal of Captain Gillmore, who had been sent for from the other gatherings, himself giving out the 47th Paraphrase, and offering up prayer. Mr. Craig came in, and, just before the sermon, told forth the unvarnished story of his conversion from infidelity. Once freed from the trammels of such barren notions, he looked back with surprise at the self-satisfaction with which he had held them. But ever the old story; not human reasoning, not affectionate entreaty, had prevailed; but a glimpse of the person of the Saviour of souls had convinced him that he was endowed with a soul, and was something more than a mere organism. It is well for men that God ever takes the conversion of a soul into His own hands. ' Not by might, nor by power, but by my *Spirit*, saith the Lord.'

"Captain Gillmore then read the 3d chapter of John. He said nothing of the mysteries of regeneration which that chapter might suggest to the metaphysical mind, but made very plain the indispensable need of a change of heart — the true regeneration; and in words calm, affectionate, copious, prayed his fellow-men and women to bethink themselves of Christ's salvation, and their own great need of that. He spoke as an educated, thoughtful, Christian gentleman so well can do, who has drawn his religion direct from the Scriptures, instead of theological tractates. The very marrow of the Gospel fell from him. After the service was concluded, we returned, hoping to gain an entrance to Dr. Eadie's church.

"The street in front of the church was crowded; and there, under the bright moonlight, hundreds were listening to a Christian layman who had been speaking to them for some time. Within that limited space, bounded on either side by the Free and Established Normal Schools, there were five different assemblies, all willing to hear the truth, and seeking to worship the living God simultaneously. We do not look upon this as the first beginning of revival in the Cowcaddens, but rather as the first fruits of much that has gone before. There has been work and prayer in the Cowcaddens for this, how heartily or inadequately God knows. But in addition to the agency already on the ground, a band of visitors from the College Church began there in winter was a year; and foremost among them was Professor Douglas, who, besides his professional duties and other claims on his attention, found time for missionary work there. And for three months this winter special prayer has been made for a revival in that quarter of the Cowcaddens. A little company of householders — a cabman, an ironfounder, a stonemason and his wife, and another young married woman, who have lately begun to follow Jesus — have all been laying this petition before the Heavenly Throne. Longing eyes were gazing upwards for some signs of the coming shower. Mr. Hammond had been little more than a week in Glasgow when he gave two services in Milton Free Church, and then other two; and now on Sabbath he is called back again to the very same quarter. Would it be presumptuous to claim, or would it be stupidity to ignore this as Heaven's acknowledgment of prayers uttered and prayers embodied in action? The Lord deals with His people as one man with another. He throws down the challenge, 'Prove me now herewith, if I will not open you the windows of heaven and pour you out a blessing, that there shall be room enough to receive it.' Such challenge was never given that it should not be taken up. Mr. Hammond has fired the mine. Christians must now be up and quit themselves like men, and in this thing do the will of the Lord. Prove Him."

The letter of a converted man, a wealthy merchant, " often seen on change," will repay perusal.

"I scarcely know how to word this letter, I feel so excited and gratified since our meeting this morning. Oh grant, heavenly Father, that the prayers then addressed to a throne of grace for me, a poor perishing sinner, may be registered in heaven. As I already told you, I belonged to a class of Christians who have a name to live and yet are dead. Revival meetings I scouted, called them quackery — excited people, and that all would end in smoke. I went upon Friday night last (and my motives were more curiosity than anything else) to hear you in Hope Street Church — the first revival meeting, but I hope not the last I shall attend. I closely observed all, and went home determined to hear more of Mr. Hammond. I, as you know, was at Mr. Arnot's yesterday; and when I heard all the voices sing, ' Come to Jesus, come to Jesus,' I felt that that was easier said than done, and so it is. Yet how easy to those who will only accept Him! Oh, that wonderful passage, ' Behold, I stand at the door, and knock; if any man hear my voice and open the door, I will come in to him, and will sup with him.' You know what God showed me after we had conversed and prayed. I had expected Jesus to open the door, but I have now found out that I must do it; yea more, I must bid Him welcome — a full and free welcome — no mere show of friendship, it must be genuine. Oh, pray that I may be kept from falling back to my old self-righteous ways, and that I may experience more of that peace which, I feel, has now begun. And Oh, I pray that God will touch my heart with love to Him, that I may speak in love, and commend in love that blessed Jesus who loved me with an everlasting love. Oh, pray for me that I may be able, having named Christ, to depart from all iniquity, that I may walk with Christ and be an ensample, so that men may take knowledge of me that I have been with Jesus. Pray also for me that, when I speak of Christ to others, He will bless my efforts, that all the glory may be his. Accept, dearest friend, my warmest thanks for a debt of gratitude I can never repay, whilst I remain, always yours."

The Wynd Journal, whose editor is pastor of the Wynd Church, has the following :

" One thing of vast importance he has achieved for the present and the future, in opening new centres of power in the city, and securing the co-operation of men in the ministry and out of it, who come to the work with fresh resources. With such an enlarged basis of operations, and such an increasing band of enthusiastic volunteers, it should not be difficult, by God's blessing, if not to take the city, at least to take its strong places, from which an effective evangelism may seize on the population in detail.

" The inquiry meeting is the real line of battle in this campaign. Many, no doubt, go away from the first meeting with their consciences awakened or their hearts renewed, who either shrink from the publicity of the inquiry meeting, or prefer on other grounds to enter their closet and shut the door and pray to the Father who seeth in secret and will reward them openly. But there are large numbers who have no place for retirement, who have no counsellors at home, who are too deeply distressed to leave the place where they have been wounded, or who fear to move away lest they should lose or miss the blessing. It is a scriptural method to ask on the spot, 'Men and brethren, what shall I do to be saved?' But if this is our real line of battle, it is here we must concentrate our forces and bring up our reserves. It is here we need wisdom and tact and readiness and power. Here we are not so much serving batteries of terrific fire, but in hand to hand encounter, ready to give quarter and to heal the wounds that have been made. Yet in meetings of two thousand or even four thousand people, (as in the City Hall,) when more than the half may wait to an inquiry meeting, it is absolutely needful to preserve order and to keep command. There should be no difficulty in providing beforehand a sufficient number of judicious Christian friends for the largest inquiry meeting that can be held, so that the dangers arising from indiscriminate conversation, and possibly from very erroneous teaching, at the most critical and most impressible period in spiritual life, may be as far as possible prevented.

"So long as inquiry meetings are held in Churches, there should be no difficulty in providing a sufficient superintendence and an adequate supply of assistants, both male and female, for private conversation and prayer. Every Church has its office-bearers who ought to be ready to undertake this work, and who have, in Sabbath School teachers, and in the Membership, surely a number sufficient for this purpose. Elders, or other office-bearers and capable persons should be appointed in a large meeting to keep order at different points, and to see that the anxious get into conference with believers who are ready and able to help. If there are not enough in a Church ready, especially in the beginning of such work, to engage in this department, it should not be difficult to get assistance elsewhere. But even if on an emergency there are not enough of known and trustworthy persons present for the number of the anxious, let these be gathered together and addressed together — a method that has its own peculiar advantages.

"At the meeting on Friday, in Hope Street, Mr. Hammond read the following letter from a lady:

My Dear Mr. Hammond, — I cannot allow another day to pass without sending you a few lines, to thank you for your earnestness and anxiety in trying to bring me to Christ. I can now say with David, 'I sought the Lord and He heard me, and delivered me from all my fears.' It is more than three weeks since I first heard you in College Church. I have ever since that felt deeply convicted, and at times despaired of ever finding peace, but the Lord in his mercy pointed out to me very simply the way of salvation. I well remember the day when you first besought me at the door of Finnieston Church to come back, and you would speak a few encouraging words to me, but I refused you three times. I was anxious to hear without being seen, and thought to slip quietly out when you were speaking to another. I have been at most of your evening meetings since, and often longed to be able to say with many of those around me, I had found Christ. Tuesday morning last I felt more distressed than I had ever done, so much so that I began quite to despair of ever finding peace. I thought there is no hope for me, and had almost resolved to go back to the world; but at night I felt quite determined to give myself to Him, and prayed as I never had prayed before. I went to my bed at night, resting myself on my Saviour, feeling I had given myself to Him, never doubting. I awoke in the morning singing these sweet lines—

> 'Here 's my heart, Lord, take and seal it,
> Seal it from thy courts above.'

I said to my husband, 'I am so happy, I feel the Lord has pardoned all my sins.' The burden of sin I had so long felt was quite removed. We wept together for joy, and I can now say, 'Happy day, when Jesus washed my sins away.' May the Lord bless your unwearied labors, in trying to bring souls to Christ. I shall ever remember you with gratitude as having been the means, through the grace of God, of saving my soul from death. Pray, dear Mr. Hammond, that my faith may be strengthened, and that my dear children may be all lambs of Christ's flock.—*22d March*, 1861.

"On Saturday last, the meeting in Hope Street was crowded as usual. Among the audience were many of that class, for whom much solicitude has been expressed, in well-meant efforts to amuse them on Saturday evenings, in concerts and other dilletanti entertainments. We beg to submit whether the agency of the prayer meeting, with its stirring addresses, and devotional exercises, is more calculated to elevate the masses, or the low buffoonery exhibited by the very men whose daily and nightly work, in saloons and elsewhere, is to degrade the people, and especially the youth of our city : which of these may reasonably be expected to prepare the better for the hallowed day of rest? We may easily prepare a people who will resemble the godless nations of the Continent, if we employ similar means as are used by their parental governments, who provide them shows, to keep them from thinking of truth and right ; but we shall not, by these means, furnish the future with the scenes or subjects of another ' Cottar's Saturday Night.' "

A leading paper of the city contains a very pointed and clear summary of the classes represented in the religious interest, and the phenomena of its progress. After speaking of the persons, scenes, and Christian fidelity rewarded, these sharp distinctions are made :

"There have been *mockers* in our meetings. A few of these, it is to be hoped, have been awakened, and with agonized souls led to Jesus, and obtained the sprinkling of His blood ; while others, it is to be feared, have had ' their bands made strong.' ' Now, therefore, be ye not mockers, lest your bands be m strong: for I have heard from the Lord God of Hosts a consump tion, even determined upon the whole earth.'— *Isaiah* xxviii. 22.

"Others, again, under the shaking of the heavens and the earth, (*Hebrews* xii. 26,) have, as it were, *turned in their graves*, and become again as still as a stone ; the Lord, to all appearance, having poured out upon them the spirit of deep sleep and closed their eyes.—*Isaiah* xxix. 10 The day of redemption is also the day of vengeance. —*Isaiah* lxiii. 14; *Hosea* iv. 17.

"Some mistaking a sound theological formula for the *living Christ*, and complacently wrapping themselves therein, have not been afraid to call the movement *the work of the Devil*. I fear these words of the Lord are applicable to such : — ' For judgment I am come into this world, 'that they which see might be made blind ' — *John* ix. 39; and of the prophet Jeremiah — ' For he shall be like the heath in the desert, and shall not see when good cometh.' — *Jeremiah* xvii. 6.

"There are others, again, so deeply wedded to order, Church organization, the routine of officialism, they cannot easily believe the waters of life astir beyond the margin of their boundaries. Surely it would be well for such to remember these words of the prophet : ' For as the heavens are higher than the earth, so are my ways higher than your ways, and my thoughts than your thoughts.' — *Isaiah* lv. 9.

"There are others, again, who, apparently from an almost incurable tendency to make idols of those whom God has honored, are doing what they can to provoke the Lord to jealousy — to bring ' leanness ' both upon themselves and others.

"Now, is it wrong to say these things grieve the Holy Spirit? Does not something of the ' fearful delicacy ' I have referred to lie here ?

"But there is a bright side, for the evidence flows in from many sources that a true and deep work of grace is going on over the length and breadth of the city.

"Now there are two facts that are patent to observing Christians. The one is the simultaneous outpouring of the Spirit on many lands ; the other, the remarkable variety in the agencies He is employing. In the first fact we are presented with a phenomenon of a truly Divine sublimity ; and it at the same time enlarges our apprehensions of the glory of Jesus Christ who has on His hands at this moment for intercession, millions of sinners awakened by the Spirit and brought to Him,—another fact this, overwhelming to our finite conceptions, though keeping out of view the inconceivable grandeur of His universal reign.

"What inroads appear to be made on officialism and routine! What new forces called into play beyond the domain of an ecclesiastical organization! May it not be there has been a too deeply-seated idea among many that all blessings would and *must* come through the consecrated channels of Church order and authority? Why, it would appear that there are phases of the ministration of the Spirit not 'dreamt of in your philosophy.'

"As to the evangelists themselves, one of the striking features among the more prominent of them is the absence of the official in their bearing, and the saliency of the human—a certain unmistakeable something, which inspires confidence and wins the heart, which says, 'We are one with you, our whole heart is yours,'—the marked and beautiful combination of faith, love, and humility—a spirit stooping to everything, that, if by such means, souls may be won to Christ. There is little wonder these men are blessed, and secure a large place in the hearts of the humble children of God.

"To be an ordained minister of the Gospel is the highest honor that can be put on man; and who shall estimate the value of a faithful and loving ministry? It is incalculable. But wherever the felt dignity of the office encroaches upon or supplants the sense of its responsibility, or blights the tender love or humility that ought to characterize the ministers of the gospel, there a great evil has been done, and an element is in operation inimical to a season of revival.

"I am very reluctant to say anything that might give offence, but I have a fear that the pride of office, of position, of a thorough clerical training, may be one reason why God, in so many places, is choosing the 'weak things, the despised things,' &c., &c., to effect the mightiest results. If it be so, then to lay aside everything unfriendly to the sweet brotherliness of spirit, that so widespread an outpouring of the Spirit is designed as it is fitted to foster and maintain, seems a very imperative duty on all who take an active part in the work of revival; and I know not a better place for the cultivation of such a spirit, than in those union prayer meetings, where ministers and others can come and go with such perfect freedom. These meetings, to my mind, are a practical exemplification of the cxxxiii. Psalm, and tend to keep among us the Spirit of God."

CHAPTER VI.

A Tour on the Continent — Letters from Geneva and Milan — Letter from an Officer of the man-of-war Exmouth, concerning religious interest on board — Presentation Meeting in Glasgow—Meetings at Miffat—London—Liverpool—Voyage in the Great Eastern—Conversions among the soldiers.

Mr. Hammond, worn down with his labors, left them the fore part of April, 1861, for a tour on the Continent. We introduce a pleasing interlude to the directly revival narrative letters, from him, published in Glasgow papers, from an officer on board a man-of-war, and others:

" ST. JEAN DE MAURIENNE, SAVOY, FRANCE,
April 16, 1861.

" MY DEAR ——, I am now to start for the top of Mount Cenis, and thence drive to Turin, 6,700 feet above the sea, before night. I send you a copy of leaf from my Journal, but I I have not time to read it over :

"*Geneva, Sabbath, close of afternoon.*

" Here for hours I have lingered upon the top of the Hotel de la Metropole. I trust it has not been a Sabbath spent in vain. The good people in Scotland will perhaps say, why not away to church? I shall be at church this evening, but there was no English service this afternoon. I have been reading the 148th Psalm. From this elevation, and with such scenes spread out before me, it is now inspired with a new richness of meaning. I can but comply with the command, 'Praise ye the Lord from the heavens; praise him in the heights' — Ps. cxlviii. 1. Surely David must have gazed with delight upon Mount Lebanon. Would that he had seen Mount Blanc upon such a day as this, and watched it as I have done through its ever-changing hues, now towering above the clouds, and now casting aside the misty veil, discovering to our wondering eyes its lofty grandeur. In front of me, covered with hundreds of boats, lies the charming lake of Geneva, its clear pellucid waters without a ruffle, asleep in the arms of the grand old mountains. What an emblem of the Christian at 'peace,' with the everlasting arms of his God about him! Clothed in white, like a guardian angel, upon the left stands Mount Jura. Nothing is wanting to complete the beauty and glory of the landscape. Such a quiet, delightful Sabbath it has not been my lot to spend on earth.

"All thy works shall praise thee, O Lord, and thy saints shall bless thee. They shall speak of the glory of thy kingdom, and talk of thy power." — Ps. cxlv. 10, 11.

But the hum of voices below recalls my enraptured thoughts, and I look down upon the hundreds of people in groups walking to and fro. No Mount Blanc with its variegated hues of crimson and purple for them; no expansive peaceful lake gladdens their grovelling souls; no holy, sacred day of rest for them. Some are on their way to the theatre, while others are killing time as they best can. How few of them have had their thoughts led from nature up to nature's God! And though, doubtless, some of them are possessed of minds capable of enjoying the beautiful and sublime, yet how few of them have a title to the 'mansions in the skies,' and can exclaim as I have done many times to-day —

> 'I love by faith to take a view
> Of *brighter* scenes in heaven;
> The prospect doth my strength renew,
> While here by tempests driven.'

I see on many of the houses balconies for promenading, and I have wondered there are not more people upon them, to admire the matchless grandeur and beauty of the work of the Great Architect of the Universe; but is it not a great wonder that *we* so seldom look away with the eye of faith to the heights of Beulah and the Delectable Mountains?

> "To spend one day with thee on earth,
> Exceeds a thousand days of mirth."

Truly this has been a day spent with God. 'How marvellous are thy works!' 'Thou art glorious in holiness, fearful in praises, doing wonders.'"

" The following letter from Mr. E. P. Hammond," says the Glasgow Scottish Guardian, "addressed to a friend, was received the other day, and as it is known that a lively interest in his movements is felt by many in Glasgow and elsewhere, it has been thought that the publication of it would afford gratification to his friends:

'Milan, Lombardy, April 18,
and Genoa, April 22, 1861.

'My Dear ———, You see I am now in northern Italy, almost underneath the Alps. We left St. Jean de Maurienne last Tuesday, by the diligence, for Turin, via Mont Cenis. The day was all that could be desired for Alpine scenery. Such a sky looked down upon us as is seldom seen in Scotland. My seat was behind the driver over the *coupé*, therefore the highest and best of all on the diligence; my companions English and American; our party composed of all nations nearly — French, German, Norwegian, &c., &c. Our ascent, till we reached Lans le Bourg, was gradual, the scenery constantly changing; the mountains threatening to impede our further progress; but, as our fresh relay of horses plunged boldly on, they seemed to retire and allow us to pass. Thus winding among them, on we went. One village after another was passed. All the Savoyards came rushing out of their cottages as crack, crack, went the whip, not needed, however, to indicate our approach. One sou, thrown upon the ground to the children holding out their hands for money, was sufficient to make a large file of them, four thick. After a good dinner at Lans le Bourg, we began the ascent of Mont Cenis. Eight pairs of strong mules were attached in front of the horses. And now, up, up we go over one snowy peak; and yet another and another rises in view of Alps in front, Alps to the left, Alps to the right, Alps closing in behind. The sun is now bidding us adieu for the night, tinging with his parting light the peaks with gold and crimson. How mysterious and varied thy power, O King of Day, in this Italian sky! Be it cold snow, or hard rock, all beams with splendor at thy magic touch! Who can help thinking, at a time like this, of the Sun of Righteousness, and of the joy that pervades human hearts when illuminated by His genial life-giving beams? No sooner had the sun taken his departure, than the pale moon appeared to cheer us on our way. We then had an American sleigh ride, with jingling bells at the horses' necks. The passengers and baggage were divided; the horses and mules, no longer in pairs, but tandem, wearily draw us up, and we seem going up, among the stars, for some of these appear as if resting upon the gigantic shoulders of the mountains. Miles below, in the dim moonlight, are the fading lamps of the villagers. At first the snow was soft, and so loose that it had to be dug through to prevent the horses plunging; and so, after this pioneer work, we found ourselves as if passing through a street with marble walls, and had it not been so cold, we might have believed ourselves in Geneva. But soon we emerge from our high-walled streets, and are slipping along on the tops of our so-called marble houses. Is it possible that all this change has taken place in one day? At St. Jean de Maurienne, a few hours ago, the sun was intolerable — the apple and peach trees in full blossom; but now all our Scotch plaids are not sufficient to keep off the bitter frost. But have I not in Scotland felt a change as perceptible as this, in passing from one congregation, where hearts were glowing with love, basking in the rays of the Sun of Righteousness, eagerly drinking in the simplest gospel truth — to another, where the atmosphere was chilling, freezing like hoar frost, the very breath indicating that few warm sympathizing hearts were present to pour ardent prayers to God for a blessing upon themselves or upon God's servants? Ah! how different the effect upon the preacher in such a case! While thus musing, we were gliding swiftly along over the smooth snow. In the distance we see lights and hear bells. What is to be done? Another party is coming from Turin, and how are we to pass them? Far off from that beaten track the snow is soft, and the horses know it, and are loath to leave the path; when compelled to do so one of the horses goes floundering deep down, and it takes all the rest to drag him out. No wonder, for he was wallowing in the soft snow bank forty feet deep, and all his own efforts would only have plunged him the deeper. I thought of the poor sinner who has wandered from the 'narrow way,' plunged in hopeless despair; and without the strong arm of Jesus to rescue him, he must perish.

'It was one of those days and nights in which one seems to live a lifetime. All the way upon the sledges I sat alone with the driver; the rest of the party were keeping warm inside. The distance seemed about eight miles. The cold was piercing; the poor beasts shrank, and at times seemed inclined to turn back. A noble mastiff of the St. Bernard breed kept close alongside, ready to lend us timely assistance. But no avalanche came thundering down upon us, as one had done a few days before, suddenly destroying six travellers.

'The sight of the telegraphic wires led us to realize that we were still breathing the air of earth ; for even over those everlasting hills, England, Scotland, and Italy were interchanging thoughts. These wires are now speaking of wars and rumors of wars, yet, also, is their work one of peace. They have made many hearts in Britain and America to rejoice, with the news of the success of the down-trodden Italians struggling for freedom and liberty of conscience. They have told of God's Word, no longer chained in the cell of the monk, but freely circulated among the people; and the day is not far distant, when they will herald the glad tidings of the unshackled preaching of the gospel to the millions who are now ignorant of its precious truths.

'After passing over a considerable extent of table land, the moon all the while smiling upon us, and the stars glowing above the unbroken snow, began the descent. At first it was fearful indeed. The mules and the horses, all but two, were discharged. Down *such* a declivity, I suppose, we should go carefully, to say the least ; but the method seems to be to take it at a bound ; besides, we were late, and the driver seemed to have more of the 'go-ahead' in him than even we Americans ever think of possessing. He placed no restraint upon the furious horses. We had left the moon on the other side of the mountains ; and, to add to our gloom, the bright lamps attached to our sledge were suddenly extinguished by the fiercely raging winds. More than once I seized the reins, but it was to little purpose ; it only occasioned a fresh crack of the whip from the driver ; and I almost wished I was oblivious to passing events, like some of the loud sleepers inside. At every turn we seemed to plunge into the yawning chasm below. Huge clouds were now hurrying across the mountain sides, as if in mourning for us. No joyful songs now enlivened our party. Sunny Italy lay spread out before us, but no sun to reveal it to us. At last we stopped at a dwelling house, and I resolved, if possible, to spend the rest of the night there, and walk down in the morning. But it was a part of but one room, and in it there were at least thirty mountaineers, who, overtaken by night, had thus far toiled up the mountain, and were sitting about in that miserable room, some playing at cards, some smoking, and the rest snoring. We soon reached the diligence, and were glad of a warm seat, and a warm climate, too. But the sun had been hot the day before, and the wheels sank down, and there, to my joy, we were forced to wait till mules were brought to our assistance. Meanwhile the earth rolled on its axis, and the sun began to streak the east with its light; the hills behind were changing their hues; the dark drapery of the mountains was flung aside, and these lofty Alps now seemed rejoicing to meet the sun, and with the heavens were declaring the glory of God, and showing forth His handy work. An Alpine village, far down below us, was sending up its morning smoke, telling of labor begun. Clouds, like sheets of snow, hung below us.

'We were entering Turin an hour or two after sunrise. But those grand old mountains had far more attraction for me than that city, though within its walls were Victor Emmanuel and Garibaldi. I could not keep my eyes away from them; I was constantly looking back to have one more last gaze. For a moment I wondered if there would be any sights in heaven more grand and beautiful. But, oh! I remember that it is written, 'Eye hath not seen, nor ear heard, neither have entered into the heart of man, the things which God hath prepared for them that love Him.'

'I fear I have wearied you with this long letter. I must therefore reserve my impressions of Turin, Milan, and Genoa till another time. I have some balls and some relics to show you, taken from the battle-field of Magenta, near Milan. A young student from Como was with me, and took great delight in pointing out the position of the French, Austrian, and

Italian troops — the traces of the battle — the houses marked with musket and cannon shot; and with much feeling he pointed to the cross raised to commemorate the burying place of the thousands who fell in battle. On reaching Genoa, I found myself much exhausted, and unable to proceed on my journey. I began to fear that my last work was done in Glasgow. But the Lord has been good to me. The Rev. D. Kay, a missionary of the Church of Scotland, who has been like a brother to me, took me to his own house, so that I am now quite myself again, and am to leave Genoa for Leghorn to-night (Monday, April 22,) by boat, and to-morrow shall be on my way to Rome.

'With much love to ——, and my many dear friends in Glasgow,

I am, your affectionate brother in Jesus,

E. P. HAMMOND.'"

At the Daily Union Prayer Meeting in Elgin Place Chapel, the following letter, addressed to the meeting by Mr. Hammond, was read:

" Rev. Dr. Stewart's,
LEGHORN, ITALY, 23d April, 1861.

" My dear Brothers and Sisters in Jesus, — My promise to write you is not forgotten; not a day has passed without my thinking often, often, of that dearly loved daily prayer meeting. The happy hours passed there I can never forget. It was there that I often found my strength revived for the evening. (Isaiah xl. 31.)

" For many years in America I was in the habit of attending a daily noon prayer meeting, and it seems like losing my dinner, to be deprived of the privilege now.

" What a contrast was presented to my mind, when last Thursday I entered the great and wonderful Cathedral of

Milan, with its three thousand marble statues, between the scene before me and that daily witnessed in your union prayer meeting. There were dozens of priests in long robes, chanting and speaking in an unknown tongue; were they not in a place bearing some resemblance to a Christian Church, we might have thought them acting some solemn part in a theatrical performance. And who were the auditors of this grand performance? About twenty unhappy looking creatures, most of them beggars; more priests and monks and friars than all the rest. Disgusted with all this delusive mummery, I fled away to the top of this marble cathedral. From that dizzy height I looked away across the snow-covered Alps, and shining Mount Rosa, and thought of you, a band of real worshippers of the meek and lowly Jesus, with here and there, mingling among your number, heavy laden souls, not listening to some avaricious priest, as he says, ' Come to the *Confessional*,' but to the gentle voice of *Jesus*, the Great High Priest, who hath appeared to put away sin by the sacrifice of himself, saying, ' Come unto *me* all ye that labor and are heavy laden, and *I* will give you rest.'

" Artistically, the cathedral is, perhaps, the finest in the world. No one, possessed with a love of the grand and beautiful, could help admiring this wonderful structure, with its forests of spires, adorned with six thousand six hundred and sixteen marble statues, and basso relievos, each of them supporting a colossal statue of some of the apostles or saints.

" Images of Jesus everywhere! but in whose heart was there the form of Jesus enthroned as the hope of glory? Semi-heathen temples on every hand! but among all their worshippers, who of them possessed souls ' fit temples ' for the indwelling of the Holy Spirit? Ah! how I longed to rush into the thronged streets and tell them of Jesus, of salvation through Him alone, and of temples not made with hands! But had I done this I should have been dragged away to prison, or to some pestilential region, where an infectious malaria would have put an end to my existence.

"But, since the union of the Italian States, the Bible has been freely circulated, and the pure Gospel is preached under certain restrictions.

"At Genoa I found rest needful; the heat was intense, and my head seemed much affected. The Rev. D. Kay, a missionary from Scotland, was like a brother to me, and in three days I was so well as to be able to speak for him twice on the following Sabbath. At the close of the evening service we had an inquiry meeting, and there is reason to believe some that day were awakened, and by the Spirit of God led to Christ. We went down into the harbor the night before, and induced some to come, who were intending to spend the Sabbath in visiting the celebrated Pallavicini Gardens.

"At Leghorn I have just spent one day and night with Dr. Stewart. Most of you are already familiar with his successful and untiring labors."

"Port of Civita Vecchia,
45 Miles from Rome, April 24th.

"While writing the above, Mrs. Stewart came and took me away to the weekly female prayer meeting. The 'little flock' in Leghorn are longing for a revival, and wished to know all about the work of the Lord in Glasgow and Scotland. About ten meet weekly to pray for the outpouring of the Holy Spirit. They request your prayers on their behalf. We had an inquiry meeting. Two remained for conversation, while the rest in an adjoining room were engaged in prayer. I told them all that they must meet daily, and not only pray, but work and speak individually to the perishing thousands around them; and some of them with tears promised to do so. It was a most precious little meeting. I found myself quite moved by it, and, I trust, received a fresh baptism of the Spirit, consecrating myself anew to the glorious work of winning souls to Christ.

"After visiting Pisa, with its leaning tower of the twelfth century, its marble Cathedral supported by innumerable fantastic marble pillars, the Baptistry, and Campo Santo, we returned to Leghorn, and visited an American man-of-war, the Susequehanna. Dr. Stewart had preached on board, the Sabbath before, and found the Lieutenant a most devoted man. It was delightful and touching, as we spoke of the sympathizing love of Jesus, to see his whole emotional nature, as the tears filled his eyes and his hand instinctively pressed my own. He took us down to the place of their prayer meeting. 'I could not live without this prayer meeting,' said he. 'It is here that Jesus stands in our midst, and says, as to his disciples of old, 'Peace be unto you.''"

At the Ewing Place Daily Prayer Meeting, on Tuesday, letters were read from Mr. Hammond. At St James's Hall, London, Mr. Hammond had addressed from 1500 to 2000 people; a good number of inquirers remained. He was to speak in Crown Chapel the following evening. He adds,— "Nearly 3000 soldiers go in the 'Great Eastern,' on Monday, from Liverpool. What an opportunity for speaking for Jesus. Pray for us."

"H. M. S. 'EXMOUTH,' Naples, 28th May, 1861.

"*My dear Mr. Hammond*,— This very day last month I bade you farewell on board the French Steamer; and though we have not the pleasure of your bodily presence among us, yet we trust that the same Spirit, which rested so abundantly upon you, has been communicated to, and is now abiding in, many a grateful sailor's heart on board. Ever since you left, we have kept up the nightly prayer meetings and addresses, and propose to continue to do so, in God's strength, as long as we can. I could fill sheets of details in telling you the simple story of those who have found peace with Jesus. Some of these were the worst characters on board the ship, and now their lives are living witnesses of the great change which the Spirit of God has produced on their lives and conversation.

"One man, a *Sepoy* sailor, was so bad and wicked, that he had been turned out of one sailor's mess after another, and none would at last receive him, so that he lived in the *black-list mess* constantly. He swore dreadfully, and was too bad for sailors to associate with. That man now has come down every night; his life changed; given up swearing; amended his ways; and the wonder of everybody who knew him. He attends the evening school regularly, that he may learn to read his Bible; then comes in to us; and if you only saw how he looks at the Bible, and turns over the leaves as if he would devour the contents, (though he can't read), yet it would melt the hardest heart. Another young fellow, one of our servants, was turned away for being a drunkard. He now tells me, that he made a collection of the very worst oaths he could hear, and entered them in a book, so that he might never forget them, but make use of them as he might see fit. That young man has now become changed; leads a new life; and engages in prayer with others on Sunday afternoons. An African sailor, born in Antigua, though he has a black skin, has now a white heart, cleansed by the blood of Jesus; and the simple and beautiful, nay, *eloquent* prayer I and others heard him offer up to God, the Father of the black as well as the white Christian, refreshed my soul as well as the souls of others. One man, a Cornish man, is very sincere in his pleadings, but his ignorance of our language is a great drawback to his expressing the desires of his heart.

"On Sunday afternoons we meet with those who are desirous of engaging in prayer. Some come down who desire to pray, but when the time comes they can't express the longings of their hearts before others; but, I have no doubt, they will derive encouragement from hearing their fellow sailors praying, and will receive the Spirit of prayer from on high. They all pray in private, but are nervous before others.

"Lieut.——, and I, felt that we had need of their prayers, and it was our duty to encourage them, and give them an opportunity of praying with those who felt the necessity of cultivating the spirit of prayer. We addressed them once or twice on prayer, and then intimated that we would set apart means of re-establishing their bodily health, and fitting you for going among my countrymen and others to proclaim '*the glad tidings of great joy,*' and win souls unto Christ. Our hearts are lifted up in thankfulness to our heavenly Father, who, in his providence, sent you for a few days amongst us, to arouse sinners from the torpor of death, to sing the songs of Zion and rejoice in God their Saviour. I feel that my own soul has been much refreshed by your presence among us, and fresh vigor has been infused. The great wall of formalism has been broken down, and I have been enabled to go and talk to sailors in a way which I have never done before. The same has taken place with Lieut. ——, who is one with me in everything which we do for the salvation of souls.

"At one time I proposed writing you sooner; but afterwards thought it better to defer it, until we saw whether the impressions made on the hearts were of a transitory character or not. I have to apologize for not writing the letter you proposed, to the scholars attending some of the Sunday schools in Glasgow; but when I thought over the matter, I felt that I could not make it so interesting as you could, and have given up the suggestion, leaving it for you to tell them about the sacrifices offered up in the temble of Serapis, as well as the sacrifices which are now offered up on board the Exmouth, by those who, at times gone by, sacrificed to other gods. You can tell them how God directed you to Naples, and the means by which He sent you on board the Exmouth to rouse sinful sailors from the sleep of death, who, until your arrival, had been sacrificing unto other gods, and living sinful lives, and doing very wicked works. How you now hear, that some of those wicked sailors are blessing the God who sent you here, that His Holy Spirit might be poured out upon them, changing their hearts, and leading them unto the Lamb of God. You can tell them that we have a sailor among us who comes from Paisley. This man, in his young days, had been taught to sing praises unto God, just as they are taught; and now he comes down every evening with his tune book, and pitches the tunes, and has become our precentor. After a hard day's work he delights to tune his heart to God — that God to whom we all sing praises, and who gives us singing hearts as well as praying hearts. His mess-mates may laugh at him but he does not care, for God has brought him among us to assist us in praising God, in singing psalms, and hymns, and spiritual songs — making melody in our hearts unto God. You may tell them how those on board, who have given their hearts unto Jesus (but can't read), are now learning to read, and attending an evening school after their day's work, that they may be able to read God's word for themselves — those epistles and gospels which were written for them, as well as for everybody who would receive them. You can tell them, how hard work it is for a grown-up person to learn to read, and how much easier it is for a boy and a girl; and how their hearts are more disposed to receive the things of Jesus, because they are not so wicked as a grown-up person, and have not committed so many or so great sins. That Jesus loves little children, and invites all, but especially them while they are young, to come unto Him, that they might be happy on earth, and be happy when they come to die; for after death they will see Jesus and dwell for ever with Him in heaven.

Your ever affectionate brother in Jesus."

The following letter was handed in by a friend of the writer, and shows one blessed result of obeying the command to "sow beside all waters:" —

"*My Dear Sister,*—I wish to tell you of a man who came on board this ship a few days ago. He preached to us, and I never heard a man so earnest in prayer. He has touched the hearts of many on board. My flesh trembled, and every nerve shrank, so that the people took notice of me. It was nothing but the Spirit of God that was pouring into my soul. I cannot tell you how I felt, but ever since I felt happy. The good man who had spoken to us was going away that evening, but some of us prayed him to stay a day or two with us, and he remained for two days. He is a true Christian. He came from America to Glasgow, during the time of the Revival there, and preached in many churches in that city. He came to this place to preach the Gospel to every one. He has again left for Glasgow, from which place he proceeds once more to America. His name is Mr. Hammond. Dear Sister, there are two of our officers who have had a prayer meeting on board every night, for many long months, but there have been few who have encouraged them by attending. They prayed to God that he would turn the hearts of those on board, and the Lord, you see, has now answered their prayer; for it was the Lord who sent that good man amongst us, who has given many of us to see the dangerous way in which we are going. Ever since he came here the meeting-room is filled. And Oh, dear sister there is a great change in me. For many long years I have been travelling on that ' broad road ' which leadeth to everlasting misery. But now I see that I have been going very far wrong. I have got my eyes opened. I have found out Him who is a way from the broad to the narrow road, and in Him I have found peace — a peace I would not want for all the world. Let the world say what it may, I will serve the Lord. Your loving brother."

Naples, 12th May, 1861.

A writer, who has been often mentioned in these pages, alludes to the effect of the absence of the principal agent:

"It was thought in some quarters, that with the departure of Mr. Hammond there would be a lull in the revival; but, so far from that being the case, it has assumed a more determined aspect. As might be supposed, the effervescence which agitated the surface of society with the first appearance of an interesting stranger, has at last subsided, and now we see to what high-tide mark the religious life in the community has risen.

"Since his return from Italy, he has been with us rather more than a fortnight; part of that time has been given to making excursions to Ayrshire, Stranraer, and Helensburgh, for evangelistic purposes. Throughout the last week of his stay in Glasgow, he daily conducted the Union mid-day prayer meeting, and in the several evenings gave a special service successively in Wellpark, St. Mark's, Anderston, and Hope Street Free Churches. To the praise of Him who is the FAITHFUL WITNESS and the AMEN, the labors of this servant have been acknowledged to the very last; the Lord making His glory to appear in the conversion of souls by the Word preached."

Before leaving for America, a soiree presentation meeting, presided over by Robert M'Cowan, Esq. was held in the City Hall, containing 4000 people, which was packed; and it was believed three times that number would have been present, had there been room. We give, as a very fair and suggestive specimen of the tone of the speeches, an extract from the editorial review of the meeting by Dr. J. Smith, LL.D., Editor of the Glasgow Examiner.

"The demonstration was significant as well as triumphant. We see in it a stranger from America, two years ago unknown to fame, winning the highest honors that even Glasgow can confer. Mr. Hammond came among us a stranger. Some of our most eminent clergymen welcomed him to their pulpits. His addresses excited a very wide interest. Hundreds professed to have been led to attend to their spiritual interests by his discourses, and crowded audiences were always present to listen to him. As he labored incessantly for weeks without fee or reward, and in the face of not a few rebuffs from a portion of the public and the press, many thought that something was due to his disinterested labors in a public way, and hence the proceeding of Thursday evening. We have never been among Mr. Hammond's unqualified admirers, and have not hesitated to state what we reckoned objectionable in his manner and matter; but we are not less prepared on that account to magnify the grace of God in him, and to acknowledge the extraordinary interest he has awakened, and the great amount of good he has achieved. After the eulogies he received on Thursday, from several of our best known clergymen and laymen, any testimony we might be inclined to give in his favor might well be reckoned superfluous. But we cannot but notice the generosity of the speakers, and the profound enthusiasm of the audience at Thursday's meeting. One who has not yet attained the rank of a licensed preacher, who is only attending to his preliminary studies, has awoke such echoes in his praise in the City Hall as were never awoke before."

Referring to his curiculum, Dr. Smith adds:

"We mention this because not a few revivalists have been popular though they had none of the advantages of previous education, or any training for public work. We mean no disrespect to them when we say, that the man who has all their qualifications for usefulness and a proper training besides, occupies a much more advantageous position, and is likely to sustain his popularity better among certain classes of society. Educated persons among his audience do not require to be told, that the speaker is one whose mind has been thoroughly trained, and who is versant with ancient and modern literature. None but a person of classic taste and training could have given the same interest to the narrative of his recent travels in the classic land of Italy. We surely do not need to argue that, other requisites being equal, the man trained to think and speak must have a vast superiority over others, however earnest and zealous such may be. The rapid sketch given by the Chairman as to the career of Mr. Hammond, as a revivalist, was very satisfactory, and the Chairman had the advantage of speaking, not only from undoubted authority, but from a personal and intimate knowledge of him. As a people, the Scotch are proverbially cautious in receiving strangers; but in this case they have such testimony, both public and personal, that they can have no hesitation, and have shown none, in welcoming him as a true man, and devoted servant of the one Master in heaven. Anything more satisfactory and decided than the speech of Mr. M'Cowan in favor of Mr. Hammond, it is impossible to conceive. The speech of the Rev. Jacob Alexander was very cordial and suggestive. He welcomed Mr. Hammond because he had developed the lay agency to a larger extent than ever — he had especially enlisted students in the work of evangelism — he had originated children prayer meetings, — and especially he had taught many to sing hymns who never sang them before. In defence of the revival movement, he brought in a very happy illustration from spring. An ill-natured person might crush the crocuses and snow-drops, and dam up the streams, and declare that there was no spring. But the mighty movement was being felt throughout the vegetable world, and would by and by burst into beauty, despite the allegations of ill-conditioned persons. And so in this movement. Men may deny it, but they cannot keep back the resistless influence at work in the natural or spiritual world."

From Glasgow Mr. Hammond went to Moffat, and thence to London. At the former place a meeting was appointed, especially with reference to his passing the Sabbath there, on his way to the Metropolis. Such was the crowd at this watering place, that the throngs went from the church door to the open air; and the divine influence, which had rested so largely upon Scotland, was manifestly present among the people.

Among the meetings in London, a large one was held in St. James's Hall, respecting which, Dr. Campbell, of the British Standard, writes:

"Mr. Hammond has just been in London, where we have enjoyed the pleasure of several interviews with him. He went off yesterday, to Liverpool, whence he proceeds in the Great Eastern, which is chartered by Government to carry out 2,200 troops, besides a body of Cavalry, to Canada. Amid such a crowd, a voyage of the old stamp, extending to seven or eight weeks, would have afforded some scope for hopeful labor; but nothing can be done in the brief period of nine or ten days.

"We may observe that he preached in St. James's Hall, last Sunday evening. Although his design was not announced till Friday, so well had the thing been managed that there was a large congregation. Having opened the service in the ordinary manner, the Rev. J. Alexander, of Glasgow, made an admirable address, replete with the purest evangelism. Mr. Hammond then discoursed for nearly an hour, in a strain peculiar, remarkable, and exceedingly fitted to be useful. Nothing could have been more void of glare, claptrap, and meretricious display. Nothing could be more unpretending and unambitious. It was throughout stamped by 'godly simplicity.' The grand object was clearly the salvation of men and the glory of God."

In Liverpool, also, meetings were held, a notice of which we take from the Liverpool Mercury:

"The Rev. E. P. Hammond, whose labors have been so signally successful in different parts of Scotland, has been holding a series of special services in Liverpool, previous to his departure for America in the Great Eastern. The first service was held on the 23d instant, in Canning Street Presbyterian Church, of which the Rev. J. R. Welsh is the pastor. The next meeting was held on Sunday evening, in the Rev. Dr. White's Church, Islington. Both services were numerously attended, and in the evening an earnest and affectionate address was delivered by Mr. A. F. Thistlethwayte, of London, who has been laboring in connection with Mr. Hammond. After the addresses, about 300 persons remained for conversation concerning religious subjects. The next service was held in Dr. Raffles's Church, Great George Street. The Rev. J. R. Welsh, who introduced Mr. Hammond, having alluded to the objections often urged against revival services, observed that he did not believe that error would be owned of God; and showed that the labors of such men as Messrs. Brownlow, North and Hammond, had resulted in the conversion of numerous souls. The Rev. Dr. White gave an interesting account of the glorious results of the revival under Mr. Hammond's labors in Annan, Dumfries, and other places. Mr. Hammond then delivered an earnest address, calculated to arouse careless souls to a sense of their spiritual condition, at the close of which a number of anxious ones remained, with the object of seeking spiritual advice. On Tuesday evening, at seven o'clock, an out-door service was held in front of the chapel, and addresses were delivered by Mr. J. W. Bonham, of America, and Mr. Thistlethwayte, of London. During the meeting, a man came near the speakers and begged one of the hymns, stating that he had resolved to destroy himself, but was just then arrested by the sound of the preaching. At the service in the chapel, a very brief address was delivered by Mr. Bonham, who was followed by a young man from Scotland, who gave an interesting account of his conversion. Mr.

OF THE HOLY SPIRIT. 199

Hammond then delivered a very earnest and affectionate address, which was listened to with very great attention, and produced a practical effect on the minds of those present, a number of whom remained at the inquiry meeting. Some were deeply anxious. Last night a further meeting was held in Great George Street Chapel, when Mr. Hammond delivered an address, and two young converts related their experience. Previous to the inquiry meeting which followed, the Rev. Dr. White urged upon those present the necessity of immediate decision for Christ. A large number remained for inquiry, many of whom went away rejoicing in the Saviour."

The homeward voyage, in its secular and religious interest, can be given in no better form than by a letter from his pen, addressed to the Daily Prayer Meeting in Glasgow, and printed in a Glasgow paper:

"GREAT EASTERN, July 2d, 1861.
"My dear ——, Here I am, away off the banks of Newfoundland, amid fogs and icebergs, and yet my thoughts revert to you and the dear people on Scotia's shores. I have had a letter thought out for you ever since we left Liverpool, but it is not so easy on board ship to get these thoughts put down on paper. Sea-sickness has not been the excuse, for I have not seen one on board thus afflicted. But I have been hard at work day and night distributing thousands of tracts and about twelve hundred Bibles, and holding meetings.

"I cannot but think that the many prayers offered for a blessing to attend us on our voyage have been answered. We have had large and deeply solemn meetings every day since Sabbath (30th.) We could not see our way to commence these meetings till then. We had first to secure the consent and co-operation of the chaplain on board, and also of the captain of the ship, and of the two Colonels of the 30th and 60th Regiments. All this was accomplished by one of the officers of the 30th, a decided Christian, to whom Captain Blackwood, whose letter was read in your daily prayer meeting, introduced me. This dear officer has been most active. He and a few others have met every day in my room for prayer. Some days we have had two and three meetings. There is no place where the voice can reach all at once. Sometimes the wind is so strong that I find it impossible to speak long; my voice soon gives way.

"Last night we had the first regular inquiry meeting. I gave it no name, but, after addressing them, just went down among them at once; nearly all remained, and many were the anxious questions asked. Would that I could have had a hundred working Christians to have gone among the soldiers, to take them by the hand, and kindly point them to Jesus. I thought of those who used to be so active in the union prayer meeting, often remaining till five and six o'clock to bind up the broken-hearted. A number of Romanists were among the awakened. About half of the 30th, I am told, are of that persuasion. I suppose I have given away at least five thousand tracts and books, which are perused for hours at a time by the soldiers. Only one man refused to take a tract or book. Some of the officers are in an anxious state of mind, and have been in my room on their knees, seeking for peace in Jesus.

"It has strengthened me to remember, that the dear friends in the daily union prayer meeting have been remembering us at a throne of grace. We have often been in danger, but not in despair. Yesterday morning we were near a collision with the steamship Arabia. There was a dense fog, and we were near running into several icebergs. We saw four or five immense ones at the same time. One of them was much like Edinburgh Castle. Many were in great alarm the night before last, by the sudden stoppage of the engines, and the sight of the huge iceberg right ahead. Several did not retire to rest all night. Most of these 'monsters of the northern deep' were prowling about, in near the same place where we encountered one two years ago (June 6th), 180 miles off St. John's, Newfoundland. That terrible scene has often come up before my mind during the past few days. In thinking over the wonderful dealings of God, and His goodness to me, I am often led to exclaim, 'What hath God wrought!' How little did I know what was before me, when on 1st June, 1859, I set sail from New York, to be absent for only a few months. I trust I have been led to renew my vows of consecration to the service of Jesus.

"While writing the above, a Roman Catholic came to ask me for a Bible. His very looks indicated that he was anxious about his soul. His lip quivered as he said, 'I have had no peace since I heard your address on Sabbath last. I am a great sinner. What shall I do? I have been worshipping images too long — all the time neglecting Jesus. Pray for me.' We knelt and prayed. It would have melted a hard heart to hear him asking for mercy. I am confident he has found Jesus, and will at the last be found in Him."

"Friday, July 5th.

"It is a glorious morning. We have just entered the Gulf of St. Lawrence. We shall soon be at the mouth of the river. It would have done your heart good to have seen our meeting last night. It was something like one of our old meetings in Hope Street Free Gaelic Church. It seems that nearly all the three thousand were listening. The power of God's Spirit was felt, and the inquiry meeting that followed showed that many were awakened. It was truly touching to see some of these strong soldiers wounded by the 'sword of the Spirit.' I thought of the words, 'Thine arrows are sharp in the heart of the King's enemies, whereby the people fall under thee.' Though half of the 30th regiment are Roman Catholics, all came to the meetings and read the tracts. If one could get a

congregation composed *entirely* of Romanists I am inclined to
think that, with *earnest — burning — heartfelt* words, relying
on the Spirit of God, he might confidently expect as great a
harvest as from an ordinary Protestant audience. But should
he begin to discuss some of their peculiar doctrines he would
lose power over them at once. But let him come to them as
an ambassador from heaven — telling them in plain words of
their enmity and of their danger in fighting against God, and
proclaiming reconciliation through Christ Jesus, and his words
will not fall to the ground. Christ and Him crucified is the
preaching that must find its way to the heart.

"I fear I have wearied you with this long letter. I shall
write you again when I reach home. Not a day passes but I
think of the daily union prayer meeting in Ewing Place Chapel. Please remember me to them. Tell them the Lord has
answered their prayers, — that souls on board the Great
Eastern have been saved. This very moment a strong man has
left my state-room, seemingly having just given himself to
Jesus. He had been anxious for some one to speak to him for
a month. One young man has been awakened since he heard
dear Mr. Radcliffe, in Ireland. So tell them to pray on. Pray
without ceasing. Your affectionate brother in Jesus."

The New York Observer reports of Fulton Street
prayer meeting :

"A gentleman said he had in his hand a letter from a
passenger on the Great Eastern. It was from one whose voice
he had often heard in this prayer meeting. On the passage
over they had prayer meetings every night, and many had been
converted. Some of the converts were British soldiers on their
way, under Government orders, to Canada. This gentleman,
whose labors had been so much blessed, had been very useful to
many souls in England, Scotland and Ireland. Wherever he
had been multitudes had been brought to Christ.

"Another gentleman arose and said that he had been a witness of the success of the labors of this man who had been mentioned for four months in Scotland. Whenever it was known that he was to be present and speak at a meeting, hundreds would come to hear. He had heard him in Glasgow, Edinburgh, and other cities and towns. It was wonderful how the Lord owned and blessed his humble, unpretending labors. Go where he may and labor as he will, souls are converted. So it has been on the Great Eastern. The leader reminded the meeting that often it had been a subject of prayer, that revivals might go with the voyages of this great ship."

To complete the glimpse of the great awakenings during the last few years in Britain, we append a general view of the Irish revivals, by James Massie, D. D., LL.D., Secretary of the Irish Evangelical Society; and, also, by the Rev. J. Dunham Smith, of Kingstown, Dublin:

ORIGIN OF THE AWAKENING.

" The religious movement, which in the northern part of Ireland has awakened such general attention, has now become a *fact* in the history of the times as well as of the country. Its origin, at first obscure and for a time doubtful to many, can now be traced in perfect harmony with the principles and character of the Christian dispensation. The gradual development and extension of the mental and spiritual phenomena, by which the work has been distinguished, have secured the thoughtful attention of many devout Christians, and demand yet more prayerful consideration. Whatever may have been the proportion and relation of human agency in its progress, the most honored instruments in its administration will gratefully acknowledge a power unseen and a presence all-pervading, which are doubtless infinite and divine. 'Where is the wise? where is the Scribe? where is the disputer of this world? Hath not God made foolish the wisdom of this world?' 'But God hath chosen the foolish things of the world to confound the wise; and God hath chosen the weak things of the world to confound the things which are mighty;' 'that no flesh should glory in his presence.' Most suitable is the acknowledgment of one, to whom great favor has been shown as a successful laborer in the Revival. 'I believe that, like the mighty stream, it has arisen from a number of springs concealed, it may be, in the bosom of the mountains of Antrim, where for a season they continued to gush forth, seen only by a few, until now they have met in the valleys, and are pouring their floods on the churches, sweeping sin and cold-hearted formalism before them.' How many have laved on the banks, or sailed on the bosom, of a flowing river, admiring its swelling tide and picturesque effect, and deriving all the advantages conveyed by its ceaseless current, who have never inquired in what locality it took its rise, or in whose demesne its chief spring first gushed forth! 'There is a river, the streams whereof shall make glad the city of God, the holy place of the tabernacles of the Most High.' Yet it was not inconsistent with the state of a devout mind, or a sanctified vision, to trace 'the waters' which 'issued out from under the threshold of the house eastward,' to follow the way, when brought to 'the gate northward,' to behold the waters which ran out on 'the right side' 'at the south side of the altar.' It was, doubtless, with wonder and gratified thanksgiving the prophet accompanied the man, whose line 'measured a thousand cubits,' once and again, till he was brought 'through the waters,' ' to the ancles,' ' to the knees,' ' to the loins;' and till it proved 'a river' he 'could not pass over'—the blessing was abundant, 'for the waters were risen—waters to swim in, a river that could not be passed over.' The enlightened, the believing, and praying Christian will watch and long for the plentiful effusion of the Divine Spirit, until 'it shall come to pass, that everything that liveth, which moveth, whithersoever the rivers shall come, shall live.'

"Every student of the Sacred Scriptures knows well that many great and exceeding precious promises have been given, that God, in the Gospel of His Son, would work, 'not by might, nor by power, but by His Spirit;' and that His Spirit shall be so abundantly poured out from on high, that the wilderness and the solitary place should be made glad for his influences. 'And it shall be in that day, that living waters shall go out from Jerusalem; half of them toward the former sea, and half of them toward the hinder sea; in summer and in winter shall it be.' The conviction has been deepening in the mind of the church, not only that this rich blessing has not yet been enjoyed, in the fulness of its promise, but, also, that the promise has only failed, because it has not been duly pleaded, or expected in faith — that for all these things, prayer should be made to him continually; since, 'Thus saith the Lord God, I will yet for this be inquired of by the house of Israel, to do it for them.' Special seasons for prayer have, therefore, been observed, and concert in prayer has been maintained by companies of the devout. It has been confessed and lamented, that the Holy Ghost has not been duly honored, and that his gracious operations have not been so fervently and constantly implored, in connection with the ministrations of the Gospel as should have been. Hence, therefore, times of humiliation and earnest supplication have been consecrated by many who are the Lord's remembrancers. Nor have they passed, without the happy experience of the richest personal enjoyment as seasons of refreshing from the Divine presence. The extended awakening which occurred last year in the commercial cities of the United States, and the myriads who were brought to decision, and to join themselves to the Lord in transatlantic churches, were, doubtless, preceded and accompanied by much believing and importunate prayer. Tidings of these things came to the ears of the church in Britain, and were diffused into remote and obscure places. Contemporaneous with the work in America, has been a silent but gracious manifestation of renewing and saving power in the mountainous regions of Wales, and some isolated parts of Scotland. These fruits have been consequent not less upon the labors and prayers of lay Christians than of faithful pastors. The Rev. W. Arthur has well described the result; 'when the true spiritual element of man is shed upon and around him, and the Divine breath flows into his soul insensibly and with spiritual power; then, when the Spirit is poured out, as Joel prophesied, and as the pentecostal Christians experienced, the servants of God seem to breathe their native air; men, who before languidly supported a certain kind of religious existence, are borne along over their daily temptations as upon eagles' wings; the besetments of their temperament abate like ailments in returning health. They answer to the call of duties, whether in the family, in business, or the church, with a joyful sense of help; and it is 'easy' then 'for the soul to be true.''

"This state of life in the members, and power in the services of the church, is never unaccompanied with fruitfulness in her labors. Then mothers tell with streaming eyes how their wilful boys have begun to lead a new life; tried and broken-spirited wives begin to see their husbands strangely seeking God; men of cold and selfish temper are found with full eyes in the sanctuary, and with new benevolence doing good to their neighbors. It is then we hear of the proud becoming lowly; the churl, liberal; the wild, sedate and wise; and many a fair and happy transformation from sinful to Christian living, which, as it circulates in the neighborhood, stirs some other heart to say, ' Is it not time for me also to seek the Lord?' and thus Christian conversions go on spreading from day to day, until the number of the newly awakened is such as to make a perceptible impression upon the community.'

"The earliest personal trace of the origin of the present spiritual movement, in the county of Antrim, is given on the testimony of a gentleman who had friendly intercourse with the individuals concerned. Mrs. C., an English lady, visited Ireland in the spring of 1856, and spent the following summer and autumn in the town of Ballymena. She thought the people cold and indifferent about religion, and was often much cast down, because of their spiritual deadness. She visited the poor in their cottages, and read the Scriptures to them, and prayed with them, but in most cases they considered the time thus occupied as lost. Occasionally she called on the rich, with the intention of speaking to them on personal religion; but they inclined to say little on that point, and often contrived to change the subject of conversation. On the whole, she considered, the rich gave her a much colder reception than the poor. Her patience was greatly tried; but she persevered, and *expected* a blessing to follow her weak efforts. During the summer her friend, Lieut. A., who gives his whole time and substance to the work of God, came, and preached with great earnestness. He was favorably received by Presbyterian clergymen, but especially by Mr. M., of Ballymena, who invited him to his pulpit, and assisted him in getting up meetings elsewhere. Mrs. C. feared that God had not as yet acknowledged her anxious labors; but she knew not of one little seed she had dropped, a few days before she left Ballymena. She had some time previously visited two ladies, who liked to talk about religious matters, but especially delighted in controversial squabbles, and found them engaged discussing pre-ordination, free-will, &c., with a young man named J. McQ. Having listened to them for some time, she sought to impress upon them the absurdity of such a fruitless discussion. Neither party seemed to her to have a higher object in view than to see who could best argue. The young man was an entire stranger to her; so that she addressed herself chiefly to the ladies, and spoke to them on the importance of seeking a personal interest in the Saviour. Her words took deep root in the heart of J. McQ., who left, ruminating on the truths brought before him. He determined to lead a new life, and prayed to God for assistance. He was a poor young man, with a wife and two children, and was employed in one of the mills near Connor. He advanced in spiritual matters, reading the Bible, and 'George Muller's Life and Labors in Bristol,' till the spring of 1857, when two of his Sabbath-school class were converted to God. He thus spent much time in prayer, seeking a companion to assist him in the work of the Lord. One came to him in the person of J. McW. These two met often in Kells for special prayer, and asked God directly for what they wanted. He was graciously pleased to hear them. One belonging to the Sabbath-school class came and joined their little prayer-meeting, which then numbered three. In a short time after, two more found the Saviour, and joined themselves with them. Thus their numbers gradually increased. In January, 1858, a child in one of the classes in their little Sabbath-school was so overpowered, that its body was prostrated, and it suffered greatly in consequence. This astonished them, as it was the first they had ever seen or heard of; but still they went on with their prayer-meetings and Sabbath-school, and God blessed their efforts in a remarkable manner. In May, 1858, they could number sixteen or seventeen who had experienced the blessed change. This gave them great courage; and in spite of some petty opposition in the shape of sneers, &c., they continued to ask and to receive. Faith grew. Hope brightened. 'The power of prayer' began to be known, and felt, and seen. The spring communion came on. Throughout the extensive parish, consisting of some thousand families, it was generally known that, lately, persons had been turned to the Lord among them — some moral, and some wildly immoral. A few had heard of a similiar triumph of divine grace beyond the Atlantic. The services were peculiarly solemn. The Master's presence seemed to be recognized, and His call heard. A great impulse was given to consideration and scriousness, intensifying and extending these general precursors of conviction and revival. The old prayer-meetings began to be thronged, and many new ones established. No difficulty was now to find persons to take part in them. The winter was past; the time of the singing of birds had come. Humble, grateful, loving, joyous converts multiplied. They, with the children of God, who in that district have been revived — greatly refreshed by the Divine Spirit — are now very numerous. There were, on an average, sixteen prayer-meetings every night in the week, throughout the bounds of that one congregation — *i. e.*, about one hundred weekly. The awakening to a sight of sin, the conviction of its sinfulness, the illumination of the soul in the knowledge of a glorious Saviour, and conversion to Him — all this operation, carried on by the life-giving Spirit, was in the Connor district for more than eighteen months ; a calm, quiet, gradual, in some cases a lengthened process, not commencing in, or accompanied by, a 'smiting down' of the body, or any extraordinary physical prostration, more than what might be expected to result from great anxiety and deep sorrow. Thus, it is worthy of being noticed and remembered, that the present American Revival began in 1857 ; so did the Revival in Connor : — the one began in the month of September, so did the other : prayer — fervent, confiding, and unceasing, was the prominent characteristic of the one and of the other : laymen — six in the one case, and four in the other — were the prominent agents in commencing the work in the one country as well as in the other."

TIMES OF REFRESHING.

" A great change in religion has come over many parts of our Irish land during the past twenty years. The light of Divine truth, mingled with the Spirit's power, has extended over numerous spots, now radiant with conversion, where the Lord Jesus Christ is no longer as ' a stranger in the land,' or ' a wayfaring man that turneth aside to tarry ' only ' for a night.'

"So signal and surprising is the present awakening, that we are like men that dream a pleasant dream. Now is our mouth filled with laughter, and our tongue with singing. As streams in the south, after mighty rains of refreshing, return to their deserted channels; so in the hundreds of sanctuaries in our land, once almost desolate of power and life, there is a river of salvation, the waters of which make glad the city of our God.

"I feel humbled and astonished that so much slight has been cast upon this glorious work, and that, too, by some good men. Whilst the Lord has been making hundreds of churches, once dead or in a Laodicean state, each one a Bochim — a place of tears — and whilst over five counties, prayer — the Spirit's own breath — has been made without ceasing, numbers of professed Christians and ministers are still standing at a distance, or coldly speculating concerning it. Some who believe in the work as a revival of religion, and rejoice in it, yet compromise and apologise respecting the physical phenomena, as if *these*, without reserve, should be condemned. I am not ashamed to confess to a different mind. I have seen too much, not to say, in regard to many bodily cases, ' This is the finger of God.'

"With Dr. Carson, I have no doubt that the physical agent, whatever it may be, has been sent by God; and for a specific purpose. Such was its effect one night in Coleraine, he remarks, that it was like the day of judgment, when sinners will call on the mountains and the rocks to hide them. ' It struck terror to the heart of the most hardened and obdurate sinner. The whole town was in a state of alarm, business was forgotten, and the revival was the only subject of conversation. A French invasion could not have produced so great a panic. I have seen much of the accumulated misery of bodily disease and mental distress; but I never saw anything to be compared to the harrowing scene in the Coleraine Town Hall. It would be quite impossible to imagine any agency more powerful for drawing the attention of men to the state of their souls. I heard many people mocking and scoffing, before that night, about the revival; but when I saw the same parties examining the cases in the Town Hall, their mocking was at an end, and they looked like criminals whose hour was at hand. No other sort of a revival could have had the same effects. If one half of the inhabitants had been converted in a minute, in the ordinary way, the other half would not have believed it — they would have laughed at it as a vision. It would have had no effect upon them.

"Exception has been taken to excesses and extravagances. Excesses and extravagances may be expected, where so vast a surface lies open before the enemy of souls. 'Tares' are usually found wherever there is 'wheat;' 'mire and dirt' will be flung up by the deep 'sea' of spiritual conflict with Satan.

"But I have seen the most hallowed results in the minds and lives of persons, who were stricken under circumstances where no natural cause could be traced.

"I said to a young man in the North, who had been lying in a stricken state for three days, —' Did you ever wish to be stricken?' 'Never.' 'Did you ever dread it?' 'Never.' 'When it occurred were you in a heated atmosphere?' 'No.' 'In a crowd?' 'No.' 'Under an exciting sermon?' 'No.' 'How did you feel when lying in a stricken state?' 'Of the external world I knew nothing. Internally I felt a dreadful load of sin.' 'Had you never suspected it before?' 'Never. I had always thought that I was a Christian, and others thought me to be a Christian.' 'How was your mind occupied during the long period in which you were stricken?' 'I had a dreadful conflict. The idea of being a Christian was like a voice within contending that I was such; but the dark load of sin on my soul, like another self, declared that it was *not*. I felt utterly lost, and, laying aside the notion that I was a Christian, as a sinner I cried to God to have mercy upon me.' 'How did your relief come?' 'On the third day I heard the archdeacon pray, 'Lord lay not this sin to *to his own charge*, but lay it to the charge of Him whose blood cleanseth from all sin.' That substitutionary truth concerning sin and its removal by Christ, I at once embraced, and the dreadful sense of its curse was gone; and then, though my bodily strength was completely prostrate, I felt a peace of mind which passeth all understanding — a joy unspeakable and full of glory.' 'Should you ever lose that sense of peace and joy, how would you feel?' 'Oh! I *could* not lose it: if I were to, I should feel humbled, yet still I *should have Christ*.'

"One thing in this case struck me most forcibly, and, I may add, solemnly. I said, 'As a supposed Christian, you were in the habit of the daily perusal of the Bible?' 'Yes, daily; but I read it because I wished to *know* it, and because it was only consistent for me to study it, and, also, that I might understand its truths in relation to surrounding controversies; *but*,' he added, 'I know that I never *loved* it — that I never, until now, had any sense or intelligence of its true value and blessedness.' Alas! I thought, how many are like this! they think they are Christians, they appear such to others, but they are not so in reality.

"And now, turning from this case I have the most precious remembrance of two little girls, both of whom had, along with some others, been stricken in a school. They were very poor, and very young — one nine and the other seven years of age. I said to her, 'Mary, you do not love the Lord Jesus Christ, do you?' Thinking that I had denied the fact of her love to the Saviour, the tears broke down her face, and her hands were clasped in the greatest earnestness, whilst she replied, 'O sir, I *do* love the Lord Jesus Christ! I do, I *do* love Him!' 'How long is it since you commenced to love him?' 'O sir, ever since we first began to seek Him.' 'Nay, nay, dear,' said her little companion, a thin, pallid-faced child of dark intelligent eyes — 'Nay, nay, dear; *we* did not first seek the Lord Jesus. *He* it was who *first* sought us.'

'Wonderful! I thought. What 'praise' is this that I

hear thus from the mouths of babes and sucklings, and what truth! How sound its theology! How suggestive and comprehensive! I said, 'Mary, would you like me to pray with you?' adding, 'Remember you must pray for each other.' Ere I had risen from my knees, this little disciple taking me at my word, began in a low, soft tone to warble such a prayer as I had never heard. She prayed for her companions, then for her poor neighbors. She said, 'Lord Jesus, thou hast come into our hearts with thy love; wilt thou not go into all their hearts with thy love?' She then extended her requests for our country, that all its people may know the Lord Jesus; and to the whole world, that the poor heathen especially may soon hear of Him and love Him. Having prayed most fervently for the whole human race, she concluded by saying, 'And now, Lord Jesus, (or, dear Lord Jesus,) I have nothing more to say. Amen.'

"Do you ask, whence this great change in religion? I answer, from the outpouring of the Spirit of God. And especially of late, on the truth faithfully preached. God has not set aside but revived the preaching of His word. He has taught, that the preaching which He honors is not that of mere philosophy, but of Christ. The one may be attractive and costly, as the offering of Cain; but the other, like the acceptable service of Abel, is valuable for the simple manifestation of the 'blood.' But whilst such as Paul must preach, and Apollos water, it is the work of the Elijahs of the Church to pray down the increase.

"My earnest prayer, then, is, that God, in mercy to our condition, may deepen this work, and extend, it. Especially blessed would it be, if it were to come to our own beloved city — so come, that all the little streams and pools of our separate and divided life in religion may be lost in one vast flood of Divine awakening, of spiritual union, of life abounding in all true Christians, and sincere love towards all saints. May the Lord the Spirit give it! and may He lead His people to desire it, and to seek it!"

The Standing Committee of the General Assembly of the Presbyterian church in Ireland give a comprehensive and suggestive summary of this mighty work of God, in their official report.

After mentioning that 357 open-air services had been held during the year, and that 50,000 persons had thus heard the message of the Gospel, it states :

" 1. Persons of both sexes, of all ages, of different grades of society, of various denominations of professing Christians, including Unitarians and Roman Catholics, have been at once convinced of sin, and apparently converted to God.

" 2. These spiritual emotions have been accompanied, in a very large number of cases, by physical impressions, producing bodily infirmity, and continuing, in some cases, for hours, and in others for days, and usually terminating in peace of conscience, and sometimes in ' joy unspeakable and full of glory.'

" The two great truths on which the converts prominently, and almost exclusively, dwell, are — the sinfulness and utter helplessness of men, and the all-sufficiency of Christ as a living, personal Redeemer.

" 4. No heresy has been started in this new and unusual state of religious excitement. The whole movement, in its various aspects, tends to give striking and vivid illustration of the great doctrines of the Gospel, as they are set forth in our Catechisms and Confession of Faith.

" 5. The effect produced by this awakening on the life and character of those who have experienced it, is decidedly evangelical — a deep sense of sin, especially of the sin of having neglected the great salvation, fervent love of Christ, intense brotherly kindness, earnest desire for the conversion of sinners, habitual communion with God, and delight in His Word, worship, and service. These attributes of character are assuredly the fruit of the Spirit, and these are the characteristics of multitudes who have lately declared themselves the servants of Christ. The drunkard has been made sober; the libertine, chaste; the blasphemer and Sabbath-breaker, devout; the worldling, constrained to think deeply and penitently of his sins, and to flee from the wrath to come. These are surely trophies of Divine grace, and many such trophies as those have been raised to the honor of God since the commencement of the present revival."

The number of hopeful conversions cannot be estimated, till Christ " makes up his jewels." And the wonderful ingathering declares, that the Spirit works by no rule of our wisdom, but must be gratefully and humbly accepted, come when, and in what way he shall please ; and points the dull eye of our faith to the hastening time, when " kings and queens shall lay their honors at the feet of Immanuel."

CHAPTER VII.

The Commencement of Labors in Boston—Services in the Salem Street Church—Statements Respecting the Work—Letters from Young Converts—Revival in Portland—Letters- Interesting Cases of Conversion.

Upon Mr. Hammond's arrival in America, he began to labor in Pownal, Vt., and other places, finding it difficult to realize the first intention to rest and recruit exhausted energies. He received invitations to labor in different fields, when, incidentally visiting Boston, early in September, he preached in the Salem Street Church. Interest was apparent, and prominent pastors of the city urged the continuance of the meetings, and took part in them. Rev. Geo. Dunham, who had supplied the pulpit in the pastor's absence, wrote the following sketch for the Congregationalist:

"Some cases of thoughtfulness had existed in the congregation and the Sabbath school, for months previous. And there was considerable tenderness and disposition to prayer, also, in some members of the church at the time. Such were prepared to hail his coming as a harbinger of mercy, and to welcome him as one sent from God laden with blessings. Such were ready to co-operate with him in his contemplated labor.

"After a few of the first evenings, the people gathered in such numbers, that it was found necessary to open the large audience room; and, from that time to the present, the lower floor has been filled almost uninterruptedly, and in several instances it has been packed full—galleries, organ loft, and aisles. The congregations have been uniformly still, solemn, and deeply interested in the preaching of the word. The character of the preaching and addresses has been the simplest, most plain, and direct possible. The topics, only such as are often thought old and threadbare; the City of Refuge, the Prodigal Son, the love of Christ for lost sinners, their danger of endless punishment, and such as these. The manner of the preacher is generally subdued and tender, sometimes full of melting pathos, and sometimes rising to a good degree of eloquent majesty.

"It seems very evident that God is in the assemblies, doing His great work, convicting sinners, and delivering them from bondage and death. A meeting for prayer is held at 7 o'clock, in the lecture room, for half an hour, which is often full, and always solemn. Latterly, a meeting of young converts is held at the same hour, in another room, when as many as fifty or sixty assemble to exhort, pray and sing, with some old Christian counsellors to assist them. At half-past seven the preaching services commence, and nearly an hour and a half is occupied in this by Mr. Hammond, occasionally assisted by other clergymen. The audiences have been profoundly still, and often deeply affected.

"The great and peculiar feature of the movement is found in the inquiry meetings that follow the preaching. At the close of this service, all Christians that are willing to converse and pray with anxious sinners, or to unite in praying for them, are invited to repair to the lecture room, and take with them as many, who are willing to be conversed with personally, as they can persuade to go.

"The meeting is opened with singing, and some short addresses and prayers. At this point it is always instinct with interest and solemnity. It afterwards becomes informal and social, the brethren and sisters speaking a few words of inquiry, counsel, or encouragement to each other, and searching out such as are yet strangers to the peace of God, conversing with them, striving to deepen their feeling, and point them to the Saviour; they kneel together in little groups about the room, and in adjoining rooms, and pray individually with such as are willing to be prayed with. These personal and close dealings often culminate at once in hopeful conversion. Many souls have been led at once directly to Christ, and have obtained a sweet relief. Sometimes eight or ten groups will be conversing and praying together at the same time, in low and earnest tones; and, instead of the confusion that might be apprehended, the effect is not unlike the order of a Sabbath school recitation. I believe no night has passed now for a considerable time, when some have not been reported as having consecrated themselves to Christ, and obtained evidence of forgiveness. The number hopefully converted are probably as many as one hundred, and there are still many thoughtful.

"Christians from many miles around have come in, to mingle with the rising tide of religious influence and feeling, and have found it good to be there. The work seems still to be increasing in depth and power, and there is strong hope of still greater displays of divine goodness and saving grace."

It was hoped and believed, at one time, that the work, so similar to that in Glasgow in its commencement, would, as there, sweep over the city, bringing thousands within its embrace.

Might not the fact, of the hopeful conversion of more than one hundred souls, have been used to move the hearts of the Christians of Boston, to more wrestling prayer for a mighty outpouring of the Holy Spirit, and earnest pleading for the salvation of the perishing?

Whatever may have been unusual in any of the methods employed to reach the people; and even if, as some may affirm, mistakes were made through human infirmity, lessons we are ever learning;—that it was the work of the Spirit, and infinitely better than the uniformity of spiritual dearth and death, no observant, living Christian will doubt. God greatly blessed the souls of men, and vindicated the power of his simple gospel, and faithful endeavors to save.

Of an open air meeting on the Common, the Boston Journal contained this notice :

" Rev. Dr. Kirk conducted the services, and, after a few remarks, stating the meeting to be one in which all denominations could unite in seeking religion, he opened with prayer, and introduced Rev. E. P. Hammond, who followed with an impressive discourse for nearly an hour ; and, with simple statements of the vast amount of evil daily practised by us, impressed his hearers with the truth of their sinful state, and invited them all to seek the forgiveness and grace of God."

For a farther history of the revival, we have a sketch, from the pen of a reporter of the Traveller, of a meeting held Oct. 5th :

" Rev. Dr. Kirk, who was present, then rose and addressed the large company before him. Every eye was fixed upon the speaker, and the deepest solemnity pervaded the entire audience. He commenced by saying, ' What a sight! What are you all here for ? What do you want ? ' After a few words upon the immense importance of the occasion, he asked those present who hoped they had recently found the Saviour to rise. A large number stood, including whole seats of young men and some young children. He then prayed for them, and afterwards addressed those present who were seeking the Saviour in his usual impressive and earnest manner.

"Rev. Mr. Hammond then requested Christians either to assist him in conversing with inquirers or to repair to an adjoining room for prayer. An interesting scene then followed. The whole company were at once engaged in praying, talking, and praising God. In one corner were four or five ladies kneeling and praying around an anxious soul. In another was a group of little children, who were addressed by an elderly man and exhorted to give their hearts to Christ.

"In another place, was a young man rejoicing, who a few days ago was a Catholic. He was busily engaged in conversing with a Catholic woman. Rev. Mr. Hammond soon came along and conversed with her. She said she would like to give her heart to the Saviour, if she could do so without renouncing her faith. Said he, 'Don't you worry about that. Isn't it your duty to submit to Jesus?' 'Yes,' said she. 'Then do it.' The three then kneeled down. Mr. Hammond prayed and she prayed that Jesus might forgive her sins. We left them in that situation.

"A few feet distant from the last group, was a young lady of remarkable intelligence stating to those around her how, a few nights since, she had given her heart to the Saviour. She said she dared Mr. Hammond to affect *her*. She didn't believe in the Holy Spirit. Something which was said, however, touched her, and she felt deeply. She prayed to God if there was any Holy Spirit to show it to her; and that night, with her sense of sinfulness weighing her down, she gave her heart to Christ. We have never seen a happier person.

"Close by, was a woman of fifty years of age, who, with tears of joy running down her cheeks, was relating to others an account of the great change which had taken place in her feelings. In another place was a group singing, and adjoining this were a half dozen praying for a weeping sinner. All through the three rooms were little companies similarly situated, and the whole scene was one which can never be forgotten by those who witnessed it. Mr. Hammond was all over the rooms conversing a few minutes with all. His custom was to make the anxious soul kneel and pray with a number of others, and in this way consecrate himself to God.

"The work seems to be going on with unusual power. Rev. Mr. Field, the pastor, who has just returned from his vacation, enters into the work heartily, and unites, with all his soul, in the efforts making to lead the impenitent to the Cross."

In looking over correspondence, we read a letter to the mother of the Evangelist, from which we take a passage of experience, which will touch the Christian heart:

"I am seeking to get low before a holy sin-hating God, so that He may use me for his glory — in leading sinners to Him. I must lie in the dust, or nothing will be done by me. He will set me aside. I have not much power given me yet. It must be, because I am not in a right state to receive it. O Lord! prepare me to be filled with the Holy Spirit! This is my constant prayer."

We give extracts from letters written by young converts, to afford a further glimpse of the awakening, and illustrate the usefulness of the inquiry meetings in producing conviction, while the already anxious are led to Christ; and also to record the fact, that all classes are included in the number of those savingly brought under the influence of the means of grace, from Romanists and seamen, to Protestant children of the church:

"Hundreds of happy hearts here, in Boston, and in all its schools, will ever have occasion to bless the kind Providence which directed your steps to America and your words to our hearts. I am not going to weary you with my own experience, happy though it has been, but simply glance over a few interesting cases which you may wish to remember. One which occurs to my mind is very near and dear to me. 'T is that of a young French lady. Doubtless you will remember her as being, with us, a constant attendant on the meetings, where she took an active part in leading sinners to the Saviour. Her father is a Roman Catholic, but she was brought up in the Universalist belief. Ever ready for novelty, and, perhaps, anticipating some amusement, we went, together with sister Lettie, to one of your Sabbath evening prayer meetings. Your solemn words of warning, coupled with the relation of an anecdote 'The Sinking Ship,' induced us to stay to the inquiry meeting. You came and asked each of us, 'Do you love Jesus?' The abruptness of your manner arrested our attention. The solemnity of the question, and its direct application to ourselves, served to awaken sleeping conscience, and deep conviction was the result. The lady before mentioned was very deeply anxious, and felt that she was a lost sinner, unless she believed in Jesus. Prayer was new to her; and, when asked to pray, it was affecting to hear her simple heartfelt words, in broken English, asking for a new heart. She found her Saviour that very evening, and immediately set forth in the service of her Master, in which she has been engaged ever since. The evenings previously devoted to the ball-room, the theatre, or some other alluring pleasure of the world, are now spent in some gathering of God's people, or some way equally acceptable to them. Perhaps you will call to remembrance, too, a young gentleman, whom you conversed with one evening, after the exercises. He had been in earlier days a Protestant, but during his stay at a college in New York, where he graduated with the highest honors, he formed the acquaintance of a company of young men, who persuaded him to become a Catholic. He did so, and for many years adhered to his new belief. He was the means of turning his brother, also a Protestant, into his error. He went so far as to study for the priesthood. He came to Boston, and, by some providence, attended your meetings. Very soon, as you know, his voice was heard in the large congregation, telling how God, through your instrumentality, ' *had brought him out of the horrible pit, out of the miry clay.*' How he had '*put a new song in his month, even praise unto our God.*' A short time he was allowed to serve his loving Master ere he was called to receive his reward.

"Returning from one of the evening meetings, he was overtaken by a heavy rain storm, and on the day following was taken sick. Typhoid fever soon set in, and in a short time his happy spirit had fled — fled to join that of his mother, who had died broken-hearted, to think that her eldest boy had forsaken the religion of his childhood. Before he was called away, he was the means, under God, of lifting the veil from the spiritual eyes of a young lady friend of mine, once a firm, bigoted Catholic, but whose eyes, now opened, can never be closed. He was buried under Protestant rites, the minister, who attended his mother's funeral, performing the same office for her repentant child. His name was *James Henry Bridge.*

"One more case, which I think will interest you, and I will trespass no longer on time so precious as yours. One Wednesday evening, you may have noticed a party of sailors, who came into the meeting, partly intoxicated. One of them, a young man, was conversed with by you, and although no impression seemed to be made on him, you prayed earnestly for him. The evening following, he came again, impelled by an invisible power. At the close of the meeting, his hardened, sinful heart seemed to be touched, and as a first step towards reformation he signed a pledge, in company with Deacon Chipman, a duplicate of which he carried to sea with him the next day. Some time afterwards, he returned, and immediately found his way to Salem Church. He could hardly find words to express his thanks to the members and you, in particular, for your kind interest in his welfare, and for your words of counsel. He brought six of his shipmates with him, all Catholics. A prayer meeting is now established among that Catholic crew, and one of those ten dollar libraries is in circulation.

"I would I had space to tell you of some of the other blessed results of your labors here, but I have not. Numbers are joining the church; eighteen had at one time joined ours, and sixteen at another. Next Sabbath, it will be *my* privilege to do so, together with E——, and two or three other young ladies, all recent converts.

"We often sing those hymns 'We're travelling home to heaven,' and 'Just as I am,' and never without a thrill of grateful emotion, and sweet thoughts of those happy Autumn days—the beginning of a new life to many souls.

Yours in Jesus.

A lamb of the great Shepherd's flock, in the Sabbath School, thus expresses her reason for the hope she found in Him:

"I am a little girl, only eleven years old, and I have felt for a long time that I have a very wicked heart. Sometimes I would try to be good, and love Jesus; but my heart is so wicked, I thought I would wait a little longer till I was a few years older, and then I would give my heart to Jesus. But, when I went into the inquiry meeting, and you came to me and talked so kindly — talked to me about Jesus, and prayed with me — I felt very unhappy, and that I was a great sinner. I wept and prayed for some days; then Jesus came and wiped my tears away, and I am very happy now. I can trust Jesus at all times, for He is my friend. Blessed Jesus! that washed my sins away! I used to say my prayers, but now I can pray from my heart, and it makes me so happy to put my trust in Jesus. I love Christians; love to hear them talk about Jesus; and I love sinners too. I want them all to come and give their hearts to Jesus. Pray for a little girl, that she may always trust in Jesus.

"Boston, October 16, 1861."

The Recorder published this additional letter from a boy of thirteen years, read, with the above, in the Old South Prayer Meeting:

"I rejoice that I have found peace in Jesus. I have been born again. I am three days old when I write this letter. I will tell you how I came to the Lord. The first time I came to hear you was the second Sunday you were here, and I then felt that I was a sinner. I came the next Sunday, and as I was passing out a man took me by the hand, and asked me to come to the inquiring meeting. I told him, I could not, and went away. But, as I went to bed, I could not have any peace, and I resolved the next night to go into the inquiring meeting. I went and sat side of a man who conversed with me about my soul. After awhile two of my playmates came where I was, and told me that they wanted to speak to me in private. They took me into a side room by the desk. They prayed for me and talked with me, and then told me to pray, and *down on my knees I gave my heart to Christ.* I said Lord be merciful to me a sinner. Take me 'just as I am.' Since that evening I have felt peace in believing. I can read my Bible so that I can understand it, what I could never do before. I have talked with my playmates, but they laugh at me and call me all manner of hard names, but I shall never give up praying for them. I will pray for them till I see them giving their hearts to Christ."

From Boston Mr. Hammond went to Portland, Maine. Rev. Mr. Moore, of the Union Church, where meetings were held for a week, summing up results in the Christian Mirror, gives the following statement at the close of that period:

"*First*, Increased attendance every night upon the preaching of the word, until the house was entirely filled,—with seats furnished in the aisles for the accommodation of the listeners.

"*Second*, The opening of an afternoon prayer meeting, which, on the last afternoon of the week, filled the large vestry with worshippers.

"*Third*, The holding of an inquiry meeting in the vestry, at the close of the preaching meeting, which nightly increased in the number of inquirers, until the closing service of the week, when the vestry was filled with Christians and anxious persons.

"*Fourth*, The conversion of a number of precious souls, who are now rejoicing in the love of the Saviour, some of whom have publicly testified to the saving power of the Cross — rising in the inquiry meeting to speak of the love of Christ. Christians who have conversed nightly with the penitent believe that score at least have found the peace of pardoning love.

' An unusual solemnity has pervaded the meetings, and especially has this been the case in the inquiry meetings. There Christians were to be seen in different parts of the vestry, conversing with sinners and anxious persons, or on their knees praying with them, and with tears pointing them to the Saviour. A verse of a hymn was occasionally sung ; now and then a word of warning and of encouragement, and occasionally a short prayer was offered for some special case of inquiry, or for the presence of the Divine Spirit.

" Christian men were there with their unconverted wives ; Christian wives sat, with tears and prayers, beside their unconverted husbands; parents were praying with their children, and children were pleading with Christians to speak and pray with their parents. The utmost solemnity prevailed. Christians were in earnest; the penitent were laying hold of the Saviour by faith; and the ungodly were awed into solemnity, and melted sometimes to tears, and though they came to the meeting unconcerned, were led, before the meeting closed, to ask what they should do to be saved.

"Some dear children of the Sabbath school were weeping for their sins, and asking about the Saviour. God's spirit had troubled their hearts, and they were awakened to feel their need of Christ.

"We feel that no true, sound Christian could have gone into and labored in the inquiry meetings, without feeling that the Spirit of God was present with great power.

"For myself, I feel greatly strengthened by the manifestations of the Spirit's presence during the week past; and with all my heart, I thank God for the providence which has brought the Evangelist to our city. May his labors be still more abundantly blest in the other part of the city, until throughout our city the work of God may revive, and sinners, by hundreds, be brought to see their need of the Saviour. Especially may his labors be blest in the old Payson church, where of old, God used so marvellously, to pour out his Spirit.

"I am permitted to make the following extract from a private letter written by the Rev. Henry Hopkins, son of President Hopkins, of Williams College, from the hospital at Alexandria.

"'I believe that the slow work of expectation and instruction is the pastor's great work; but sometimes after the husbandman has toiled and sowed, and the long summer days, full of God's sunshine and gentle rains, have done their work, the gleaming fields of ripening grain would perish if left to be gathered by him alone; and he must call some one with a sharp sickle and a tireless arm, to help him bring them in and shout the harvest home. And happy is he if he find such a reaper.'"

We take further extracts from a letter addressed to a well-known pastor, in accordance with his request, which appeared in the Congregationalist:

"Portland, Dec. 11, 1861.

"Rev. Dr. Kirk — *My Dear Brother :* — You have asked me to recall and state the circumstances, that preceded and introduced the remarkable work of grace now advancing in our city. However sudden this work may appear to outsiders and superficial observers, it certainly has not come suddenly nor altogether unexpectedly on the pastor, or on the prayerful and practically devoted members of the church with which he is identified. The desirableness of a genuine revival of religion has long been the subject of social conversation — the brief addresses of the conference room have often turned on the momentous theme — and prayer, earnest, fervent and importunate, for a plenteous effusion of the Holy Spirit has been a prominent feature of our social devotions.

"We shared with all our sister churches — during the spring and summer months — the distracting and depressing influence of the war; and, at times, the idea was by some very freely expressed, that it was utterly vain to hope for a religious revival whilst the war continued. Many of our young men, besides, were either in the camp or in the field; and few families were free from the natural anxieties of parental and fraternal love. Newspapers of all kinds were eagerly read and ransacked — political lectures were attended by vast numbers — and the influence of Gospel truth was greatly counteracted by the incessant eagerness for news, and the secular current of conversation even on the holy Sabbath.

"In September last, he exchanged, by request, with Mr. Haskell, of East Boston, and had his attention called to the work of revival then in progress in Salem Street Church. He attended several of the meetings, spoke at two of them, and, on his return, reported to his people the facts that had come under his own observation. An intelligent member of Salem Street Church kept him informed of events connected with the work as they occurred, and these, duly reported by him, fanned the desire of a similar work amongst ourselves.

"Soon after the pastor's return from Boston, he learned that Mr. E. P. Hammond had been invited by a young clergyman of this city to spend a week with his congregation. The invitation was accepted. Mr. Hammond spoke each evening throughout the week, and, by the blessing of God upon his labors, much good, it is confidently believed, was done. The pastor of the Second Church attended some of the meetings, encouraged his people also to attend, and eventually suggested an invitation to Mr. Hammond to labor in the Second Parish.

"There has, since, been Divine service in our church for thirty-one successive evenings — the interest still continuing unabated — and great numbers having expressed the hope that they have passed from death unto life. In all but six of these meetings the pastor has taken an active part. He was greatly assisted and encouraged by a visit of several days, including a Sabbath, from yourself, whose ministrations were so much blessed as to induce a unanimous request from the brethren of the church for a 'second benefit.' Several other ministerial brethren have kindly aided occasionally in the public services. With the exception of ten days' absence, Mr. E. P. Hammond has been indefatigable in his labors. To his honor be it spoken, he has, in no instance, attempted to invade the prerogatives of the pastor — has readily adopted every practical suggestion as to methods of procedure — and has proved himself, in all respects, a workman that needeth not to be ashamed. The seal of Divine approval has been most unequivocally affixed to his unwearied labors. Many of our Sabbath School pupils, especially of the adult classes — already well instructed in Divine truth, have sprung at once into vigorous vitality. Young heads of families, having given themselves to the Lord — have reared their domestic altars, and resolved, in the strength of Divine grace, never to suffer the fire to go out. A pastor's Bible-class — designed especially for young converts, — is now organized and in healthful operation. The members of the church are generally quickened and revived, and very many of them taken an active part in the inquiry meeting, which is held at the close of every evening service. A daily prayer-meeting has been held at 3 P. M. since the commencement of this work.

"I must, as yet, say nothing as to numbers, though, after the most careful and cautious scrutiny, there will, doubtless, be a large accession to the church. Meanwhile, the work of conversion is going on, and the influence of the movement is beginning to be felt by other congregations in the city and vicinity.

"Pray for us, dear Brother, that the Word of the Lord may have free course and be glorified.

"Many sheets might be filled with accounts of specific cases, but these, for the present, I reserve.

Yours most fraternally,

J. J. CARRUTHERS."

John Neal, Esq., whose name is familiar to the literary world, wrote thus for the Portland Transcript:

THE RELIGIOUS AWAKENING HERE.

"*Qui S'excuse S'accuse.*"

"No large moral movement ever happens without the clearly seen co-operation of man. What we call agency or instrumentality is God's way of working through man upon man. Let us not be astonished, therefore, when God, who is no respecter of persons, appears to be working with instruments which we, in our wisdom, should never have thought of, perhaps, nor ever have supposed fitted for the work — little children, or uneducated men and women, for example.

"Of one thing we may be certain; that what God has to do with man, he will do in his own way; and we may be equally sure that what man has to do with God, must be done, *always*, in God's way, whatever man may think, or believe, or hope; and that God will never change his declared plan for our accommodation, whether reasonable or unreasonable in our judgment.

"There are many about us, who are always willing enough and ready enough to go to heaven — but they insist on going in their own way. They would like to be *safe*, here and hereafter; but they have a plan of their own, which however reasonable and proper, they will never find to be God's plan.

"If they pray, their prayers are conditional. They insist upon understanding the why and the wherefore of His purposes. They require to be satisfied upon every point, before they will consent to be saved. What should we think of a man swimming for his life, who should insist upon a clear explanation of the Westminister catechism, or the mysteries of free agency, before he would consent to grasp the outstretched hand of a fellow man, safe ashore, standing perhaps on the rock of ages?

"There is a story told of an English sailor, who having tumbled overboard, in the Bay of Biscay, got astride of a hen-coop, which had been thrown him, and floated off into the darkness. At midnight a large ship came by and a voice hailed him in French. Not understanding such lingo, he refused to go aboard, and stuck to his hen-coop. What became of him nobody knows. Yet this poor sailor did only just what thousands about us are now doing. They will not consent to go into the Ark, but upon their own terms; forgetting that God himself being unchangeable, and having once published his conditions to the Universe, *cannot* save us, but with our own consent and co-operation.

"Mr. Hammond, of whose labors and wonderful success in Scotland, we have been hearing so much — for the last year, is now in our very midst. And, if we may judge by what we have heard and seen for ourselves, here, God is with him. Let those who doubt, while refusing to see for themselves, and let all who insist upon the Holy Spirit working in a pattern, always in one way, which is always their own way, bear in mind that God never deals with any two of his creatures in precisely the same way, for any purpose. He seems to reverence their individuality, and leaves them to act here as they are to be tried hereafter, *separately.* Let all such gainsayers, whether in the church or out, therefore, go and see for themselves, and prepare to answer for themselves, if they stand in the way, or try to discourage others, or even refuse to co-operate with all their strength, humbly, though heartily."

Mr. Neal narrates a touching case of conversion in another communication, which, on account of its suggestive interest, we give entire:

"After seeing and hearing for myself, I have become satisfied that the late awakening here is worthy of devout attention. I have been present at some of the inquiry meetings, and have talked face to face with weeping adults and joyful children, and, for one, am *satisfied,* as I have said before. Take one of many cases that have come to my knowledge, and say what our duty is. Are we to stand *aloof* or *aloft,* because God hath a way of His own? or because man may seem to be unreasonably earnest?
J. N.

"At the close of the service last evening, I noticed a young lady just before me, who seemed undecided about remaining to the inquiry meeting. Once or twice she rose to go, but finally sat down. When you asked those who felt that they loved Jesus to rise and sing a hymn, she kept her seat. After the hymn I leaned forward and asked her, if she could not say she ,oved Jesus. She burst into tears. I then asked her, if she did not wish to become a Christian. 'Yes,' she said, 'but *I* shall never be a Christian. I begged her not to say so, and tried to lead her to the Saviour, by telling her how ready he was to receive her, that he was more than willing, that he was waiting with outstretched arms to take her. But she said, 'No, Christ would never take *her*, she had rejected him for three years. She had once had serious impressions, but had stifled them. During the last revival she had been somewhat concerned for her soul's salvation, but had danced all night afterwards, and since then had never felt any further anxiety about it. For three years she had been treading Christ under foot, and in all that time had never offered a single prayer, even of *words*, to say nothing of the *heart*. You came and talked and prayed with her, but still her answer was, 'I can never be a Christian. Jesus will never take me.' You asked her if she thought she was a greater sinner than Paul. She said 'Yes, for Paul *thought* he was doing God service, but she *knew* she was not.' She had ridiculed religion and these meetings, and came only to make sport of them. You prayed with her again and left her with those who tried to persuade her to give her heart to Jesus then; but she could not believe, and went home sorrowing still.'

"The next day she was invited to go to the afternoon prayer meeting. She went, and her countenance still indicated her deep distress. She said she had passed a sleepless night, but could obtain no relief When you spoke with her after meeting, she begged you, if you ever knew any one anxious for the first time, to entreat them, from her, not to delay, but to come to Jesus *then*. She thought Jesus would have taken her at first, but now, it was *too late*. She had said, that only weak-minded, nervous people were affected by this revival; now God was showing her her condition, but would not save her. She still insists that she can never be saved: that she is willing to give up everything, but can *never* be a Christian.

"God grant that she may find that it is her own heart that is keeping her from her Saviour, and that she may yet find peace in believing."

"SEQUEL.—The sequel to the case of the young lady who felt that Christ would never receive her is most interesting. She remained in that state of mind for two or three days and nights, unable to sleep or feel any peace till one night she remembered this verse,—'If we confess our sins, he is faithful and just to forgive us our sins, and to cleanse us from all unrighteousness.' Light broke in upon her. Yes, she said, I will trust Him. I will believe. I have confessed my sins, and—'He is faithful and just to forgive us our sins.' Oh! I will believe Him. I will take Him at His word. She had begun to trust Him, and she was very happy in doing so; and, although she feels that she does not love Him as she ought, and sometimes doubts whether Christ has really received her, yet she feels that Jesus is her only refuge, and she is determined to try and serve Him, hoping that she may eventually find that peace and joy which makes the Christian's life a heaven begun below."

He adds another touching case.

"A father and mother had long been praying for the conversion of their son, a young man of some nineteen years. When the revival began in the old Payson Church, an unusual spirit of prayer was given them. Their wrestling seemed now to have reference to the glory of God. They saw their boy was rebelling against the government of a just God. Though willing to attend any of the meetings, he fled from those who would speak to him of Jesus. But prayer was not lost. The Holy Spirit was at work. The spoken word reached his heart.

"Sabbath evening, Nov. 24, 1861, hundreds were unable to find standing room. At the close of the first meeting, as some retired, a few of those about the door were able to pass in to the inquiry meeting. Among the number was the son of these praying parents. He met Mr. H. at the door, and, instead of shunning him as before, he seized his hand, and exclaimed, ' I have found Jesus.' ' How do you know?' Oh, I *know* I have. I *know* I love him. I have just given myself to him." In two minutes more he was standing up in the centre of the house and telling of the wondrous change.

"When he had finished, his father, an office bearer in the church, attempted to thank God, but his tears came faster than his words. He seemed to forget that every eye of that great audience was resting upon him, as he pressed his way to the embrace of his son, and throwing his arms around his neck, he kissed him. It was a thrilling scene which brought tears to the eyes of many."

An editor, who referred his decided religious impressions to the scene, wrote a sketch illustrating Mr. H's influence over children, which, as a pleasing link in events of the awakening, we subjoin:

"About seven o'clock, on a clear still evening, we heard the voices of children in sweet and silvery tones, apparently led by a strong masculine voice. We listened for a moment in surprise and wonder, and then made our way in the direction from whence the sound proceeded, and in front of the Custom House, found the fervid preacher engaged in solemn exhortation to sinners, the singing having ceased. The scene was an unusual one for the staid and quiet city of Portland, and we were in doubt for a few moments as to how so unusual an occurrence would be received. In a short time, a large number had gathered to hear the powerful and eloquent appeal of the man of God. We were apprehensive of scoffing and jeers from the ' roughs,' who will always be found on such an occasion ; but not a word or a lisp did we hear to break the solemnities of the hour. Every one was deeply, seriously interested; and we doubt not, that some who were present were made fully and sensibly aware of their sinful condition, during the few minutes exhortation of the earnest and sincere man who addressed them. Mr. Hammond was to preach that evening in the Second Parish Church, and his design was to induce all who could to go. After his entreaty was ended, he broke forth into the well known hymn—

'Worthy the Lamb, &c.'

in which he was joined by the children with which he was surrounded, and moved forward to the church, the whole singing joyfully, and making melody that we have rarely heard surpassed. The scene was novel and startling, and the earnest appeal was responded to with great unanimity; hardly a man who had witnessed the occurrence failed to accept the invitation of the preacher, and follow him to the church to listen further."

Would the proposed limits of this volume permit, we should extend the pages of experience as recorded by converted persons, in which the work of the Spirit is clearly seen, convincing of sin, and revealing its glorious remedy, — the blood of atonement. A recent visit and conversation with the able and excellent Pastor of the Second Parish confirms the estimate, formed at the time of the " gracious rain ;"—watering the garden of the Lord, and spreading bloom and fruitfulness over it, to the abiding joy of His people, and the glory of the reigning Immanuel.

CHAPTER VIII.

A week in Bethel—An unusual scene—Gorham, among the White Mountains—A new Church—Bath—Statement of Rev. J. O. Fiske —South Paris—Farmington.

At Bethel, a romantic town twenty miles from the base of the White Mountains, and a place of considerable resort in the summer;—in the autumn of 1861, an increased spirit of prayer for a refreshing had been felt by a few Christians, and souls were converted. Having visited the scene of a revival, the pastor returned more deeply moved in behalf of his own people, and called a company of Christians together to meet Mr. Hammond. The resolve was unanimous to enter the harvest field, securing the help of the Evangelist. A meeting was held of great power; the people were on their faces before God.

The pastor wrote, early in January, after the daily meetings had been in progress nearly a week, to the Christian Mirror:

"God is pouring out His Spirit upon us in Bethel. Many hope that they have been 'born again.' Many are asking what they shall do to be saved. Our meetings are solemn, well attended, well sustained by the prayers and efforts of God's people, We find Mr. H. a devoted servant of the Lord Jesus Christ, a man of prayer that prevails with God, &c. He will remain with us but a few days longer, but the prayers of many will follow him when he goes from us, that he may be still more successful in leading souls to our ever blessed Redeemer. Happy is the pastor who can secure the labors of this humble servant of the Lord Jesus."

In the same paper, we have these additional and interesting communications:

"BETHEL, JAN. 10, 1862.

. . . . " Our meetings have been, and still are, deeply interesting. People come from miles around to hear Mr. Hammond, and many are now rejoicing in Christ, who before were indifferent, or entirely thoughtless, or who made sport of religion, and first attended the meetings for the purpose of making sport.

" But they found themselves sporting on the brink of eternal woe, and have fled to Christ for refuge.

" I will mention a few cases of conversion, hoping they will interest you, as it has pleased God thus to work through Mr. Hammond, whom we all love.

" Mr. C. long ago thought he was born again, but he was either deceived, or a great wanderer. He had long been feeding on husks, and would not return to his Father's house. He thus related the manner in which he was brought 'home':

"'I attended the meeting first out of curiosity. For two or three evenings I was not deeply impressed. I thought Mr. H. a fanatic or insane. But one evening there came a change. He requested that the hymn commencing—

'The hill of Zion yields
A thousand sacred sweets,'

should be sung. He said: 'Those who are Christians may rise

and sing. Those who are not Christians may remain on their seats. Now, if any of you who *are not* Christians rise, *you will tell a lie*. If any of you who *are* Christians remain on your seats, *you will tell a lie.*'

"'I was very angry. I thought he had no right to say who should sing, and who should not. I took my hat and was going out. I had no idea of being controlled by *him*. Then the thought, ' God drew the line before he did,' entered my heart quickly, as though a dagger had pierced me. I sat down, still feeling very stubborn.

"'That night the Holy Spirit strove with me. I felt that I was a great sinner. At the inquiry meeting Mr. Hammond talked and prayed with me. The burden was very heavy, and did not leave me till I resolved to *give up all* for Christ. Then I was happy.

"'I went home one night, feeling it to be a duty to pray in my family. I had never done so, and I shrank from it. But, when I went in, the way was made easy. My little Clara (ten years old,) brought me the Bible, and asked me to read. She had been requested so to do by her mother, who was a Christian, and I could not refuse. I read and prayed, my wife prayed, eldest daughter (fifteen years old,) and my young son prayed, and little Clara repeated the Lord's prayer ! It was the most solemn prayer meeting, and at the same time the happiest, that ever I attended. I with my three children had found Jesus within one week ! '

" In this beautiful manner was the family altar set up in a home where prayer was not wont to be made except by the mother in secret.

" Mr. R. says: ' I did not at first attend the meetings. I thought I had been about the world a little too much, to be humbugged by such a man as Mr. Hammond. But at last I went to hear what he had to say. I sat directly in front of him, that I might look up into his face. I was very bold. I looked him steadily in the eye. I *defied him to move me.* He made one of his thrilling appeals to sinners. I was not moved, but I knew I was a sinner, and thought perhaps that I ought to feel it. So I prayed that I might feel it *just a little.* I did not want to feel very bad. But I got more than I bargained for. I not only felt that I was a sinner, but that I was a *lost* sinner. I felt black through and through. I was perfectly wretched for two or three days. At last I found I could do nothing for myself; that I could not save myself. I felt that Christ must do all for me; that he was standing near to take me. So I reached out my hand and said, ' Here Jesus, I am, vile and full of sin. Take me, just as I am, do with me what thou wilt. I am lost without thee. Take me and never leave nor forsake me.'

" ' Jesus took hold of my hand, and has not let go. He has led me ever since.

" ' I have left off doing anything of myself. He does all for me. At first I was tempted, and for a moment let go his hand; and then the thought came again, ' I am nothing — I can do nothing — He must do all ; and the hand of my spirit reached out and took his hand, and I have been perfectly happy ever since.

" ' Why, I never knew what those hymns meant before, never knew what young converts meant when they told about the love of God in their hearts. Now I know. I thought I was a Christian before. But I never before knew what it was to be born again, what it was to love God. I must have been deceived.'

"Speaking of the young mens' prayer meeting, which was organized last Sabbath afternoon he says :

" ' We have had a beautiful meeting. At first we did not know what to say or what to do. It was the first meeting of the kind many of us had ever attended, and we felt that we could not do anything. I suppose God made us feel so, and afterwards he showed us what to do, and put words into our mouths, and we had a glorious meeting. I suppose this will be the way all along. God will first show us that we can do just nothing at all, and then he will show us how to do in Christ's strength, what he has for us to do.'

"Mr. R. 's faith is beautiful, so childlike. I think before, he was very proud, perhaps self-righteous. He is completely changed. He has become ' as a little child.' He is now laboring earnestly, for the salvation of souls.

" Mr. B. says : ' I was requested to meet Mr. Hammond at the depot, and conduct him to his boarding-place. I was angry. I did not want him to come here. I did not want a revival. But I could not avoid going for him. Sunday evening, when he made one of his earnest appeals to sinners, I was ready to thrust him out of the house. But when Mr. Wheelwright, our pastor, rose and confirmed all he said, I thought I should sink. Convictions came upon me thick and fast. I was miserable, and not till I gave my heart to Jesus did I find peace. To-night I stand here free ! This has been the happiest day of my life. And I will say to my young friends, come to Jesus! Come now — just now ! You will never regret it. Come, *come*, COME ! ! '

Mrs. —— thus found the Saviour :

" 'I attended meetings at first without receiving any particular impressions; but on Sunday evening I was a little more interested. My husband noticed my serious countenance, and determined in his heart to laugh me out of all serious impressions. But I had experienced no particular change, and I told him so. But in the night I awoke with a great burden upon me. I felt that I was a sinner, and I longed for holiness. I wanted Christ. I longed for the Sabbath morning to dawn as calmly as it did in days of childhood. I longed for the holy Sabbath stillness which seemed so sacred to me years ago. And I prayed that my sins might be forgiven, and felt happier, and then fell asleep.

" When I awoke, morning had dawned ; and the stillness *was* holy. The sacredness *did* return. I roused my husband, and asked him if it did not seem different to him. But he could perceive no change. I went to the window. The sun was just rising. A halo of glory seemed to surround all things.

"'The beauty of the scene thrilled my soul through and through. Everything seemed changed — so much more beautiful than ever before. I was happy. My soul was at rest, and in harmony with all God's works. My husband looked at me. I suppose he saw the change in my countenance, and said:

"' Do you really believe?' and by the grace of God I was enabled to say — ' I do — I do!' Since then my husband and his daughter have both found Jesus, and it seems as though we had just began to live.'

"As she told this her face was radiant with happiness, and I could not doubt that she had found the ' pearl of great price.'

"A number of young men who went to make sport were arrested by the power of God's Spirit, and have come to Jesus, and are completely changed. I wish I could have room to tell you more; but this is enough to show you how wonderfully God has been working here.

"If we could only retain the influence of the Holy Spirit, in the great measure in which it has been poured out upon us during the last two weeks, this would be a ' Bethel ' indeed. Pray for us that the work may go on."

The Independent, of New York, published the following, from a physician, formerly of that city:

"Hundreds remain for the inquiry meetings. Weeping is often heard in different parts of the Church, and large numbers, who but a few nights ago were deeply convinced of sin, are now rejoicing in the love of their first espousals.

"Yesterday afternoon our people, of all denominations, were seen flocking to the Universalist Church to listen to a ' discussion on the subject of regeneration,' but as the Universalist minister affirmed his belief in the necessity of the new birth, there was no dispute, but a most solemn and impressive meeting. Mr. Hammond often repeated the words, 'ye must be born again,' and during his address the tears in the eyes of not a few indicated, that the Holy Spirit was leading some to feel the desperate wickedness of the heart. Much prayer had been offered for a blessing upon the meeting, and the children of God felt it had not been in vain."

Rev. Mr. Wheelright, who had a very deep experience of the law and Gospel of Christ, at one of the meetings overpowered with a view of the sinner's final doom, gave remarkable force to other exhibitions of this awful reality, by the weeping testimony with which he sustained the most startling presentations of a scriptural message, from which there is a liability to recoil, by both preacher and hearer. With him anxious sinners found no refuge, no quarter, as they sometimes do under Christian influence. The church also, stood by the pastor.

From Bethel Mr. Hammond went to Gorham, a village among the White Hills, — " peace reposing in the bosom of strength " — where the Rev. Geo. F. Tewksbury, was laboring without a sanctuary and without a church.

Soon after Mr. T. wrote to the Mirror these hopeful words:

"GORHAM, N. H., JAN. 11, 1862.

"The work of the Lord is evidently revived in Gorham, N. H. A series of religious meetings have been held during the past week, every afternoon and evening, with increasing interest and encouragement. Bro. Hammond has been laboring with us most faithfully and earnestly, and his labors have not been in vain. As the result, many are awakened and some are rejoicing in hope as new-born souls. The first cases of hope were in the Sabbath school, where the interest commenced. Professing Christians also are quickened, and much encouraged to renewed prayer and effort, working together in a spirit of union and harmony. The meetings are crowded every evening, and the public mind is generally stirred. And such is the spirit of inquiry awakened, that many remain at the close of the meeting to be conversed with on the interests of their souls.

"The prayers of your Christian readers are earnestly desired in behalf of this place, where so many of the people have been, and still are, under the poisonous influence of infidelity and false teaching.

"Yours truly,

"G. F. Tewksbury."

As the result of the merciful visitation of the Spirit, a church has been formed, and a neat, pleasant temple dedicated to the worship of Him, "who touches the hills and they melt, who taketh up the isles as a very little thing."

We select the narrative of a conversion very clear and striking :—

"When you came to Gorham, last winter, I was unable to attend the first meetings. This I regretted very much, for I was very desirous to hear what the Scotch preacher had to say. Not that I thought I might become interested about my own soul. Oh, no. I thought I was as good as my companions, and those around me. I never thought what a wicked heart I had. One evening I went to meeting with some of my friends.

When we entered they were singing, 'I'm glad salvation is free.' I had heard it sung a great many times before, but never thought it meant anything in particular; but then I felt that it meant a great deal. Salvation is free for you and me, for everybody. So strange that I had never thought of it before.

"In your discourse you repeated Scripture; one verse was, 'He that believeth on Him is not condemned, but he that believeth not is condemned already.' 'He that is not with me is against me.' I never meant to be against Jesus, but surely I was not with Him.

"I stayed to the inquiry meeting; you and several other Christians talked with me that night. I went home, and to rest; but there was no rest for me. I arose in the morning, determined that there should no one know my feelings. I did not want them to think I had any interest in the meetings. I resolved not to go again. But the next night I went again, in hopes that I should hear something that would drive away these feelings. At the inquiry meeting, you prayed that thorns might be planted in my pillow. I thought there was no need of that, for they were there already. I continued in this state four days. Oh, what a proud, rebellious heart I had, when Jesus was so kind, and willing to wash all my sins away. At last I went to my room, resolved not to leave it until Jesus had forgiven my sins. I took my Bible and began to read. I soon became calm; I prayed as I never had before; my sins were all swept away. It was so sudden, I could not realize my senses, but I was so happy. Oh, I do not wonder that you love to speak of that dear Jesus who died to save us. I hope you will remember me in your prayers."

The city of Bath, whose population had never the reputation of being excitable, but staid in character, and devoted to the business of a sea-port town, was stirred with scenes of unearthly interest, during the months of January and February, 1862. The beginning and phases of the remarkable religious interest is recorded by the pen of the able and judicious pastor of the Winter Street Church, Rev. J. O. Fiske, in a communication to the Christian Mirror:

"You ask for some brief account of the recent work of God's grace in this city; and we ought to be ready to declare with gladness what God has done for our souls. I may say then, that, last autumn, an increased seriousness was manifest in some of the congregation, and a more earnest prayerfulness actuated many in the church. In November, a day of fasting and prayer was observed by our church, with reference to the state of religion among us. The public meeting that day, which continued for four hours, was largely attended, and will long remain as a memorable occasion of the special presence and power of the Holy Ghost. The first week in the year, we assembled with the Central Church daily, in a prayer-meeting for the outpouring of the Holy Spirit. The third week in January, there was commenced in our church a series of evening meetings, at which solemn, earnest, pointed addresses were made by Edward Payson Hammond. These meetings were held uninterruptedly every evening for four weeks. In the afternoon a prayer-meeting was also held at two o'clock every day, which was continued, either in our church or in some of the other churches or vestries of the city, for nearly four months. These meetings were very largely attended, the house being usually, during the latter part of the time, completely full. Almost all the evangelical ministers of the city attended these meetings, and were exceedingly active and devoted in them. There was no denominational jealousy, no friction, nor difficulty of any kind, growing out of this union of all who love our Lord Jesus Christ in sincerity. At all the evening meetings, and after those in the afternoon to some small extent, there were meetings for religious conversation and inquiry. In the evening often five or six hundred persons, or more, would remain for these conversations. A portion of these would often be professors of religion, conversing, and in quiet tones often praying, with those who were anxiously asking what they should do to be saved. Some of these inquiry meetings presented scenes of very solemn interest. Many were weeping, many rejoicing, many anxious, many finding their Saviour ready to forgive them even as they were in the act of prayer. Prof. Chadbourne, of Bowdoin College, Rev. Mr. Carpenter, of Houlton, Rev. Mr. Howard, of Farmington, Rev. Dr. Tappan, and other clergymen rendered us very valuable assistance in the midst of these solemn scenes, by their addresses, sermons, prayers and conversations. Twenty-six heads of families, in my own congregation are among those who have begun lately to entertain a hope in Christ.

" From the very first, special attention was given, in meetings Saturday and Wednesday afternoons, and in the other meetings, *to the children*. They were all very deeply interested, and one of the best features of Mr. Hammond's labors among us, was his unintermitted skillful and *believing* zeal for the conversion of children. Quite a number of these lambs of the flock we hope have passed from death unto life, and a few of them between the ages of twelve and seventeen years, have been received into our church. No meetings that I have ever attended have been more delightful and solemn, than some of these childrens' meetings.

" As the fruits of the revival, *thirty-two* were added to our church at the communion in May, and *twenty-four* more last Sabbath. We are expecting quite a number of others on subsequent occasions; some have gone to other places, and will,

I trust, become connected with churches there. The Central church, the two Methodist churches, the Baptist, and the Freewill Baptist have all shared in this work ; and some of them have had large accessions to their numbers; but I cannot now speak with definiteness concerning them. They all feel, however, that they have enjoyed a season of delightful refreshing from the presence of the Lord.

"Christians, I think, have learned to feel their personal responsibilities more. Let me assure you, it has been no feature of this religious awakening, that Christians, male or female, were made to feel, that they had only to stand still, and see somebody else do the work of the Lord. The deepened sense of responsibility, the earnest prayerfulness, the greater faithfulness, diligence and fertility in the use of means of grace on the part of Christians generally, have been among the blessed characteristics of this revival.

"It has also been a revival of the straightforward, unflinching, abundant preaching of the old-fashioned truths of God's word. We think God's *word* has been honored ; and when I looked upon the crowds packing every pew and standing place in our church, as the fifth week of our evening meetings opened, and all to hear nothing but what all faithful ministers of the gospel have always preached, I could but think that the notions of some, that these ancient doctrines of orthodoxy are losing their hold on the public mind, have had their day, and are about run out, were as well refuted, as we could reasonably desire. I know of no better proof of the divine origin and authority of the great truths of evangelical religion, which some imagine are almost too stern and awful to be presented, except in softened terms, with bated breath, and an apology, than their power of thus rousing and holding the undivided attention of a large community like this, where they are entirely familiar, and the amazing and blessed transformations of character which they effect. The sword of the Spirit is mightier

than any human inventions : ' The foolishness of God is wiser
than men ; ' and after such scenes as we have witnessed here,
we all have a re-assured confidence that the gospel, as we understand and teach it, will yet be ' the power of God and the
wisdom of God ' unto the salvation of a believing world.

"Yours sincerely,

Bath, July 10, 1862.   J. O. F."

We select one or two cases of experience, which have already been printed, and made useful in awakening sinners and leading them to Jesus :

" One week ago last Saturday I stopped to the inquiry meeting, but did not feel that I was such a great sinner, and thought
I would not be converted at the time of a revival. You spoke a
few kind words to me, as did others, but I went home very
angry. I went again Sunday evening, and remained to the inquiry meeting ; I was in great distress of mind, but would not
believe the blessed promises. As I left the church, I requested
you to pray for me, also dear Mr. Page, and *tried* to pray myself, but found no relief. I slept very little that night, and was
in great agony all the next day. I wept until I was entirely
exhausted. I felt that I must do something. I *went to Jesus*
and prayed Him to take me *just as I was*, for I could do nothing more, and felt during the evening meeting that I was forgiven ; after meeting I went to Mr. Fiske and expressed my
faint hope, and besought him to pray for me that I might have
more light. I felt at peace with God, but did not feel that perfect happiness. Wednesday night I was perfectly happy and
fell asleep, seemingly clasping Jesus' hand. I feel that I cannot praise the Lord enough for His great mercy to me. I
tremble when I think of the danger I have escaped, and of the
many who are yet travelling the broad road which leadeth to
destruction.   Very truly yours."

Among the towns adjacent to the centers of efforts and blessing, visited by evangelical labors and the accompanying power of the Holy Ghost, was Phipsburg, a few miles from Bath. A precious season was enjoyed in connection with comparatively little labor; the outer wave of the divine influence from the Pentecostal scene. A number of sea captains are among those rejoicing in the love of Christ.

The following letter from one was read in a religious meeting, and from it we are permitted to make some extracts:

"BATH, March 15th, 1862.

"*My dear Friend*,—Having as I hope found the Saviour precious to my soul, I will attempt to give you some account of my experience. I am now about forty-three years old, have followed the sea all of my life, and like most others of my profession, have led a very wicked life. I have been deprived of many of the means of grace; and others, that were within my reach, I have neglected; until I grew to be a very hardened sinner; so much so, that I felt quite indifferent to all that concerned my immortal soul, and continued to live on year after year without a thought of what was to become of it, when it should be summoned to leave this world.

"In this state of mind you found me, at the commencement of the meetings held in this place the past month. I attended the meetings at first, not from any desire to be benefited by them, but for novelty of hearing a strange preacher, of whom I had heard so much, and made up my mind, that you had come among us to get up an excitement, and I for one would have nothing to do with it. Went home scolding about you, but still could not make up my mind to keep away from the meetings. Went again;—you came and talked with me as did some of the other ministers; but all your words at that time had no effect upon me. The next evening in the inquiry meeting, you came again to me after some conversation, and asked if you should pray with me. I gave consent but declined to kneel; so you prayed as we stood in the pew—you prayed, that the Lord would *plant thorns in my pillow, so that I might not sleep until I had given my heart to Christ.* I slept *some* that night, but awoke many times and felt of my pillow to satisfy myself, that there were not *thorns* in it. The next evening I could not *resist* going to hear you again; and, as you was addressing us, you presented the truth, that we, in rejecting Christ, were guilty of the greatest sin. I had never thought of this before, and it fell with crushing weight upon my guilty soul. I saw myself a sinner of the deepest dye, and went home that night resolved to seek for mercy. I tried to pray, but could not. My mouth was so completely sealed up that I could not utter a word, and it was not until the next day that I could open my mouth in prayer to God for mercy, and even then I could not give myself up entirely to Christ. I could not divest myself of the idea, that I had not something *to do* to make me more acceptable to Christ. This, of course, kept me in darkness and in sorrow. About this time our good minister, Mr. Fiske, called at my house, and, after praying with me and my family, proposed that I should pray also; this I at first declined doing; but when he told me that he feared that I was not humble enough, after much entreaty, I made an attempt to pray, but still no relief came to me. I remained in this state a number of days, and was fast settling down in despair, when one evening, after spending the whole afternoon upon my knees in prayer, I went to church. Prof. Chadbourne, of Bowdoin College, addressed us that evening, and, in the closing remarks, when urging sinners to come to Christ, he said that we should leave our own strength behind and go forward in the strength of our Saviour. I felt this was what had kept me from the Saviour, dependence on my own strength. I there and then as I sat in my seat, yielded that, and all other points, asked the Saviour to take me *just as I was* with all my *load* of sin and guilt. I saw that God would be just, if he refused to accept me and sent me down to everlasting woe; but in a *moment* I felt that Christ was able, and would save me; and that moment peace and joy took possession of my soul, light broke upon my darkened mind, and I felt that I was indeed 'a new creature.'

"It is now about six weeks since I felt that I had a hope in Christ, and I can truly say, that they have been the happiest weeks of my life. I have no wish to turn back to the world, for I feel that I have left nothing there worth going back for, but I hope by God's grace to press onward in the path of Christian duty, and finally gain the reward promised to those who remain faithful to the end.

Yours in Jesus,   Chas. N. Delano."

A little boy gives the story of his conversion as follows:

"*Dear Mr. Hammond:*—Two weeks ago last night as I was playing in the street, three ladies came along, and invited me to go to meeting. I thought I would go to have some fun, and be out evenings. That evening I laughed and made sport of those that you were praying for, and those that were anxious. I attended the childrens' meeting the next afternoon, when you gave an invitation to those who were anxious about their souls, to stop. Mr. Fiske came along and talked with me, and you came and prayed with me, and I felt that I was a lost sinner. I went home feeling very badly about my soul. I resolved to pray that night, and I did. Sabbath morning I felt a great change in my feelings, and I have felt happy ever since. I *love* Jesus. I love to read my Bible. I love to go to meeting. I love Christians. But the enemy of my soul tempted me, and tries to lead me astray, but in the strength of the Lord, I shall try and conquer and lead a Christian life."

South Paris, a village on the Grand Trunk Railroad, between Portland and Bethel, received a great and abiding dispensation of the Spirit, which, the pastor, Rev. Mr. Southworth, described, several months after the rain of God's mercy passed the crisis of its fulness :

" Everlasting praise belongeth unto God for this gracious visitation, in which a large number of souls have been hopefully brought to the saving possession of the truth as it is in Jesus.

" God for months had been preparing His people for His coming. The year 1862 was commenced with prayer. The spirit of supplication seemed to be given in unusual measures. Meetings for conference and prayer were held more frequently. The impenitent came to them and were more tender and thoughtful. God, by His Spirit, was evidently present to quicken believers, and the unconverted ; and still the clouds *delayed* to break, and pour its refreshing waters *abundantly*. At this time God seemed to impress His people with a desire to do all they could ; and, as it came to their knowledge that Mr. Hammond, the Evangelist, was greatly blessed in his labors in other places, there was a desire that he might be invited to come among us. He was invited and came. This was the 21st of February ; he staid but *two* days, but they were days of great power. The cloud of mercy which had been hanging over us shed down its mercy drops; Christians were deeply impressed with a sense of their active dependence upon God. The words of the Evangelist were attended by the demonstration of the Spirit; and, of the large congregations, few, if any, remained unmoved. Some, indeed, were not impressed favorably, but others allowed themselves to be convinced of the truth. The truth *was preached* with great *earnestness, boldness* and true *tenderness.* He sought to bring the children to Christ, and they were savingly impressed. One of the excellencies of his efforts among us was, that he preached no pleasing, delusive doctrine, by which men might be led to take up with a false hope. He preached the *Lord* and *Christ;* and sought to convince men of their sins by *showing* them *their* sins.

"Another most interesting feature of the work with us was, the inquiry meeting after the public exercises, at which many remained, and were addressed on the subject of religion. This meeting was continued for months, and proved a blessed means of grace, in which many were led to consider their lost condition. There have been not a few cases of *deep interest* — cases of conversion which have most signally displayed the Spirit's power to subdue the heart. All classes of community have shared in the work!—children, little children; business men; our most esteemed and respected women. Many families have rejoiced, and do rejoice. Forty-four have united with the church by profession. Others are designing to do so. It is not designed to be understood, that this was the result of the efforts of any man however blessed of God; but the result, when the church of God gave itself to prayer and faithful labor—were us it appeared, in an agony for the salvation of souls. With the church, in this condition, the Evangelist faithfully, prayerfully, earnestly co-operated, and, under God, was the means of much good among us. God grant that the time may soon come, when all our communities may receive a like, or still more gracious, visitation from on high. To God be all the glory."

Farmington is a delightful village in Franklin County, Maine, amid varied and sublime scenery, the seat of the widely known and excellent " Abbott School;" the birth-place and resort of the Abbotts.

Rev. Mr. Howard, the brother of the beloved and noble General Howard, of the army, who lost an arm in the battle of Fair Oaks, is the pastor of the Congregational church. He published in the local paper, an account of the glorious refreshing which came to that place in February, during which, a hundred and fifty were, it is believed, brought to Christ, besides an interest awakened in other towns:

" Will you allow me a little space, in which to speak of the present marked attention to the subject of religion in this community? The unusual meetings were commenced by a union prayer meeting at the Academy, on Monday of last week. This was attended and participated in by all the clergymen and many of the people. It was then expected, that Edward Payson Hammond, the Evangelist, would address a united meeting on Thursday evening, but the detention of the cars preventing his arrival, the meetings each day and evening during the week were conducted by the resident pastors. In spite of the unfavorable weather, the meetings increased in numbers; professors of religion were aroused and much earnest prayer was offered, that Mr. Hammond's labors should receive the blessing of God. But the blessing was not delayed till his arrival. A number of persons began seriously to ask the question— ' Lord, what wilt thou have me to do?' Mr. H. held his first meeting Sabbath evening, and the Congregational Church was crowded. His method of procedure is to conduct the exercises of singing, reading the Scriptures, prayer and preaching, without much regularity but with singular earnestness. After these services an inquiry meeting is held, to which all persons wishing to converse on the subject of salvation are invited to stop, and also such ministers and Christians as are disposed to instruct them. This inquiry meeting has been a blessed meeting. A large number of persons, of all ages and conditions in life, may be seen nightly in all parts of the house, conversing, praying and weeping, with occasional general admonition from Mr. H. and others. The unanimity among Christians, ministers and laymen, seems to be perfect. All recognize it as a work of God's Spirit, and all seem to love the evangelist, and to co-operate with him with all the heart.

"The scenes here are but a repetition of what has been witnessed in Portland, Bethel, Bath, and South Paris.

"Will not the prayers of all God's people go up for this dear brother who has been the means of bringing so many sinners to their Saviour? As he is about to leave us, I am expressing only the general voice, in saying, that our hearts are filled with gratitude and love to him, and we have no doubt that wherever God shall call him to especially labor and pray, an abundant blessing will follow."

We shall not forget an evening we spent in a meeting three weeks afterward, when, among others, a popular physician related the steps by which he was led from mere curiosity to anxiety, — from anxiety to distress, — and from anguish of soul to peace in believing.

And at the same moment a scoffer lay dead in his

home, one of a business firm that opposed the meeting; followed soon after by the most thrilling scenes of the death-bed of the wife, kneeling on her bed and begging for prayer and for mercy. Thus judgment followed blessing, the usual order of God's providence among men.

CHAPTER IX.

The Old Colony. The Church of the Pilgrimage. The Winter and Spring of 1862. Facts and incidents. Lewiston, Maine. The cloud like a man's hand. The mighty outpouring. Letters of experience. Farewell meeting. Brunswick. The College. Scenes and cases of striking conversion.

In the providence of God, the writer seeking health, went to Plymouth, Mass., in the Autumn of 1861. With all descendants of the Pilgrims in natural or spiritual lineage, he felt a deep interest in the Old Colony, with its beautiful bay, where the Mayflower rocked, — Burying Hill where their ashes lie, — and the church they planted, with sacrifice and suffering without a parallel since the days of the apostles. The Congregational Society there, during the first 180 years, had only *seven* pastors, including Brewster, who would never consent to be ordained, although in labors of love, the shepherd of the flock in the wilderness. Since the exodus from Arminianism in 1800, with the loss of all material possessions as a parish, a period of sixty years, there have been, also, seven pastors; showing that a sad change has gone over Puritan New England since the days of the fathers. Precious revivals of religion have been the repeated benediction of the Lord upon his heritage. But the 'enemy of all righteousness' seems to have had a peculiar hostility toward this Jerusalem of the new world, and every possible form of attack has been made upon the faith and peace of the church.

Errors were rife in the community, and too often the Zion, which should beat them back, had slept, while her adversary sowed the tares. For three months before the date at the beginning of this chapter, the sanctuary of God had been closed, from reasons material, and conditions of feeling; and "the ways of Zion mourned." When invited to supply the pulpit, and afterwards to remain, the conviction, which laid aside all other plans, was, that the time to favor her had come with God. The parish was visited, church fasts appointed, and the necessity of a revival kept before the people on all occasions. The aspect of the congregation gradua'ly changed to a marked seriousness, and indications of unusual interest apparent among the impenitent. But health not yet confirmed, forbidding extra meetings, and the exciting war news, between the Sabbaths, kept back the outbreak of feeling,— the outgushing of the waters of the sanctuary. At this crisis, attention was turned for help to Mr. Hammond. The church invited him to come; and he held the first services on Sabbath-day the last of March.

The work in a brief time, assumed a decided

form and power. Although he remained less than three weeks, the house of God was opened nightly for almost nine weeks; — during which were witnessed scenes of stirring interest. In the town between two and three hundred expressed hope in Christ, many of whom, at least, have continued to walk according to the gospel. The assistance of Rev. A. B. Earle, Rev. Dr. Kirk, and the former pastor, Rev. Mr. Porter, was of great value in the progress of the work; especially the earnest and abundant labors of Rev. Mr. Earle.

At the close of a sermon, during the course of the evening meetings, from the mass that filled the sanctuary, rose a stalwart man of about 60 years, and with trembling frame, cried out; "My friends, it is twenty-six years since I have been in the house of God, till last evening. I have been the vilest of the vile; and now I feel that Jesus Christ is working on me,— and he is working fast. If any of you can pray for me, I want you to do it." He soon bowed in the dust, and begged for pardon, while a daughter on each side, who had found the Saviour, wept aloud.

Upon another occasion, a member of the Church, who had found fault with the severity of the gospel message, with a flood of tears and broken utterance, declared that he had been a boarder in God's family, and sought an interest in believing prayer. Scenes like these were common for many weeks.

The following incident appeared in the columns of the Congregationalist :

"It was on the lovely morning of May 25th, that we were sitting in the chapel of the 'Church of the Pilgrimage,' at the very base of 'Burying Hill,' the Holy Spirit filling the place, when suddenly a call at the door summoned a young man to the vestibule, who had recently found Jesus. In a moment he returned, and in a flood of tears broke the hallowed stillness by saying : 'My friends, the 'Standish Guards,' to which I belong, are ordered to leave at 2 o'clock to-day. And now I want you to pray for me, that I may be a faithful soldier of the cross; and, if I fall, may die happy in Christ. *Pray for my comrades.*'

"He sat down amid the audible sobs of many; for this was the first intimation of the additional contribution to the ranks of the army from the young men of the Old Colony. Then one and another begged the prayers of God's people for the brothers and friends also called away ; and hearts and lips *did pray.*

"The meeting closed, and there was hurrying to and fro to obey the summons. A little later the armory was thronged, and the streets lined with all classes. As I spoke to the young men who had recently been converted, with a smile they said, 'We are ready to go.' Those who had been inquiring the way of life for days past, wept. Soon to the stirring music of the drum, whose roll was thunder to sad hearts, telling of the withering stroke to the affections, the Guards, attended with an immense concourse, reached the depot. Stepping forth from the ranks, a young man leaned upon his gun, and weeping said, 'Had I not been converted, I should not want to go, but now am glad to be here.' Next came to my side a fine youth with whom we had often conversed about his soul, but who had no hope, and weeping, desired to be remembered at the throne of grace. I said, go to the Bible for light, while you pray for it.

Laying his hand upon his breast he replied, 'Yes, I have it in my pocket,' and also wept. Another moment, and the bell sounded, and away the company moved amid cheers and tears, from the atmosphere of a precious revival, to aid in beating back the waves of the darkest rebellion perdition ever poured over the plains of time. Let unceasing prayer ascend for the soldier and for the government, that there may be wisdom to discern and courage to meet the issue God is forcing upon us."

All classes were reached. Men who had not entered the sanctuary for a score of years were smitten down, and gave evidence of the saving change. Whole families were taken by the Spirit from the bosom of popular error, and the town was pervaded by the Spirit of the Lord; and whatever discount man's weakness or sin may make, Jehovah vindicated the faith of the Puritans, and his glory, in the eyes of all the people. Although the pastor elect felt it his duty to leave, the tidings came of many accessions to the churches, and blessed seasons around the altars of prayer.

While in Plymouth, a call from the city of Lewiston, Maine, the united voice of the pastors of the various churches, came to Mr. Hammond, to labor in the whitening harvest field. We give a statement of the general aspect of the greatest outpouring of the Spirit, perhaps, witnessed in any one place in this country for years, until, it is believed five hundred persons were hopefully converted,—as we find it in the Lewiston Herald, from the pen of one of the ministers. The origin of the interest, is mentioned in the last chapter of this work in another connection:

"Mr. Hammond has now preached nine successive evenings in the Free Baptist Church, the largest in the place, with increasing interest, power and blessing. He spoke first to the children in Pine Street Chapel, Rev. Mr. Balkam's church, on Sunday afternoon of the 27th ult., and not only were children and young people wrought upon, many of whom have since expressed hope, (and it is delightful to see their happy faces,) but yesterday, at the morning prayer meeting, a gentleman of mature years and mental powers rose in hope, and said his heart was touched at that meeting. He spoke with great calmness, though we presume no one ever heard his voice in any public meeting before. He said he had always been afraid of the world, but now he wished every body to know where he stood, and with divine aid meant to stand, the rest of his days. Some of our readers will call to mind a stout, fat, jovial young man, whom they have often seen upon the railway, between this place and Danville Junction. He has declared himself publicly and inflexibly upon the Lord's side. There have been many cases of conversions, embracing a pretty wide range of character, and the work is apparently extending to the outmost circle of society, and including all classes.

"Saturday evening, the Free Baptist Church was packed in every part of it, above and below, by people sitting or standing, while the large vestry was also filled.

"Sunday evening the above church was filled exclusively with men; the vestry with men, women and children. The Baptist Church was filled exclusively with women. The M. E. vestry, which is very large, was filled as usual. The morning prayer meeting, Sunday, was one of deep and tender zeal. Meetings of great interest have also been held in High St. Cong. Church, during the week, of which we have not time and space to speak more particularly.

"If this work were not based upon the most thoroughly considered scriptural and theological teaching of years, it might be dismissed as the blown up heat of an hour. As the matter is, nothing of the kind can be pretended for a moment. We suppose there is as much calmness of instruction at West Point, as at any other school of learning. But every lesson given there in utmost quiet, contemplates the excitement and shock of battle. Yet not more certainly, than does the whole system of Evangelical truth contemplate a certain excitement, when it is received into the heart. It is the inevitable excitement of truth in conflict with error — of sin in conflict with holiness — of human will in resistance to the Divine will — of human depravity lifting itself in opposition to infinite purity.

"If Mr. Hammond produces excitement, it is only by the greatness of his zeal to persuade men to be reconciled to God that he does it. Besides, the farthest aim in the world from his, is an effort to *create* excitement. His simple aim is to preach with his whole soul what he believes to be the truth. The secret of his power is the entireness with which he gives himself up to the impulses of the Spirit. He always appears with his Bible in his hand; wherever he goes, the Bible seems to be the talisman of his power. If any suppose he wishes to exalt himself, they could not be more mistaken. He loses himself in the greatness of his work. And most emphatically may it be said of him, ' the zeal of thine house hath eaten him up.' If he is deluded, then the whole system of Orthodoxy is a delusion.

"We were surprised this morning, upon entering the store of one of our most able and excellent citizens of this class, to find that, last night, in the retirement of his home, he had settled the great question. He went home, and went to his Bible; he read it — read it without skipping — believed it — believed it all — felt it as the very Word of God speaking to him. We know there are others, many of them of this class, who are already convinced of their duty, and who are only awaiting a little more pressure of will, now, to become, in the most delightful sense, children of God.

"At the open-air meeting Sunday evening, when full three thousand were present, more than half were men. The ministers of the place were generally present, and for the first time at any of these meetings we noticed the Episcopal and Catholic clergymen. Mr. H. was distinctly heard by the outmost circle, as well he might be, for he has spoken so as to be heard, to five times the number in Aberdeen, and other places in Scotland.

"It was a heart-stirring sight. The evident impression of the truth showed, that it was falling on minds, curiously moulded by the Creator to be wrought upon by just such appeals."

The following interesting letter was read in one of the churches. These letters indicate the wondrous change that is daily taking place in the hearts of many of the people. Some of the leading men of business stood up in the great congregation, and testified of the power of the Holy Spirit to transform the whole moral nature:

"LEWISTON, May 12, 1862.

"*Dear Mr. Hammond:*—In very early life I was the subject of strong religious impressions, and, through the deceitfulness of my own heart, for awhile believed I had given myself to Christ. But soon I found myself deceived. Then did I refuse all confidence in experimental religion, and gladly sought to believe in the universal salvation of all. That would give me a wide scope for dancing and like amusements. I watched professing Christians, glad to detect their faults. Thus had I become careless, when Death entered our family circle, and Oh! how deep did I sink in despair. Then I promised to become a Christian, yet had no faith in Christianity. I felt that I must be wrong, and often asked myself if Universalism is true, why, in this the hour of deepest need, does it forsake me? why these dark and dreadful doubts? But I silenced conviction, looked at professed Christians, and thought myself as good as they.

"When I came to Lewiston, as I found it inconvenient to attend a Universalist meeting, I visited different churches, that I might glean a harvest of their imperfections. How faithless, how wicked was my heart.

"The first time I heard you speak, I returned home more faithless than ever, assured that 'Godly sorrow' none could have. The following Monday, you spoke of the different ways God takes to draw us to himself; one was, taking from us our dear friends. I never can tell how it pierced my heart. It seemed, you was to give me a last and final warning — that I must repent now, or be for ever lost. After meeting, before I could leave the house, you spoke to me — asked if I loved Jesus? I was ashamed to be seen conversing with you — ashamed of my own feelings, which I could no longer conceal. You prayed with me but I could not kneel. You left me, saying you would return soon, but I waited for no second interview. That night I sought my pillow, but found little rest. Satan seemed to say 'folly, all folly,'' for — 'as in Adam all die, so in Christ shall all be made alive.' But I could not keep away from the meetings. The next evening I sat back by the door to see if I should feel the same. But there was no peace for me. I did not stop to the inquiry meeting, but went home and tried to read my Bible; it was a sealed book. I no longer tried to drive away my feelings, but hoped they would deepen.

"The next day I was wretched. I felt that God would never forgive me; that I had committed the unpardonable sin,

OF THE HOLY SPIRIT. 267

in once having professed to love my Saviour, while my heart was in rebellion against Him. I resolved I would test my feelings. I would not go to meeting, and see if my feelings would be the same. But on all around seemed written,

   ' Till to Jesus' work you cling
    By a simple faith,
   Doing is a dangerous thing,
   Doing ends in death.'

"I read my Bible, and tried to pray that if there was such a thing as a change of heart, God would not suffer me to rest till I had found it. Then came a dear friend, and with her arms around my neck, said she had found Jesus, and it was so easy. I was discouraged. I had spent miserable days and sleepless nights, and now to be told it was 'so easy.' That night I went to meeting, stopped to the inquiry meeting, conversed with several, but found no relief. I met with a friend, who had during the week written me a letter, begging me to give my heart to Christ. I would not tell him what kept me back, and we left the house in company with other ladies who had just passed from 'death unto life.' Their company only made me more wretched. I felt I was *lost* — there was no hope for me, and I would no longer seek what I could not obtain. I finally resolved to tell my friends the sin of my youth, which I feared God would not forgive, and what I had ever after thought of Christians. They were talking, but I know not what they said, for I was lifting my heart to God as I had never before, repeating the words,

   ' Just as I am, though tossed about,
    With many a conflict, many a doubt,
    With fears within, and foes without,
     O Lamb of God, I come.'

"Then peace, such as I had never known, came to my soul.

It seemed like going from darkness to the light of the noon-day sun. I no longer doubt Christians, but with them hope to spend an eternity of bliss."

The additional instance of sovereign rescue from the edge of ruin is that of a young lawyer, whose family name is familiar in the national Senate, and throughout the State, T. A. D. Fessenden, Esq.

A daily paper reports the touching occasion of his solemn narration of his conversion, as follows:

" Mr. Fessenden detailed at some length the story of his conversion, which enchained the attention of the large audience, and came home to many a heart. Mr. F. spoke nearly as follows : —

"'I cannot refrain from saying, that it is repugnant to my natural feelings, to speak of myself; but in the hope that it may possibly, with God's blessing, be the means of some little good, I will speak. I feel impelled to speak for the cause of Jesus, and of my late experience, though my words be feeble. My story is a simple one. But a short time since I had supposed that I was possessed of a strong will, of good nerves, and of a clear judgment. I did not think I was emotional, and I remarked to a friend with whom I was conversing, and who mentioned that Mr. Hammond was creating an excitement, that if he could raise any emotion in me, I should like to have him, for it was dull, and had been so long since I had felt emotion, that I should like to feel it. One Sunday evening it entered my mind that I would go and hear. I went and listened intently, but it was with no expectation that it would afford me any pleasure, except that of hearing one who, from report, appeared to be an earnest and impassioned speaker. I listened to him and went away. I descanted to my friends upon his power of illustrating, and told them that he drew upon his travels for his figures of speech. I was utterly indifferent so far as my personal state was concerned. Some time after, I attended again, and listened attentively. I fastened my eye upon the speaker, and for some moments his gaze was riveted on mine, as he addressed me in tones of impassioned earnestness to come to Christ. It was thus I began to think, is this real? Is it necessary? Is it a duty we have resting upon us? But when the sermon closed, I walked down the aisle, and out of church alone. I thought then, there is no necessity of my stopping here to talk with these people ; it will do well enough for persons not in the habit of thinking for themselves, but not for me. I concluded that I would not go again; but, on reflection, I said, I will go, I am not afraid to hear the man. I went. I was interested in the sermon ; I was interested in the experience of Mr. Wight ; I was interested and moved by the affecting prayer for physicians and lawyers, more particularly, perhaps, because I had been introduced to Mr. Hammond during the day, and thought he might have me in his mind, and my heart was somewhat softened ; but I did not heed the invitation to stop, but steeling my heart I walked to the door.

"'I was overtaken by him. He urged me and a friend who was with me to remain. He said my old father was praying for me, and kindly pressed me to stay. He asked me to promise him that I would pray that night, but I refused the promise, and said I would see him the next day. As I walked down the still street my feelings overcame me, and I wept ; but when I neared my home I endeavored to crush out all my feelings of remorse, so that I might enter the presence of my wife calm and unmoved, for I would not let her see, that a man in the prime of life could be so wrought upon, and appear so unmanly. I sat down, but my grief came over me, and I covered my face with my handkerchief. She sought to comfort me. I choked down my sensations for the moment, and said, ' This is excitement — it will pass away'; but she replied, 'It is the Spirit of God struggling with you,' and begged me to yield to its influences. I was softened. I asked her to pray. She did so, and asked me to pray, and for the first time since I was a young boy, I knelt and prayed. The next morning, Mr. Adams met me. He talked a moment with me in the street, and I invited him to my office. He then talked and prayed with me, and I tried to pray. He left, and during that day I was overwhelmed with mental anguish. My sins were before me. The memory of my past life came vividly to my mind, and temptations and suggestions of all sorts pressed upon me to shake off these delusions; but I prayed constantly and fervently in my mind that the Spirit of God would not leave me, but would continue to strive. That evening I attended meeting, and heard the story of the Son of God; that He came to save the lost; that for our sakes he was treated as though a guilty rebel; of his agony upon the cross; and when I listened to the words of the dying Jesus, in the extremity of agony, 'My God! my God! why hast Thou forsaken me?' my heart melted. I stopped at the inquiry meeting, and on my knees I promised God, that, if he would forgive my sins, I would take sides with Jesus — that I would stand up for Jesus — give my heart to Him, and would trust to Him and be His. I was at peace. Hence I am willing to stand up and speak to you to-night. This may seem to some a simple story, but appears a solemn reality to me.'"

Another wrote:

"DEAR MR. HAMMOND: — When you came to Lewiston, I went to hear you simply because you were famous; for, though calling myself a Christian, I was proud and self-reliant, and had had no sympathy with what I scornfully called 'revival excitement.'

"The first evening I heard you speak, you showed me that, at best, I was only a 'boarder' in the Lord's family. I was startled and angry. I went to hear you talk to sinners, and not to test, by *personal experience*, your power of awakening *cold hearted* professors. I tried to get out of the house, but it was so crowded I could not; stopping at the inquiry meeting, Satan advised me as my only refuge, to feel disgusted; and I went home *trying* to think I was; all the next day and the next, I quarreled with my conscience, and, by convincing others, tried to make *myself* believe that the revival was fanatical and absurd; not a thought, in those days, of the struggle that was going on in the hearts around me; not a prayer for the precious souls that were embracing or rejecting Jesus; only a wilful desire to forget my own duty.

"But as I listened, a week ago to-day, in the High St. Church, to a letter you read from a lady in Portland, and to your remarks concerning it, I could no longer shut my eyes to the fearful wrong I was doing my own soul, and, through you, the cause of Christ; I knew then, just how Peter of old felt after he denied his Lord.

"Jesus forgave me, as I trust, and took me back to his arms once more; but I knew I ought to go and tell you, and ask you to forgive me too; it was so hard, I thought I *could* not; so I tried to help you at the inquiry meetings, and every way I could think of, but it was no use; if I attempted to speak to an anxious one, I thought how I had stood right there, and actually laughed at you, a little while before. I couldn't pray for you, even, for I kept thinking, 'If thou bring thy gift to the altar,' &c., and last Sabbath evening I couldn't bear it any longer, so I went and told you; then I could sing and pray, brother; I couldn't help it."

Rev. Mr. Adams, of Auburn, across the river from, and practically a part of Lewiston, gives his own clear account of what God has wrought:

"The special religious interest, in the two towns of Auburn

and Lewiston, came upon the mass of our community as suddenly, no doubt, as the freshet that sweeps along our river in the early spring. And yet it was not sudden, for just as the snows that whiten the mountain tops in November, and cover the plains, and fill the valleys, give token of the coming flood, so have there been for months past, from as far back as November, certainly, awakening providences, burdened Christian hearts, pleadings and tears in secret places, now and then a case of conversion, and, as we have since found, a deepening thoughtfulness with many of the unconverted.

"Whether, however, all this would have issued in a general awakening, apart from the special means employed, and which God has so evidently blessed, may well be doubted. Some time in March, a union morning prayer-meeting was commenced with us, in which the interest and the prayerfulness of Christian people found utterance, and the new awakened ones found encouragement and help.

"Just at the close of April, Rev. Mr. Hammond came to labor among us, at the invitation, and with the full and hearty concurrence, of the pastors in the two towns. For a period of nearly four weeks, he maintained, in concert with the pastors, a series of evening meetings, and devoted himself with a singular and unremitting zeal to the work of saving souls. Rarely, I am sure, is the truth of God preached more forcibly and pungently. Rarely do men find themselves pressed by a more determined urgency, or plead with more fervently and more tenderly, to give up their sins, and accept the Gospel salvation. The meetings, held mainly in the Free Will Baptist Church in Lewiston, and (less frequently) in the High Street Congregational church in Auburn, were invariably crowded, hundreds standing through the evening, and hundreds going away to prayer-meetings elsewhere. All was subdued and still. The Spirit of God was manifestly present. The inquiry meetings that followed the more public service—though it is hardly proper to distinguish between the more public and less public, where the numbers in both cases were so large—were scenes of marvelous interest. Christians, young and old, were seen conversing with their unconverted friends, pleading with them sometimes with many tears, kneeling down with them, in their pews where they were, and pleading with God on their behalf, and from time to time new witnesses bearing testimony to the pardoning mercy of God.

"Besides these evening services, meetings have been held for the children, Wednesday and Saturday afternoons, attended by large numbers of children as well as by many other persons. There Christ has been preached first and foremost, and they have been appealed to as if it was really believed that they might be converted, and converted now; and when we have seen hundreds of them troubled under a sense of sin, when we have seen them bowing before God, and pleading with many tears, when we have seen many subsequently peaceful and radiant with Christian hope and joy, when we have heard their testimony for Christ, and have seen them pleading with their friends, and pleading for them, when we have seen in them, from day to day, the transformed lives, and the fruits meet for repentance, we have said, this is just what we might have expected. This is in precise accordance with our own previous theory of things, and is just what the Gospel and the promises of a gracious God warranted us in looking for.

"As the results of this work thus far, some hundreds—I do not know how many—profess conversion. Among these there are people of all ages and conditions. Some have been very hard cases, young men of profligate lives, and yet for the most part, and so far as I know, young men who have been followed in all their wanderings by the prayers of Christian fathers and mothers. Some are men of position and influence. Many are heads of families. Many are children, from sixteen years old downward. In our own Sabbath school Concert, last evening, a large number, I should hardly dare to say how many, rose to testify their choice of their Saviour, and their consecration to his service.

"There are two or three things suggested by this recent experience of which I should like to speak, but I can only allude to them. One—the indispensableness of a more direct, pungent, close home style of searching than generally obtains among us. There is, says Dr. Chalmers, a time to reason and there is a time to affirm. The reasoning time is always with us, but the time of bold, undoubting, urgent affirmation we too rarely reach. A very large share of Mr. Hammond's power lies in this; that what other ministers prove he assumes, on the marked testimony of the Bible, and treats as incontestible and urgent fact. And if any man takes exception to the style of that brother, as making small account of established principles in logic and rhetoric, I answer, so much the more in favor of my point, for with all this drawback he effects a lodgment of truth, and sways men by it a hundred fold more than you do, with all the closeness of your logic, and all the felicity of your illustration and appeal.

"A second point—which I can only suggest—has reference to that most neglected class, the children. Most neglected class, I say, notwithstanding the Sabbath-school and all its appliances. What minister gives them their fair proportion in the instructions of the pulpit! What minister, even in times of revival, arranges meetings for them, and preaches to them, and pleads with them, as he does with those who are older! 'Were half the breath thus vainly spent'on adults given to those whose hearts are yet tender, we should see blessed results.

"A third point—and one on which your correspondent presumed to say a few words at the recent meeting of the Suffolk South Conference, in Park Street Church—is a *determined urgency* in dealing with individuals. We have seen the value of this in the present revival. People who could get through the sermon and the prayer meeting little moved, were brought up by the conversation meeting that followed, and by the importunities of Christian friends. Men of judgment and culture, who had been awakened, and who might be left, if any might, to consider and decide for themselves, had been followed up to their homes or their offices, and pressed with the truth there, and, when they admitted it, met with the call, 'Come, then, let us kneel down before God right here, now, and confess our sin and plead for mercy,'' and all the urgency of Christien zeal, and all the tenderness of Christian love and sympathy was brought to bear upon them to help them. But I have no time to go farther, nor have you room for me. I only say in closing, 'the Lord hath done great things for us.' May our future lives yield some harvest of gratitude and faithfulness.''

We have in the Daily *Journal* a review of the revival, in addresses made at a closing service on the evening of the 12th of June:

" The Free Baptist Church was crowded to overflowing, Wednesday evening, on the occasion of the last union meeting in which Mr. Hammond, the Evangelist, is to participate in this place, for the present, at least. Every part of that large church was filled—the galleries, sittings, pulpit, aisles, doorways and entries: and hundreds went away without being able to obtain even a standing place,—the interest in the gathering being heightened by the fact, that it was a farewell meeting to Mr. Hammond, on the occasion of which his numerous friends had determined to present him with a suitable pecuniary acknowledgement for his invaluable labors.

" Rev. Mr. Lowell conducted the meeting, and made the opening remarks, for an abstract of which, together with a synopsis of the remarks of others, we are indebted to Rev. Mr. Tufts. Mr. Lowell said, that he had been most favorably impressed by Mr. Hammond, and that it was a matter of gratitude he had come among us, and aided the ministers here in the good work of bringing hundreds of souls to say,

'I love Jesus, yes I do, I know I do.'

He thanked him in their behalf, in behalf of anxious souls still inquiring, and in behalf of others not yet determined in their minds to seek the Lord—hoping that the good word, spoken to them from time to time, would be as good seed, so that in the future they may turn back to these meetings as the beginning of serious thoughts, and as blest of God through Mr. Hammond, whom the Lord was pleased to employ as the means of their conversion.

"Rev. Mr. Butler said, he would bear testimony to the wondrous things he had seen of this servant of God, who a few weeks ago came among us unheralded and unknown. At first he was distrustful of Mr. Hammond's measures; but that feeling soon passed away, and it need not be said what had been done. It took hold on eternity, and that alone could tell what God had wrought in this revival. Like Napoleon, he held himself to no rule of action; but like that leader, he hurled his legions with great effect against the enemy. So had Mr. H. plead God's word, and many sinners had been plucked as brands from the burning. He hoped this work would go on. He rejoiced that family altars had been increased, and that many fathers and mothers could now throw their arms around whole households. He hoped, that, when generations had passed, this audience would rise up in praise of this revival. He thought it would be matter of rejoicing among the angels and saints in glory, in the ages to come. He was glad to be present and bless God with others for this revival; not only for what it had done here, but for its influence in other places. He spoke of a good work begun near by, and hoped hundreds would be gathered in. He deprecated the objections of some against the conversion of children, as though they would not hold out. He spoke of his own experience and observation of twenty years to the contrary. He rejoiced in the jubilee, and hoped it would be the beginning of endless joy—a foretaste of that great gathering in heaven where all would be happy and joyous.

"Rev. Mr. Wood said, of all the assemblies of life we might look to this as the most precious. In the eternal world, where we take higher degrees of glory, we shall see this was a pure work, wrought by God's Spirit. What but love could do such a work? He blessed God, that Mr. H. had come among us, that a work of grace had been accelerated, the church blessed, and souls saved. We had been taught to love each other as never before. He spoke of the influence of this work at Bangor, that Mr. Small carried the Spirit home with him, and that a revival had commenced there with flattering prospects. He hoped all would labor on in the work, and not think it finished.

"A. D. Lockwood, Esq., said, he did not expect to speak, but would say with other Christians, that he enjoyed this gathering. We had come together for no ordinary purpose. He could speak of the love of Jesus. At eighteen he had experienced religion, and during all the trials and perplexities of business it had been his support. Nothing like a trust in Jesus could sustain the sinking heart. He urged the business men of Lewiston to come to Jesus, embrace religion, and be prepared in time for eternity.

"D. M. Ayer, Esq., said, he could not resist saying a word for Jesus. Though not entirely free from doubts, he could say Jesus was precious to him, and that a load had been taken from his heart. He was determined to conquer the obstacles before him. He was happy in duty and in the love of God; that so far he had had supports in business he could not otherwise have had. He urged all to come to Jesus.

"Rev. Mr. Balkam said, he would bear testimony to what had already been said of the efficiency of Mr. H.'s labors. He said that two sisters in his church assured him, if he would invite Mr. Hammond to come to Lewiston, that all pecuniary obligations should be met. His people at first were not in favor of the invitation, but soon thought better of it. He approved of the measures adopted by Mr. H. Since the smoke of the battle had cleared away, and results had been seen, his appreciation of him and his work had risen, and he rejoiced with others that a new era had dawned.

"Rev. Mr. McMilan spoke of the evidences that God was here, and that the love of Jesus ruled in many hearts. He rejoiced at all this. In eternity hundreds of converts in this revival would shine as stars in the crown of Mr. H. He hoped the work would not stop when our brother left us.

"Rev. Mr. Adams spoke of the difficulties of the ordinary pastor in winning souls to Christ. He did not share in the apprehensions of some, that Mr. H. would impair the friendly relations between pastor and people. He believed that his object was to bring souls to Jesus and not to himself. He suggested that other Christians strive to become better Christians, and adopt modes of action more aggressive, come into closer contact, and not be satisfied with planting their weapons at a distance and firing them occasionally, but to draw near the enemy and grapple with him. He thought Christians had learned much within a few weeks, and he thanked God for it. He closed by addressing himself to that class who had not yielded to God, some of whom had attended the meetings, but apparently to little or no effect, asking them if they were willing to go on as they are, to call the question settled, to have it said that Mr. H. had come here, labored, prayed, plead and besought them to come to Jesus, and they rejected Him, grieved the Spirit, hardened their hearts against God, and would not yield?

"Mr. Fessenden said the scene before us was inspiriting. He had stood before larger assemblies, but never before one of this character. He had seen large assemblies do honor to men from abroad, to victors, heroes and civilians, who had done well for their country, but never had he seen anything of this kind before. He felt a pleasure tinged with sadness as he stood before that great audience; and he would take occasion to express his attachment to Mr. H., who was soon to depart from us. Before passing to that, he wished to allude to what had been said by a clergyman present, that he had no fear that Mr. H. would lead any from their attachment to their pastors. He believed that no bad effect would arise from it; that he could speak only for one, but in his opinion great good would come from it. He felt it so himself. He believed the bonds would be strengthened by such measures. He believed that he had experienced a great change in that respect. It has been said that Mr. Hammond was aggressive, and had taught Christians they should be aggressive. That is true; the church should be aggressive—it is the church militant.

"No one had ever followed *him* to the portals of the church, to urge him to go back and listen to what might be said, and to remain in the inquiry meeting, till Mr. H., on a certain evening a few weeks ago. God in sovereign mercy had blest his soul as he trusted, and he thanked him to-night that he made Mr. H. in any way to contribute to the result of which he had spoken.

"Mr. F. alluded to the peculiarity of the occasion, that Mr. H. came here a short time ago, not as a distinguished warrior, or great statesman, claiming the praise of meritorious service, but as a simple soldier of the banner of the Cross. He would not recount his labors, they were familiar to all. He spoke of his success in winning the hearts of children to Christ, of his earnestness in seeking the unity and co-operation of ALL Christians. The argument, the illustration and the appeals he had made to the same. The laborer is worthy of his hire, but we do not asssemble to-night to pay a debt of wages to Mr. H., but to thank God, and assure Mr. H. of our attachment and affection, and to present him a slight token of our regard. The reward of his services in the cause of Christ, he will, we trust, find in another and better world.

"In addressing Mr. H. he said, 'that in behalf of all who had spoken to-night, and in behalf of a large circle of appreciating friends, who had contributed a purse of money as a token of their respect, and who now welcome you again to our midst, for a day, I present you this, which you will please receive as an indication of our esteem, and with our prayers for your prosperity and success in the years to come.'

"Mr. H. replied in a most affecting manner, thanking Mr. F. for the token, and repeating the expressions of gratitude to the many friends who had given him evidence of their esteem. He did not take to himself any praise for what had been accomplished, but attributed it to God, and under him, a large share to the ministers, who had all co-operated with him in the kindest manner in the work. He referred to several things of a most happy character. He spoke feelingly of the children and gave them some timely counsel. He read from Paul's farewell address to the Ephesians, with great effect. For want of room, we are obliged to omit his remarks. But they were characteristic. The audience were in tears, and all hearts moved.

"The silence of Rev. Mr. Tufts on the above occasion was attributable to his reporting the above.

"The remarks were interspersed with the singing of familiar and inspiring hymns by the large audience."

We providentially visited this pleasant city, and beheld and heard much of the results of the great revival. We saw hundreds, a large portion of whom had sweetly expressed hope, rise together and sing, "I love Jesus"—a spectacle never to be forgotten—following as it did, the graphic experiences of several who felt that they were "brands plucked from the burning." This work of grace opened a new era in the history of the town—and God alone can trace its streams of influence in their own sweep to eternity.

In early summer, in obedience to the repeated call of Christians in Brunswick, the beautiful seat of Bowdoin College, and twenty miles from Lewiston, the Evangelist entered upon a course of systematic effort there, to concentrate and *use* for the salvation of souls, the faith and working power of the churches.

There had been a burden on the hearts of some connected with the College, both for it—consecrated to Christ by prayer—and the people of the town, perhaps never known without a blessing near.

Dr. Adams' large and beautiful church was soon thronged; and with him, on the platform, were gathered the Faculty of the College.

One of the Professors of the College writes to a religious paper:

"Mr. Hammond has now been with us two weeks, and the Holy Spirit has been present to set his seal to the words of truth uttered by him. Many among us are rejoicing in Christ, and we may add, the work is increasing in power, reaching the hearts of the strong men. At almost every meeting, some of the students in College stand up for the first time, to speak from the fulness of their hearts of what God has done for them. A number of these students, in company with others, assisted in conducting several meetings the last week, in the outskirts of the town. Last Friday, P. M., Mr. H., accompanied by Rev. E.

P. Whittlesley, and a number of college students, recently interested, and others, went over to Bowdoinham, eight miles from Brunswick, to hold several meetings. One was held in the open air. And the interesting account which these young men gave of their recent conversion, caused many men to wipe away the falling tears. Yes, the good Spirit was there, and we hope to hear of blessed results connected with this one visit to Bowdoinham. A childrens' meeting was held in the afternoon, and also a meeting in the church in the evening.

"Saturday last, Rev. A. C. Adams and Rev. Mr. Balkam, accompanied with about 300 youth and children from Lewiston (the greater part of them young converts) made us a visit of a few hours. An open air meeting was conducted on the common by Mr. H., immediately on their arrival. It is supposed 1500 persons were present. A very solemn impression was made at the meeting by one of the students, who stated in his address, that he came to the first open air meeting held by Mr. H., six days ago, an *infidel* and now he stood up, in the same place, a witness for Jesus. From the common, the children went to the church. It was the afternoon for the childrens' meeting; and it was deeply interesting to listen, while several of the boys from Lewiston, in a calm and clear voice, told the story of their conversion. Surely, we are now witnessing scenes not unlike those when the multitude shouted Hosanna, and the children were permitted by Jesus to lisp his praises,—when He Himself welcomed them by his own tender voice, and loving hands placed upon their heads, close to his side.

"Having come on a flying visit to the beautiful seat of Bowdoin College, we found the work of God progressing with quiet but deepening interest. On Saturday afternoon, June 14th, at 2 o'clock, a meeting was held on the common. A large multitude gathered around the stand, on which were seated, with Mr. Hammond, Professor Chadbourne, Dr. Adams, of Brunswick, Dr. Carruthers, of Portland, and others.

"Dr. Adams opened the meeting with singing. Mr. Hammond then spoke for half an hour, and Rev. P. C. Headley made a few remarks in connection with the revival in Plymouth, Mass.; a converted student of the Junior class in college, followed with an earnest appeal; and Dr. Adams, Dr Carruthers, and others, impressively addressed the concourse. Tears were shed, and great solemnity prevailed. In every part, the meeting was a complete success, making all to feel, as Dr. Carruthers said, that these apostolic methods of reaching and saving men, may be now wisely employed."

Writes an intelligent lady of high position:

"The case of a blind girl, whose spiritual eyes have been opened to see Jesus, has excited much interest. We cannot describe the scene, when, with tears streaming down her large, dark eyes, she spoke of having found Jesus, and of her desire to go to the Asylum of the Blind, that she might be taught to read the Bible. Oh! ye who have eyes, and see not, remember the case of this poor blind girl, and ask, why am I blind, when I have eyes to see—eyes to read the word of God? A dear little boy of eight years died, while the meetings were in progress, and repeated often during his illness the texts he heard from the lips of Mr. Hammond. He left a little letter to Mr. H. unfinished. He and his little sister of four years, died the same night, of scarlet fever, and were placed in the same casket. And the mother is smiling through her tears, knowing her lambs are gathered home to the bosom of Jesus.

"It is impossible to calculate the length and breadth of this revival,—the number of souls hopefully converted, and the still greater numbers probably awakened, as never before, to believe in the reality of personal religion. These persons are of all classes and ages, both of men and women, youth and children. The Medical class had nearly closed its session, when Mr. H. commenced his labors, and yet some students tarried a few days and were blessed. Other strangers, visiting B., have carried away a blessing. The college is blessed. There is a deepening of the work of grace among the Christians in College, as well as in town. And a goodly number of students are rejoicing in new found hopes, and aims, and purposes to live, not unto themselves, but unto Him who has loved them and died for them. Oh! how gentle, yet soul subduing have been the influences of the Holy Spirit resting on the minds and hearts of these dear youth."

The following is an interesting story of a conversion, published in the Religious Herald :

"The spring of 1862, found me a gay and thoughtless girl. Nineteen years of my life had passed amidst Christian influences. During all these years the Spirit of God had often visited my heart, urging me to seek Christ, and devote the *morning* of my life to his service, but I had turned coldly away from all its influences, and refused to accept Christ as my friend and guide. The first meeting held by you in Brunswick, I attended merely out of curiosity. At the close of the service an inquiry meeting was appointed, but I had no disposition to remain, and went home resolved that I would not attend any more of the meetings, for I knew they would make me feel restless and unhappy.

" But, when the next meeting came, and the bells commenced ringing for service, something in their very ringing seemed to say to me '*go.*' I went, and during that evening the Spirit of God was striving with me, but I withstood its influence, and passed out of the church, *regardless* of the urgent request for any one, who would like to converse on the subject of religion, to remain. I had proceeded but a few steps, when some friends proposed returning just to see what would be said to us. We went back, but scarcely any thing was said *personally* to me as I sat with others. The next evening I did not wish to remain at the inquiry meeting, but, as all from Topsham stopped, I was obliged to   The Spirit was still hovering round, softly yet *earnestly* pleading with me, and for fear that I should manifest some signs of the deep emotions I felt, I took a seat apart from the rest. I had sat but a moment, when you (whom I most dreaded to meet and tried to shun), came along and addressed me with the simple words, 'Do you love Jesus?' I answered, not as I should. You then asked me if I wanted to be a Christian, to which I replied that I had *no* convictions. You talked a few moments, and then wanted me to kneel down, while you prayed. I *refused* to do this, but you prayed very earnestly for me, told me to read the 3d chapter of John, and left me. I tried to *forget* what you said, but the *few* simple words, 'Do you love Jesus?' haunted me. I could not *forget* them. They excited in my heart the deepest feelings. I thought how much I ought to love Jesus. How kind he had been to me since my angel mother passed away. I remembered, too, that he was my *mother's God*. That he sustained and comforted her in sickness, enabling her to leave her children in His protecting care, and made the gloomy 'valley of death' bright with His presence. It seemed as if I could almost feel her hand resting upon me, and hear her voice urging me to love Jesus, and meet her in heaven. I spent a very restless night. During the next day scarcely a moment passed, in which something did not bring to my mind the question, 'Do you love Jesus?' Everything inanimate seemed suddenly to have acquired voices, and to whisper me reproachfully, 'Do you love Jesus?' In this state of mind I attended the meetings for more than a week, keeping my convictions entirely to myself. Sometimes the sinful pleasures and follies which I must renounce if I became a Christian, appeared very attractive to me. But I felt *assured* that they could never *really satisfy* me, that there was a gulf in my heart, which nothing but the peace of Christ could fill. Pride and the Spirit of God were having a *severe* contest in my heart. I feared above all things that people should think I was serious. I plead an excuse for stopping at the inquiry meetings, that I was willing to put myself in the *way* of convictions—that many stopped from curiosity, while all the time I *wanted to be a Christian*. At this time you preached from the words, ' Why persecutest thou me?' Every word went home to my heart. The thought that Jesus, sitting at the right hand of the Father in glory, should stoop so low as to plead with sinners and say, ' Why, oh why,' affected me greatly. He seemed to appeal directly to me, and to say, what have I done that you will persecute me. I could bring no charge against the Friend of sinners. He had ever been to me a merciful God, *full* of forbearance and long-suffering, and I had repaid all his goodness by rejecting his love—by trampling under foot the blood of atonement—by resisting the Spirit—by despising heaven and putting the world in the place of God. That *why* added greatly to my unhappiness. The following Saturday I attended a childrens' meeting. As I was leaving the church, you spoke to me and asked *what* kept me from Jesus? I answered truly, fear of the world. That evening you preached from the words, ' Believe in the Lord Jesus Christ, and thou shalt be saved.' During the discourse you said, ' I see before me a young lady, who told me deliberately, this afternoon, that *fear of the world* kept her from Jesus. Oh! my young friend, you may meet those you now fear in torment, and there they may say, ' 'T was you that hindered me from being a Christian.' As you spoke, my sins arose before me in all their terrible greatness, and I saw myself lost, *forever* lost without Christ as an Almighty Saviour. Before you closed your discourse, you spoke of the willingness of Christ, and represented Him as saying ' Come unto me.' An invitation was given for all who wished to become Christians to rise. I *did* want to become a Christian, but *pride* rose in my heart stronger than ever, and for a moment conquered. The singing commenced. ' Do n't reject Him just now.' Pride gave way, and I resolved, God helping me, that I would *no longer* reject Christ, but would seek him with full purpose of heart. Looking back upon that evening, I feel that it was with me the turning point, and cannot but exclaim,

> ' O happy day that *fixed* my choice
> On thee my Saviour and my God.'

Never shall I forget the encouraging words that fell from your lips that evening. You prayed with me, commending me to the care of our heavenly Father. I went alone to my room, read some precious promise of Christ, and knelt, determined *never* to rise unless convinced that I was saved or lost. I told him, that I came in dependence on *his own promise* that he would receive sinners, and turn none away. I asked him to fulfil his word, and repeated,

> ' Just as I am, without one plea,
> But that thy blood was shed for me,
> And that thou *bidst* me come to thee,
> O Lamb of God, I come.'

The burden rolled away from my heart, and peace like a river was mine. I had imagined I should have *great ecstatic* joy, and the reality was so different that I very soon began to doubt, and the sky again became clouded. That Sabbath evening, when an invitation was extended to those who had given up all for the Lord, and who could sing, ' 'Tis done, the great transaction's done,' to rise, I remained seated. I knew that I had yielded *all*, but I had none of that rapturous joy many mention of, and the Tempter whispered that I should be acting the hypocrite, and had better wait until I was *sure* that I was a Christian. That *whisper* turned the scale, and I immediately went back into deep darkness. Had it not been for the encouraging words spoken to me at this most trying time, I should have despaired of salvation, and gone back again to the cold world. I lived in this way for nearly a week. The following Friday evening, at six o'clock, you were to meet me at the Mercy-Seat, and I again cast myself on Jesus, asking him to forgive me for denying him before the world, and solemnly promised never to deny him again. The sweet peace I had lost by disobedience returned to my heart, and I felt a calm, *resting*, *trusting* in Jesus. I confessed him before the world that very evening, by rising with Christians, and found additional happiness and strength by conversing with those who were sinners, and telling them the simple way in which I found Jesus."

Another story of God's mercy in salvation is given by one, who emerged from the darkness of error and unbelief:

"Six years ago, visiting in a Methodist family, whose every member was Christian, I discovered a beauty and value of a religious experience, I had never realized before, in softening and beautifying the character, and controlling the wayward tendencies of every nature, subject to the temptations of a city life, an exalted station in society, and worldly wealth. The dear friends' anxious solicitude for my conversion, exhibited in loving warnings, tears, and prayers, touched my heart, and more, because it was their desire, than from an owned sense of duty to God.

"Knowing what must be the effect of such unceasing efforts upon a sick head, it gave power to your words over me, through your sacrifice: thus I listened and learned, till I came to lose thought of you wholly, and accept instead, Jesus' words and promises. For days I worked hard, trying to do for myself, till one Tuesday evening, going home from meeting, a friend inquired of me my state of feeling, and I said, 'I have done every thing I know how to do; and now, if Jesus accepts me, he must take me as I am, or not at all,' not thinking it was all he required; and, as I said and felt this, my burdened heart knew its first peace. It seemed like awaking from a disturbed sleep, so quiet and calm was my hitherto troubled heart. I was not even then fully assured, but, going home, took my Bible and read the first of John, prayed with new zeal, and lay me down sweetly to sleep, as I had not for many nights before. In the morning I awoke with a song of praise in my heart, and ever since have been quietly happy, only regretting wasted time and lost opportunities of serving God. And now I must tell you this, that even my poor, weak prayers have been heard, and *God has heard my mother's cry.*"

It was the writer's privilege to go amid the memorable scenes of that deep and blessed work of the Spirit; to meet with the students when the heavenly influence pervaded the college; to stand with the pastor who has long been over the flock of Christ, in the sanctuary of God, and open air, when none could doubt the presence of the most High.

More hallowed hours, fresh and fragrant still in memory, we have never known in all the experiences of Pentecostal blessings.

CHAPTER X.

Revival Meeting in Portland—Its Origin and Object—Addresses by Rev. Dr. Carruthers and seven other Pastors from Maine—Summary of Principles.

On Monday evening, June 23d, a large audience, filling the church edifice of the Second Parish, in the city of Portland, assembled to hold a Revival Meeting, as it was called by the pastor; the first of the kind, we think, ever convened in this country. The idea originated with Dr. Carruthers, by whom it was carried out in detail, with the cordial co-operation of all the Christian people with whom he conferred on the subject. The particular evening was selected, because the following day, was the time appointed for the meeting of the General Conference of the State of Maine, and many clergymen and others could attend, with reference to the anniversary meetings of the week; and it was also hoped, that the influence of such an occasion would be pleasant and elevating, upon the churches which were represented there, during the sessions of Conference.

The plan of meeting was, with the usual religious services, to have brief addresses from seven of the pastors, in whose parishes there had been revivals during the winter and spring. At seven o'clock, Dr. Carruthers opened the meeting with a very appropriate and impressive hymn.

This was followed by reading the 4th chapter of 2d Corinthians. Rev. P. C. Headley offered prayer. After singing another hymn, the pastor spoke of the precious work of grace in his congregation, whose fruits remained to the glory of God ; and eloquently expressed his hope that these manifestations of the sovereign Spirit's power, might be the bright assurances of a glorious future for the churches of the Redeemer.

The Rev. Mr. Wheelright, of Bethel, was the next speaker. He commenced his address with much feeling, which threw a subduing influence over the audience. He said he came to Portland last November, and, as he entered this church one evening, the congregation was singing, " Oh to grace how great a debtor ! " and his heart was filled with joy at the words. He felt that God was there ; and asked, can he not bless Bethel? And cannot brother H. come and help gather in the harvest ? He went home, resolved to go to work for souls, and strive to bring them to Christ. Mr. W. then gave an outline of the efforts and results, which is found in the preceding pages ; closing with the statement, that " when he received a letter from Dr. Carruthers, inviting him to attend this meeting, he asked the young converts what he should tell the people — whether he should say the interest of months past had been all excitement. They replied, "no; tell them God is here." He believed God was in Bethel. He did not wish to call names, but loved Bro. Hammond, as he loved his own soul. God blesses earnest efforts; and the minister, who labors most earnestly, will be the most successful.

Rev. Mr. Garland, of the Second Church, Bethel, followed, remarking, that in a few words he could add, God has been blessing the town with the power of his Spirit. Mothers in Israel had been praying— one of them for several days, prayed all the time; and had just gone to heaven. The triumph of the Cross was complete. Men, not fit for the society of decent people, were converted and began to preach that sinners must be born again. Accessions had been made to the church, and others are soon to be added. It needed no human eulogies, to exalt such a work as had been witnessed in Bethel.

Rev. J. O. Fiske, of the Winter St. Church, Bath, commenced his statement of the work there, as follows: The best I can say is, to tell you what I saw in Lewiston, last evening. Seven persons, mature in years and experience, rose one after the other, and offered prayer; and then the young converts. I forgot that I was tired by eight o'clock. One man said that he had not been to meeting for years, but felt he must go and hear Mr. Balkam preach.

The sermon reached his heart, and soon he found Jesus. He rejoiced to tell them, he was witnessing similar scenes in Bath. Not unfrequently we see a reviving religious interest, and then it subsides. But the work had been deep in that city. Much earnest prayer had preceded it—some persons spent the whole night wrestling with God. He went to Portland and saw such indications as constrained him to send for Mr. Hammond; and he thanked God upon every remembrance of him, in his prayers. Mr. F. then sketched graphically the thrilling scenes, whose narrative we have given.

Rev. Mr. Southworth, of South Paris, said, every true revival must be the work of God, and it must also be carried forward by men—by preaching and prayer, and effort. The stated ministry was indispensable, but we ought to use such other instruments, as God raises up from time to time. Evangelists had their place, among the saving agencies he employed. Mr. S. spoke very earnestly and feelingly, of the increase of the spirit of prayer, of the attendance upon meetings—of the indications of God's providence and grace, which led the church to send for help. He went to Bath, and saw the personal efforts of Mr. H.—never before, saw and felt how to approach men, although he believed he loved their souls. He had the assistance of the evangelist but two days, but was taught things he had not learned before. Dr. Carruthers and Dr. Chickering also came to his help. It would take a long time to tell what God had wrought, subduing strong men, and bringing babes to Christ. A little boy was converted—asked God to bless his father—went home and erected a family altar, and still kept it up.

Another was so deeply impressed, that he said, he loved Christ, but did not know as Christ loved him. Soon the Spirit revealed Jesus to his heart. The work had been characterized by a vivid sense of guilt. Aged Christians were sure, they had never seen so pungent convictions of sin, in any previous revival. Forty-four had united with the church, and more were coming forward. He closed with an urgent request, for an interest in the petitions of all, at the throne of grace.

At this point of great interest, prayer was offered; and the congregation sang a hymn.

Rev. Mr. Howard, of Farmington, was rejoiced when he heard of this meeting. Edwards declared that one great means of promoting the work of God more than a century ago, was to report its progress, to people unvisited by the divine presence. He thought it might save souls in Portland. The past winter he came to P., and saw strong men bowing to Immanuel, and longed to transfer the scene to Farmington. He went to Bath, and was called up at dead of night, to pray with two persons. Returning home, he asked his people what they should do, to develope and deepen the interest apparent among them. They replied, something must be done. Br. Hammond was invited to come and help them. The snow-drifts blocked up the roads, so that he could not get there. But Christians prayed and worked on—and were encouraged by a letter from young ladies in Bath, saying, that they had resolved to pray, till the blessing came to F. Neglectors of the sanctuary, were seen at church. He felt, in preparing for the pulpit, that he must present more distinctly and boldly, the doctrine of an eternal hell, and feared he had neglected this duty. The evangelist came, and the work swept through the place. Rev. Dr. Tappan rendered timely assistance, and conversions occurred in connection with his earnest words. The fruits of the revival continued;— mutual love, and good works.

God has followed mercy with judgment. A company of men used to scoff. One of these was smitten down last week, and died, "making no sign." His wife was taken with the same fatal disease, diptheria, and such scenes, as attended her death, can never be forgotten. She knelt on the bed, leaning on her father, and asked him to pray for her. She had known that the Spirit was in the place, but trifled with, and grieved him. She begged for, and we hope found mercy.

An old man rose in meeting before he left, and asked God to send down the Holy Spirit on this meeting; and if we did not grieve him away, that prayer will be answered—it will.

Rev. Mr. Balkam, of Lewiston, said there was no rule for the Spirit's operations—striking providences had prepared the way. With the rising religious interest, a desire was expressed by those who had witnessed the work in Portland and Bath, that Mr. Hammond should be invited to hold a series of meetings. One of the pastors, who had been greatly burdened for the city, felt the suggestion was in answer to prayer, and united with his ministerial brethren in extending the call. During four weeks the daily meetings were thronged, sometimes filling two churches the same hour.

Mr. Balkam dwelt with great force upon the outlying masses, which could only be reached by these special efforts, and of the immediate answers to the prayers which were offered in the vestry, while the word was being preached above. The lateness of the meetings, was unavoidable. Thousands were brought under conviction of sin, and had there been a sufficient number of Christians to speak and pray with the anxious, he believed there would have been thousands instead of hundreds, converted. The work had reached all classes, from the most refined and educated, to the most degraded. When the question of compensation arose, he was assured that there would be no difficulty after the people were once interested, and he was happy to say that they had not forgotten in Lewiston, that the evangelist, as well as the pastor, was worthy of his hire.

Rev. Mr. Adams, from Auburn, a part of Lewiston in situation and business interest, and separated only by a river, was the next speaker. He said he could not, like some who had preceded him, speak of any special, visible preparation among his people.

The work with them was sudden and powerful. He had long felt, that, owing to his ill health, he could not carry on the extra meetings attendant upon a revival of religion, without foreign aid. Mr. Hammond's first meeting for children was one of great power. At the close of Mr. H.'s address, hundreds of children, among them two of his own, remained at the meeting, many of them weeping for their sins.

And, when told of Jesus' love for them, they did n't know any better, than to think they might then believe in Jesus, and be saved; and the result has shown that many of them were then accepted of Christ.

When he met Mr. H. in Boston last fall, he urged him to devote himself to the great work of preaching to children; and he was now more convinced, that he could not spend his time more profitably.

Prof. Chadbourne, of Bowdoin College, Brunswick, spoke with much feeling of the yearning for the pastor's office, which the touching narrations had awakened. He then sketched in outline the powerful work in B., including the college. The evangelist could do little without the pastor. To God belonged all the glory of salvation. With hesitation he gave his influence in favor of engaging the services of Mr. Hammond last winter, for the way was not then open. But he blessed God for what he had wrought in connection with them. The work of conviction was deep.

When Mr. H. proposed an open air meeting, he feared the result, but when, a few days after, a student spoke of an arrow of conviction having then pierced his heart, he had nothing more to say.

We had heard much about the way being prepared in other places, but he believed the Lord also prepared instruments for this evangelistic work. God had been preparing Mr. H. for this work. When a freshman in college, he was the same humble earnest laborer, and often as he accompanied him among the mountains, he had been rebuked, to hear him talk with the people about their souls, and asked them if they loved Jesus, as easily as he would ask the way to town.

From the beginning, the exercises were deeply interesting. The waves of hallowed influence would sometimes seem to lift the people from their seats— so marked was the moral power of the occasion. Though not designed at all for the purpose, it indicated the office of the true evangelist, whatever defects in the methods of labor might appear to the eye of observers, disposed to criticise closely the individual peculiarities of any man. The effect of this demonstration was visible during the week of conference, and will be good and wide-spread among the churches; and may lead to the appointment of similar meetings in our smitten land, under the discipline of Jehovah's hand for our sins, preparing it to breathe the prayer from the depths of Zion's humiliation before her king,—

"O Lord, revive thy work!"

The following propositions we think, are established in the pages of this narrative.

1. Revivals come not by any sovereign interposition, apart from the responsibility of the church, in securing the salvation of men. In every case, so far as we can trace the history, Christians, at least a small company of God's people, have "set their faces to seek the Lord,"—often by fasting and prayer,—then have used the means, personal effort, and calling in such aid as God's Spirit led them to accept.

Usually, while some have expected a blessing, the work of grace has been carried forward under God, by a minority of the nominal membership of the church. That is to say, a majority have floated on the tide of feeling, or been indifferent. A part only, have manifested living sympathy with Christ in his travail of soul, and efforts to save the perishing. So that, the believing should neither "make haste," nor wait till the church as a body are awake.

2. The inquiry meeting has been especially blessed, and for reasons very simple and influential. The minds of the people are in the best possible condition for hopeful effort in leading to Christ, when the truth is freshly laid upon them, in an atmosphere of prayer, pervaded by the influence of the Holy Spirit, and the difficulties to be met, stand clearly before the conscience.

Besides, the opportunity itself developes and brings to the surface, conviction which had been hidden for months or years, because no personal effort in their behalf had called it forth. And farther, the sight of a single anxious sinner will affect the inactive Christian more than many sermons; and often make, also, impenitent observers thoughtful. No other means of promoting a revival has been more signally successful. This demonstrates the affirmation of one who has had much experience in revivals, "that God is always in advance of his church." Christians are not watching and waiting to be "led by the Spirit."

3. The masses of every community, who do not attend the sanctuary, and are overlooked to a great extent in the ordinary means of grace, have been reached alone by unusual methods to gain the listening ear; such as inviting them to come, and open-

ing a temple or hall freely to them; or in the open air, bringing to bear upon them, the agencies of salvation.

4. Children can be converted,— and oftener than otherwise, are made the first fruits and earnest, of a glorious harvest in the kingdom of God. The command of Him who took them in his arms, rings over the generations since that hour, but imperfectly heard and heeded by the church of his love, "suffer the little children to come unto me, and forbid them not."

5. The simple gospel, presented directly and earnestly to the conscience, is "the power of God unto salvation." In no instance has a revival or conversion been traced to logically powerful or elaborate sermons as such; but oftener than otherwise to the repeated text of God's word; a fearless, tender appeal, or a tearful declaration of what God has done for the soul. Sermons and the pastorate are indispensable, but successful, in proportion to the Scriptural simplicity, and adaptation of the truth and labor, in the ministry and laity, to the common thought and experience, accompanied with believing prayer.

6. The power of a revival, and consequently its extent, depend very much upon the united efforts and hearty support by Christians, of the plainest and most searching exhibitions of the truth of God. If his seal of approval is apparent, and thus recog-

nized, cavilers and scoffers are left to the lightnings of Sinai, as well as to the tears of Calvary, with no refuge or hiding place in the church of God. We think this point of primary importance. "The terrors of the law," have their place in the gospel messages, and cannot be ignored without fatal loss of power. Love must alarm, as well as beckon.

7. It is also clear, that, while we are not called upon to deny the imperfections and mistakes in the human agencies, and to have no desire for their removal, it is obligatory upon Christians, to accept whatever God sends to promote his kingdom, using it with all bold and hallowed prudence, and prayer. And his seal may be seen in the Holy Spirit's saving presence, overruling the weakness of man for the glory of God, in securing the travail of the Redeemer's soul.

8. One of the principal means of success, in special efforts, is the Scriptural method of dealing with souls, in seeking and expecting an immediate decision, upon the claims of Christ. We think no single source of power in the harvest-work, greater than an urgency of appeal to the impenitent, with a full dependence on the sovereign Spirit, not to leave the sanctuary or the place of entreaty, without the choice of God,—the submission of the soul unconditionally to Him,—pressing upon the sinner the command, "Choose you this day whom ye will serve."

9. Another fact, and peculiarity of the evangelistic labors described in the pages of this volume, is the directness of the effort to the sinner's case. No preparatory sermons to the church were delivered; but relying on the few engaged in the Master's service, and the truth as it is in God's word, with the quickening effect upon all Christians, which their efforts to save, and the tears of the anxious will have; the labors of even a day or two have resulted often in the conversion of many souls. This was Richard Weaver's, and also Reginald Radcliff's successful method, in Scotland and England. And this suggests the question: whether an expectant and decided measure to test and develope feeling in our congregations, by pastors, would not often be the outburst of the gracious work of the Spirit. Manifold are the ways of the Lord in saving men, and revivals in their origin conform to this fact, in the economy of his grace.

10. The question sometimes raised, why were convictions of sin—of personal guilt—generally deeper, formerly than now, we think answered in the narratives of conversion. It is not because, as a young clergyman recently remarked, men, in the progress of theological thought, pass " more easily and gracefully into the kingdom;" but on account of superficial views of the natural heart and its only means of cleansing. The best indication that the Holy Spirit's work has been chronicled, is the poignant

sense of sinfulness expressed by nearly all who gave evidence of conversion.

Those who have been "slain by the law, and made alive by Christ," have a clear and well defined experience, and love to hear all truth, receiving with docility and profit, that contrasted and awakening statement of the sinner's lost condition; "He that believeth shall be saved and he that believeth not shall be damned." Any other gospel, i. e., messages mainly of love and clemency, or of guilt, judgment and retributive wrath, are a partial exhibition of truth. Paul declared, solemnly, "Knowing the terrors of the law, we persuade men." God's ambassadors and witnesses, need to feel more deeply the words of the faithful, tearful Doddridge:

> "The watch for souls, for which the Lord
> Did heavenly bliss forego;
> For souls — that must for ever live
> In raptures or in woe!"

The sainted Bogatzky expressed the living Christian's holy longing, a century and a quarter ago; a fitting close to the records we have given of the past:

"Oh that thou wouldest rend the heavens, that thou wouldest come down, that the mountains might flow down at thy presence . . . to make thy name known to thine adversaries, that the nations may tremble at thy presence." — *Ias.* lxiv. 1, 2.

> "Awake, thou Spirit, who of old
> Didst fire the watchmen of the Church's youth;
> Who faced the foe, unshrinking, bold,
> Who witnessed day and night the eternal truth,

Whose voices through the world are ringing still,
  And bringing hosts to know and do thy will.

" Oh that Thy fire were kindled soon,
   That swift from land to land its flame might leap;
   Lord, give us but this priceless boon
   Of faithful servants, fit for Thee to reap
   The harvest of the soul ; look down and view
   How great the harvest, yet the laborers few.

" Lord, let our earnest prayer be heard,
   The prayer Thy Son Himself hath bid us pray;
   For, lo ! thy children's hearts are stirr'd,
   In every land in this our darkening day,
   To cry for help with fervent soul to Thee;
   Oh hear us, Lord, and speak,— Thus let it be !

" Oh haste to help, ere we are lost !
   Send forth Evangelists, in spirit strong,
   Arm'd with Thy Word, a dauntless host,
   Bold to attack the rule of ancient wrong ;
   And let them all the earth for Thee reclaim,
   To be Thy kingdom and to know Thy name.

" Would there were help within our walls !
   Oh, let thy promised Spirit come again,
   Before whom every barrier falls,
   And, ere the night, once more shine forth as then !
   Oh rend the heavens, and make Thy presence felt,
   The chains that bind us at Thy touch would melt !

" And let Thy Word have speedy course,
   Through every land the truth be glorified,
   Till all the heathen know its force.
   And gather to thy churches far and wide ;
   And waken Israel from her sleep, O Lord !
   Thus bless and spread the conquests of Thy Word !

" The Church's desert paths restore,
That stumbling blocks, which long in them have lain,
May hinder now Thy Word no more ;
Destroy false doctrine, root out notions vain ;
Set free from hirelings, let the church and school
Bloom as a garden 'neath Thy prospering rule!

www.ingramcontent.com/pod-product-compliance
Lightning Source LLC
Chambersburg PA
CBHW030747250426
43672CB00028B/1289